Marrying & Burying

also by Ronald L. Grimes

SYMBOL AND CONQUEST

BEGINNINGS IN RITUAL STUDIES

RITUAL CRITICISM

READING, WRITING, AND RITUALIZING

MARRYING

&

BURYING

Rites of Passage in a Man's Life

Ronald L. Grimes

Westview Press

Boulder • San Francisco • Oxford

Copyright © 1995 by Westview Press, Inc.

Published in 1995 in the United States of America by Westview Press, Inc., 5500 Central Avenue, Boulder, Colorado 80301-2877, and in the United Kingdom by Westview Press, 36 Lonsdale Road, Summertown, Oxford OX2 7EW

Design and composition by Westview Press

A CIP catalog record for this book is available from the Library of Congress
ISBN 0-8133-2459-9
ISBN 0-8133-2460-2 (pbk.)

Printed and bound in the United States of America

The paper used in this publication meets the requirements
of the American National Standard for Permanence of Paper
for Printed Library Materials Z39.48-1984.

10   9   8   7   6   5   4   3   2   1

Life itself means to separate and to be reunited, to change form and condition, to die and to be reborn. It is to act and to cease, to wait and rest, and then to begin acting again, but in a different way. And there are always new thresholds to cross: the thresholds of summer and winter, of a season or a year, of a month or a night; the thresholds of birth, adolescence, maturity, and old age; the threshold of death and that of the afterlife—for those who believe in it.

—**Arnold van Gennep**
The Rites of Passage

[The course of a man's life consists of] the movement ... from a fixed placental placement with his mother's womb, to his death and ultimate fixed point of his tombstone and final containment in his grave as a dead organism—punctuated by a number of critical moments of transition which all societies ritualize and publicly mark with suitable observances to impress the significance of the individual and the group on living members of the community.

—**Lloyd Warner**
The Living and the Dead

The failure of anthropology to deal with the experiences of ritual participants—private, subjective, psychological, conscious, and unconscious—is an enormous barrier to our understanding of the subject.

—**Barbara Myerhoff**
Celebration: Studies in Festivity and Ritual

TO TOM F. DRIVER

Contents

PART FIVE   PRACTICING

Acknowledgments

The trajectory of much scholarly writing is centripetal. We academics approach our subjects from the outside, creeping up on them from the circumference, our noses pointed toward the vibrant centers of things. Even on occasions when we are in fact insiders, we act as if we are not. After years of writing about ritual from outside its boundaries, I am assuming the posture of an autobiographer. Now I must make my way from inside to out. Because the task requires gazing along another vector, it puts a kink in the neck. Hoping not to be trapped in my own ego, I proceed centrifugally, cutting a path from center to circumference.

Now that *Marrying & Burying*'s publication is assured, I feel a kind of idiot gratitude to those who disliked or rejected it. Irritation can motivate almost as effectively as the desire to tell a story can. Some of the negative responses are memorable. A colleague remarked, "You are not old enough to write this kind of book." A friend confessed, "If I had just read this part of your manuscript and saw you walking down the street, I'd cross to the other side." Another advised, "Looks like washing dirty laundry in public. Wait a year or two and then decide whether to publish it." More than one editor justified nonacceptance in plain-spoken language: "Autobiographies don't sell unless you are a movie star or a politician." Another justified her press's rejection by observing, "It's too intense. Besides, the public is not interested in self-revelation."

I thank colleagues in the Department of Religion and Culture of Wilfrid Laurier University, where much of the writing originated, and the Department of Religious Studies at the University of Colorado in Boulder, where much of it was completed.

The labor of writing has been so protracted that I have sought more than the usual number of readers along the way. Many have ruminated and commented on fragments of the book. My appreciation goes to William Doty, Sam Gill, Char and Sonya Granskou, Darrell Grimes, Sherry Grubelnik, Bob and Julie Harwood, Beverly Irons, Hugo Martínez-Serros, Robert Moore, Art Read, Sue Stortz, Tod Swanson, Pat Watt, and Dan Webster.

Cathie Huggins and Dennis Huggins convinced me that *Marrying & Burying* was of interest outside the academic world. Their appreciation and encouragement marked the moment when I decided to write for a larger, nonacademic audience.

I am especially indebted to readers who wrote critiques of entire drafts of the preliminary manuscript. Some of them spent long hours calling me to task, reminding me of what I had forgotten, querying my intentions, and insisting that I not give up. My gratitude goes to Madeline Duntley, Barb Matson, Claudia Putnam, Ted Tollefson, and Stephanie Walker for their sustained labor.

I thank the staff of Westview Press, especially Polly Christensen and Jane Raese, for their exceptionally competent handling of a complex manuscript. Jan Kristiansson did a superb job of copyediting. Spencer Carr, senior editor, took unusual risks in arguing for the book's publication. Without his support the book would have remained a manuscript, an orphan without legitimacy.

Carolyn Heilbrun's reading was wise and invaluable. She provided succinct and compassionate criticism. Her capacity for hearing women's voices is already evident to the reading public. Her ear for a man's voice is no less finely tuned.

Susan Scott tolerated *my* telling of *our* stories with remarkable equanimity. In addition, she kept me from domesticating our family's domestic ritualizing, and she midwifed the book. My gratitude to her is boundless.

Marrying & Burying is dedicated to Tom Driver, friend, teacher, and companion in the search for fully embodied, ethically responsible ritual.

Portions of the material on the Ritual Studies Lab appeared in *Ritual Criticism* (Columbia: University of South Carolina Press, 1990) and are reprinted here with permission.

Since some of the characters in these stories more than coincidentally resemble real people among the living as well as the dead, some of the names have been changed to protect both the innocent and the not so innocent.

Ronald L. Grimes

BEGINNING

In Spanish there is a saying, "The opposite of a funeral is a wedding." Marrying and burying are a venerable old couple. They love, fight, and deserve each other. These two moments in the human lifecycle are indissoluble. I let the pair stand for the whole. "Marrying & burying" is a euphonic shorthand for major lifecycle transitions. The cycle includes more than weddings and funerals; it also comprises births and initiations.

Lifecycle transitions are larger than the rites that mark them. Birth, marriage, maturation, and death are complex religious, biological, social, and psychological processes. They engulf the rites that people use to define them, such as namings, weddings, initiations, or funerals. Ritual is a means of greeting, deepening, condensing, and negotiating these transitions. It is a way of ordering a process that might otherwise seem random or hopelessly entangled. It is a means of enhancing change so that its meaning is not forgotten or overlooked.

In some societies, bridges between the phases of a life are crossed without benefit or obligation of ritual. In others, transitions sag with the weight of ceremony. North America is ritually impoverished. A small proportion of its economic, intellectual, and imaginative resources are committed to ritual. The time and money devoted to rites of passage are paltry.

The four moments—birth, coming of age, marriage, and death—constitute a scenario, a schematized plot that lives are supposed to follow. A scenario is a conventionally expected sequence of actions on the basis of which groups or individuals improvise the performances that constitute their lifestories. This fourfold scenario is not automatic or natural; it is constructed. The scenario could include other moments. For example, a plausible one might include six phases: birth, coming of age, *employment*, marriage, *retirement*, and death. The moments could be ordered differently. Suppose your parents were the sort who considered you a child until you married. Their scenario would contain the four

1

moments but in a different order: birth, marriage, initiation, death. Initiation into adulthood would follow, rather than precede, marriage.

In actual, rather than abstracted or idealized, lives some of the anticipated episodes in the lifecycle never occur. Your aunt doesn't marry but chooses to remain single; your uncle has no funeral because his body was lost at sea; your niece will never become socially a woman because she has Down's syndrome. In actual lives the so-called great transitions sometimes turn out to be not so great, and minor, unnamed ones become major. Your colleague's greatest transition is finishing her Ph.D.; your best friend's most crucial turn is the failure of his marriage.

So even though this book's structure reflects the expected four moments, it does not follow them in the expected order. Moreover, it questions the generic scenario. It notices exceptions to supposedly universal patterns. It considers botched as well as felicitous passages. It attends to overlaps and recursive movements in the trajectory leading from birth to death. It puzzles over the ways each rite of passage can permeate or evoke another. For instance, a death can seem like a birth, or a wedding can function as an initiation.

We may all suffer birth and death, but we do not all bring forth and bury in the same way. However universal birth and death may be, the experience of them is always particular, and the rites for negotiating them, always culturally bound. So stories are better than theories at conveying their sense, since stories exceed theories in their ability to dramatize experience. So stories I will tell.

Barbara Myerhoff's complaint in the third epigraph to this book bemoans the lack of attention to ritual experience. Because most accounts of ritual were written by anthropologists, they are about the collectively held or public meanings of rites, not about their meanings to individuals. In anthropological accounts culture is cast in the role of primary ritual actor. As a result, few attempts have been made at characterizing the ritual sensibilities of actual people.

Writing about one's experience of ritual experience is troublesome. There are few good models for doing it. Much of the writing is uninteresting, because the people who enact the rites are missing from it. Characterizations of ritual action and ritual actors have been flat: This happens, then that happens, and finally something else occurs. Detail follows detail endlessly, as on a shopping list. Functionalist ethnographic accounts have typically taken this form.

A variation of the functionalist approach treats ritual as a set of symbolic codes requiring translation. Thus the style: They do this, the meaning is that; they do this, the meaning is that. The meanings do not belong to—are not embodied by—anyone in particular.

Current popular writing about ritual takes a more personal, less analytical tack. Much of it is confessional and prescriptive: This is how I ritualize; you ought to do it this way, too. The tone of this writing is not that of the academy but that of popular psychology. It is syncretistic and steeped in the how-to ethos of New Age North America. In this kind of writing the rhetoric of enthusiasm displaces the dry objectivity of scholarly description. But the rites advocated are just as disembodied, despite the rhetoric of embodiment that suffuses them.

I have tried to avoid both distanced objectivism and facile advocacy. Attempting to do so has required a community of voices: that of child, father, scholar, husband, poet, storyteller, lover, son, teacher, ritual-maker, and others I do not know how to name. The voices are occasionally harmonious; often cacophonous. But a community of voices is necessary for evoking the richness and complexity of ritual, itself a collage. The voices call upon a multiplicity of genres: stories, dream accounts, letters, journal entries, ritual scripts, poetry, rumination, argument, and invective.

Dreams and poetry can pose hurdles for readers, because of their cultural associations with therapy and fine art. A popular assumption about dreams is that they are psychic garbage and therefore not worthy of attention. Another is that they are desperate, esoteric messages best quarantined to analysts' chambers. The usual view of poetry is that it is the most rarified of verbal art forms. This cultural placement would restrict dreams to the mentally ill and poetry to geniuses, each requiring the control and expertise of professional interpreters, namely, analysts and literary critics. Poetry is thereby imprisoned (it must be kept pure), while dreams are banished to the asylum (they are too polluting). In the standard cultural portrait neither has a strong enough constitution to tolerate elbow-to-elbow contact with normal folks.

But the importance to ritual of both dreaming and word-crafting (for ritual purposes, a more accurate term than poetry) predates their segregation from ceremonial enactment. Ritual without dream and poetic language is as desiccated as it would be without song or dance. I try to reconnect ritual with some of its essential sources as well as illustrate how ritual can be a primary source of poetic speech and dreamlife. The dreams I recount are ones that share images or dynamics with rites. I make no claim to expertise in dream interpretation, only to having studied it formally and to having taken its relation to waking life seriously for the past twenty-five years. And I do not claim to be writing good poetry either, only rhythmic, image-laden words actually used in ceremonies or useful in articulating my experience of ritual. Such poetry should be judged as good or bad according to how it does its ritual work, not according to some critic's view of how well it is written. If I had some other label, I would not even call this sort of writing "poetry," because of the falsely elevated associations the word has. The poetry in *Marrying & Burying* is included to facilitate an understanding of ritual, and its relation to ritual is varied. Some of the poetry was written to be read during ritual occasions; some of it was written in response to a rite. Some of it *is* ritual, some of it is ritual-like, and some of it is only ritual as imagined. In any case, an account of either my life or my experience of ritual would be as falsified by the absence of dreaming and poetry as it would be by the absence of storytelling.

For the past twenty or so years I have been conducting research, teaching courses, and writing about ritual. The public face of my work has been largely theoretical and the idiom, scholarly. An autobiographical shadow, however, has lurked about its edges. Editors have sometimes balked at my occasional but persistent use of first-person rhetoric. *Beginnings in Ritual Studies* opens with an autobiographical account. *Reading, Writing, and Ritualizing* closes with personal reflections. Even *Ritual Criticism* includes a first-person account of my own teaching activities. Here the autobiographical shadow approaches daylight.

In university classes I argue that theories are inescapably rooted in theorists' cultures and imaginations. This rooting does not invalidate a theory, but it does anchor it in a specific time and place. So anchored, the theory is likely to be far more interesting, but it may also be far less universal than theorists suppose. Here I take my own argument seriously by playing autobiographical storytelling and theoretical reflection off each other.

Marrying & Burying resembles both intellectual autobiography and spiritual autobiography. It chronicles developing ideas and meditates on religious struggle. However, the writing is more focused on bodiliness than is typical of intellectual autobiography, and it is more concerned with practice and experiment than is characteristic of spiritual autobiography. Traditionally, spiritual autobiography has required stringent self-examination and self-critique, tasks I pursue here even though I risk embarrassing readers who may be uncomfortable with self-revelatory writing.

This book is not only about religion; it is also a religious book. In religious studies classrooms we professors distinguish teaching religion from teaching *about* religion. Teaching religion, or worse, teaching *a* religion, is against the law. Teaching about it in many states and provinces is not. However legally and pedagogically useful this distinction between the practice and study of religion may be, in my experience it is anything but absolute. The membrane separating study from practice is more permeable than we may think. What I practice at home influences what I do at the university; what I think at the university has consequences in ritual performed at home.

In universities analysis is the expected mode of discourse. At home the currency is conversation and storytelling. I do not tell stories from my life for the sake of autobiography alone. I also tell them as a way of illustrating the dilemmas that characterize passage among white, middle-class, North American males. My life is of interest only to a handful of people, but rites of passage as rooted in a concrete human experience are of considerable current interest. This interest can be summarized in a set of questions: What ritual processes typify passage in North America? Are our rites effective? What are their consequences for spiritual formation? How do they nurture or distort a man's life? These are some of the questions that drive the book.

The autobiographical elements of *Marrying & Burying* represent a peculiar slant on my life. As a result, they distort it. The narratives are selected for their relevance to rites of passage, so major nonritualized transitions are missing; so is daily life. The angle from which I shoot this self-portrait is not always a flattering one. Because that narrative concentrates on major passages, I am typically off balance. My ordinary self recedes into the background. As my crisis-driven self emerges, I am exposed—a man exercising power, defending territory, milking relationships, anticipating conflict, recollecting grief. I have no apology for such a self-portrait, since I think that being off balance and grasping for spiritual resources are typical of most people making major transitions. Rites of passage bring out the worst in us, though tangled up with the best. Such a knot of neurosis and virtue is characteristic of lifecycle transitions.

I have not always liked ritual. My early experience of it left me empty. Eventually, I responded to it with disdain. Then, I recognized how badly I needed it, and I began to cultivate it. Cultivating ritual is a major theme of the book. One could say "inventing" or "making up" or "constructing" ritual, but cultivating is a richer metaphor. People invent lightbulbs, construct office buildings, make up lists and likely stories, but they cultivate soil. The image of cultivation conjures olfactory responses and tactile images: manure, dark earth, weeds, seeds. The metaphor of cultivation reminds us of what ritual is not. It is not a mechanical activity. Sometimes I speak of incubating as well as cultivating. Ritual cannot be incubated by using manuals or attending weekend workshops. Ritual, even of the made-up variety, requires waiting; rites emerge.

The organic metaphor—ritual as grown rather than invented—can be a bit romantic. It can be dangerous to middle-class Anglo-Americans who are alienated from the soil and its literal cultivation. We risk self-deception by imagining our hands in the earth, since it is currently cultivated with magnificent agribusiness machines that maul this Mother whom most of us have never really known.

To prevent romanticizing about ritual, I use a second metaphor: negotiation. Ritual is not only something we grow but also something we fight over, fight with, and fight for. It is a political act requiring the exercise of judgment and the use of power. Ritual is a tool for forging consensus and eliciting cooperation. Ritual is a right fought over. It can be a weapon used to exploit others. Ritual is sufficiently powerful that the yearning for it ought to be accompanied by a relentless criticism of it. Ritual fails as often as it succeeds, but even in its failure it can exercise power like some dying, fiddling emperor.

Cultivation and negotiation are images that make ritual sound rich and deep, powerful and socially significant. Missing from the picture is ritual's utter ordinariness—its improvisational, patchwork quality and its imperfection. The members of Welfare State International, an English art and theater collective, with whom I once worked, sometimes speak of themselves as ritual plumbers. They use this image to balance a more elevated one they also claim: civic magicians. Like them, I imagine myself as a ritual plumber. Ritual is an ordinary activity. It ought to leave the hands rough and dirty; it should smell like it has been close to the bowels of the earth.

Two other images of ritual are important to my experience of it: "spit and bailing wire," a phrase Mom used when speaking of things precariously held together; and "bricolage," an image popularized by the French anthropologist Claude Lévi-Strauss. In Waterloo, Ontario, where I live, and in Clovis, New Mexico, where I grew up, there are two marvelous examples of motley assemblage worthy of the label bricolage. Both are bicycles—ridden, pushed, or carried by street people, both men. The bicycles sport veritable hardware stores. Every conceivable thing that might appear in a flea market or junkyard hangs on them: old radios, coils of plastic, broken squeeze-ball horns, castaway saddlebags, electric motor parts. Astonished spectators can hardly see the frame and wheels for all the utter-clutter hanging off the handlebars and fenders. These are bricolage bikes, assemblages to ride.

The sort of ritual in which I typically engage is usually of this motley sort, seldom of the high and elevated kind. It is piecemeal and local—the stuff of plumbers and unshaven men who bike to no place in particular instead of working for a living. It is less goal directed, institutionally grounded, or belief tethered than is typical of mainline North American religiosity.

Susan, Caleigh, Bryn, and I are inveterate ritualizers. Our home—not a church, temple, or vegetarian restaurant—is the space we make special by our ritual activity. The attic on Dunbar Road is an incubation chamber, a nest. It is a repository for things that don't fit the usual definition of domestic or sacred space. The attic, which insistently demands that we lower our heads or risk splitting them on a dormer's edge, is carved into niches saturated with miscellany: bells, sand, masks, keepsakes, crackers, cushions, mats, dolls, wind-up turtles, statues, a horse's skull, baskets, kites, treasure boxes, sticks, tin-can drums. These are the paraphernalia of our domestic ritualizing.

Growing up Protestant, I found the taste of ritual to be as bland as mashed potatoes without salt, pepper, or butter. As both an American and a Methodist, I craved drama, not ritual; climax, not repetition. Drama I could find in preaching, but not in the worship service that surrounded it. I expected religion to be deeply heartwarming and personally rewarding. When it was neither, I believed it had been corrupted by a secular malaise that I imagined more religion would cure. Eventually, I discovered that more religion of the denominational variety only made my disappointment more profound.

Disappointment with conventional Christianity and hope for some other perspective drove me to Zen Buddhism and meditation practice, which I have carried out erratically and doggedly for over sixteen years. I know of no more severe challenge to the search for the heartwarming and personally rewarding than Zen. I hoped to find and practice pure Zen with an enlightened Zen master. The first one I met went back to Japan and died. When I ferreted out a second, he died too. Many of the others were either shrouded in scandal or failed to wear their enlightenment convincingly. Some were in the throes of wrangling about power, sexuality, drugs, or money.

No pure Methodism, no pure Zen.

For a while I imagined one might discover Christian Zen or invent ecumenical Zen. I once heard that somebody was engaging in both simultaneously, but I decided I would only be doubling my trouble by trying to synthesize two traditions into some third, new institution. Although I have more or less abandoned institutional Christianity and Buddhism, I remain a religious animal. The perspective from which this book is written is that of an impurely religious man without the legitimacy of a pedigree. This is a book about disaffiliated religiosity and mongrel spirituality. A colleague once chided me. Declaring that he was a Christian, he asked how anyone could claim to be "spiritual" or a "religious animal," both of which he took to indicate generic religiosity. Far from being generically religious, like some no-name product in a grocery store, my religiosity is piecemeal and idiosyncratic. Though it may be multiply fractured, it is glued together tolerably well—with spit and bailing wire.

PART ONE

INITIATING

If we ignore the ritual and magical paraphernalia of New Guinea manhood, how close it all is to the standard anxiety-drenched American conception of masculinity!

—David Gilmore[1]

All this claiming of superiority and imparting of inferiority belongs to the private school stage of human existence where there are "sides" and it is necessary for one side to beat another side, and of the utmost importance to walk up to a platform and receive from the hands of the headmaster a highly ornamental pot. As people mature, they cease to believe in sides or in headmasters or in highly ornamental pots.

—Virginia Woolf[2]

1

COWBOY
CHRISTIANITY

W ho initiates the North American adolescent male? Who cares enough? Who is wise enough? Who has a tradition sufficiently rich and nuanced? Your grandma? Your parent? Your boss? Your first sexual partner? If no one does, everybody does. If everybody does, no one does.

In most societies manhood is a status to be achieved. Whatever can be won can also be lost—thus the extraordinary fragility of manhood. The white, middle-class, North American version of masculinity is in the throes of a severe crisis even though, or because, men remain in power. The nature and value of our sort of manhood can no longer be taken for granted. There is no good or just reason for construing it as a generic norm for defining the whole of humanity. The critical questioning of our gender by women and nonwhite males leaves us drenched with anxiety. Many who are currently contemplating the dilemma suspect that the prize of manhood is an empty, though highly ornamental, pot, the competition for which we should outgrow.

Theorists argue that rites of passage thrive in small-scale societies and decay or die in large-scale industrial ones. If their claim is true, I wish it were not. In many of the smaller, more traditional ones initiations transform boys into men. They do so by clearly marking the transition with ceremony. Using protracted seclusion, physical exertion, and grueling ordeals, elders inscribe traditional knowledge in the bodies of initiates, thus ensuring the continuity of generations. This is the purpose of male initiation.

By contrast, coming of age in North America is extraordinarily diffuse—accomplished more by ritualization than by rites. The distinction is important and part of a larger set of terms including ritual, ritualization, ritualizing, and rites. "Ritual" refers to the idea; "rite," to the action designated by it. "Ritual" is general and abstract; "rite" is concrete and particular. Thus, I speak of "a rite," never "a ritual." "Rites" are differentiated from ordinary interaction. They are typically concentrated, focused, and named: Christian baptism, Jewish bar mitzvah, Muslim Ramadan, and so on. Rites are recognized by practitioners and defined by traditions.

"Ritualization" is less differentiated, more diffuse. The term denotes biological, psychological, or social processes that are not generally recognized as ritual but that can be seen as such. Lovemaking, housekeeping, canoeing, giving birth, footnoting, and TV watching are among the activities that scholars have treated as ritual—"ritualization" in my scheme. Others include the aggressive and mating activities of animals as well as neurotic and psychotic human behavior. Ritualization is largely preconscious or unconscious.

Since there are no culturewide rites of passage in North American society, most men undergo initiation without benefit of rites. Instead, they experience ritualization, usually in unconscious—sometimes in excruciating—ways. They go to war, visit prostitutes, play chicken, and obtain driver's licenses. A few try to invent rites of passage. Such efforts at ritual creativity constitute "ritualizing," the deliberate attempt to incubate ritual activity. The *-izing* suffix signals ritual processes that are less differentiated than rites but more deliberate than ritualization.

For most of us there was no coming-of-age party, much less a becoming-a-man rite. I came of age years ago. I am still doing it. My initiation, like that of many men, has not been an event but a messy process. Although other men have similar stories, our initiations into manhood were not undergone together, and they have not bonded us into an age cohort or gender group, nor have they allied us with a collective of respected elders. There are some conventional markers of manhood: getting a driver's license, having sexual experiences, leaving home, getting married, securing full-time employment, doing military service, graduating, becoming a father. Any of these, all of these, or none of these may function as transition markers, but these events are not in themselves rites, much less effective ones. Often they are driven by violent, unconscious ritualization.

In any particular man's life the conventional markers may not be the real ones. If I were to peruse the list of man-making events looking for the most formative moments of my own male adulthood, I would have to revise it to include leaving home for college, two marriages, one divorce, the death of my parents, the births of three children, and the death of one of them. My initiation does not coincide with a single ceremony, and it bleeds profusely into other ritual processes.

This process whereby one rite piggybacks on, evokes, or bleeds into another I call "ritual entailment." For example, say that a father's social circumstances or psychological constitution make it impossible for him to grieve at his daughter's funeral. A year later he attends the funeral of someone else's child and completes his grief work there. The first rite "entails" the second. Because initiation into manhood continues to be worked out in the context of other rites, we make a serious mistake if we consider one rite of passage in isolation from others. The work of one rite, I believe, often continues in another.

If we search out only the formal instances of initiation, we may miss the heart of the matter. For most North American males initiation is not a moment or an event but a puzzle of shards pieced together as we tell stories about our adolescence. In some cultures young men are ritually initiated by elders who are invested with the social and religious authority to transmit the wisdom of the tradition. In ours sedate middle-aged men invent their initiations by recollecting what they suffered and by inventing what they never quite underwent. We do not lack initiatory experiences or the ritualization of manhood, but we do lack shared, effective initiation rites. The few men who are formally initiated join clubs and fraternities in which a privileged few hold membership. So our few initiation rites divide us. They do not integrate us into a common masculinity, much less a common humanity.

In my mid-thirties I began to write a book of autobiographical fiction. Many of its stories were marked by initiatory motifs. They allowed me to meditate on the ways that the child is the father of the man, to borrow Wordsworth's apt phrase. They enabled me to play with the tangle of motives that characterized my formative years. They were means of negotiating my name, claiming my vocation, and contemplating the meaning of manhood.

Originally, the main character was called Ronnie, a name I gave up as I crossed the Texas state line on my way to college. From then on I was Ron, except on legal documents and scholarly books. I would have been Roxie had I been a girl. The decision about my name was made late one night as Mom and Dad (Nadine and Milton) were strolling back to their trailer house. They were on their way from a movie at the Roxy theater in San Diego, where they were working for Consolidated Aircraft during World War II. Since I was born a boy, I was dubbed Ronnie, officially Ronald, in honor of the star of the movie Mom and Dad saw that night. His full name—infamous in the circles I travel and famous in the only remaining superpower there is under heaven and on earth—I stubbornly refuse to put in print here.

The character soon took on a semi-independent life, and Ronnie became Harley. Harley, who is between eight and ten years old through most of the stories, began to develop ideas of his own that did not match what actually happened to Ronnie. The name change marked the beginning of the fictionalizing and mythmaking that were necessary for me to understand myself, particularly my religious formation, which was shot through with biblical and Hollywood imagery.

By the end of those never-published stories the reader begins to wonder who the narrator is. Is it the grown-up Harley, telling stories about himself in the third person? Or is it Harley's father, who overidentifies with his son, because the boy and he will soon be separated by a divorce? The narrator sounds omniscient, or at least fatherly, but at crucial points his rhetoric and perspective lapse into that of an eight-year-old. Father and son, in some peculiarly mythological way, seem to give birth to each other.

Harley is not sure what it will mean to become a man, much less a religious animal, and he struggles with the question adults are always putting to him: "What are you going to be when you become a man?"

When Lash LaRue came in the flesh to the Lyceum on Main Street, he wore black. Carrying his whip curled around his shoulder, he walked onto the stage as soon as one of his movies was over. They'd promised he would. To Harley, Lash was not as big as he had seemed on the screen. There he was bigger than life. But that little guy onstage—was that really him? He was short, just about the size of a normal human being, one with short legs. A lady with long white legs held Coke bottles, while Mr. LaRue snapped their caps off with his whip. He had a blacksnake whip. He said so. That was what he called it. Harley strained to see whether it had a head or rattles, but the action was too far away to tell. He was sitting where he usually sat on Saturdays, in an aisle seat halfway down the left side so his mom could find him.

The long-legged woman wore a black bathing suit. She was probably the wife of Lash LaRue, Harley guessed, because she let him pop cigarettes out of her mouth, and because they looked into each other's eyes. But Harley could not recall what movie she was from. Maybe she wasn't his wife after all. He wished Mr. LaRue was his father. No he didn't; he changed his mind. What if he got a whipping from this guy who used a whip to stop fleeing outlaws? Wow! And Harley would have a different mother for every movie, because the black-haired, long-legged one onstage was not the only woman Harley had seen Mr. LaRue with. Why did Lash LaRue stay the same and his wives change from movie to movie?

Harley was shy. Still, he waved his hand high and even stood up when the performers asked for volunteers. But they chose a girl—of all people—to come onstage. She tried to crack the blacksnake whip but couldn't. Finally, a fourteen-year-old boy succeeded. Everybody but Harley cheered. He wished the girl had cracked it, because the boy was a bully who had declared to the world that Harley sucked. Harley had been furious. The accusation made him remember Elmer, a little calf covered with slobber and froth who goosed his mother for milk. The calf's nose was soft and wet, and his eyelashes were long. Harley got mad when people said he had long eyelashes like a girl or big brown eyes like a cow. He did not suck! And he hated being called a suck by some big bully who got to pop the whip. Harley's mom said that as a baby, Harley had bit a lot, so he knew he was capable of more than sucking. He could bite. Hard.

When Mrs. LaRue pointed to Harley, saying, "Young man, come up here," he gulped and stumbled as he climbed over legs longer than his. Eventually, he reached the edge of the stage that jutted out from the movie screen, and LaRue yanked him up onto it. The boy's blood rushed when the man and the lady both laid hands on his shoulders. He wished he could marry them. And whipping wouldn't matter. If they would just be his mom and dad.

LaRue had pulled out a gun, something he never used in his movies. The movie star was talking about his six-gun to the kids, assuring them that he used blanks, that he would never really kill people, and that children should not play with real ones. This one had no real bullets in it. He went on for a long time about safety. Even Harley was getting antsy with the moralizing.

Then Mr. LaRue shocked and confused his young audience by declaring like a ringmaster that he was going to have a shoot-out with this young man. He had chosen Harley, who was instantly filled with stage fright and on the edge of tears at the thought of shooting it out with a movie star who was better than a heavenly father who gave out golden crowns.

Harley was a puppet—led here, turned this way, pointed in that direction. The lady thrust a pistol at him, belted a holster around his waist, and strapped the bottom of it around his thigh. She topped him out with a white hat, kid-size, which Harley still has to this very day.

He and Lash LaRue faced each other across the stage. The lady, the fourteen-year-old, and the little girl who couldn't crack the whip stood near the movie star. Envy filled the fourteen-year-old. Trembling and tears filled Harley. His throat clamped shut. His belly was doing somersaults. He didn't want to kill Mr. LaRue, who was a good guy—even if he did dress in black. Who was going to be the bad guy in this shoot-out? Harley wanted the movie star for a dad; he did not want to be a Wanted guy with a price on his head.

But the lady was already counting, slowly making her way to three, at which number the two "men" were supposed to draw. One. Two. Harley's hand, unnoticed by all but the fourteen-year old, was already on its way to the pearl handle of his pistol. Desperately, he wanted to be a man. He labored to yank the pistol free of its holster and to point it in the right direction while looking deep into Lash LaRue's strangely blue eyes. He knew exactly how it was supposed to be done; he had practiced his fast-draw on the goats at home. The stiffness of his holster forced him to glance down as he grabbed the holster with his left hand so he could get the gun out with his right.

"Three."

He drew and fired. Smoke burned his eyes. His ears were ringing. The girls, and even a few boys, screamed. His heart was drumming dents into his chest bones. Lash LaRue lay sprawled on the stage, his hand clutching his stomach. Harley was numbed by the sight. For a second or two the theater fell silent as a tomb. Then Mr. LaRue peeked up at Harley, bounced back to life, strode across the stage, and hugged the boy off his feet and up into the air. Everyone was cheering when *his favorite bull-whipping cowboy whispered in Harley's ear, "Thanks, son." He patted the boy on the rear and sent all three kids back to their seats. The lady touched Harley on the head. She smiled in a way that made him, for a second time, want to marry her.*

For years Harley kept a secret that made him strong. The only hint of its content was deeply buried in a song he yodeled while strolling around the cow pens. He called it "I Am Just a Poor Christian Cowboy." He didn't tell anyone until he was almost grown that he had turned the barrel of the gun just a little to the left and shot the fourteen-year-old. No Christian cowboy should shoot a movie star, especially one who called him son.

For a faculty colloquium I let some colleagues read the Harley stories. Repeatedly, they came back to this one. Was it true? Did it really happen? They liked the drama of it. The fact that I still wore boots, even though I was an American professor in a Canadian university, made them suspect the event had happened just as I had told it. They knew I had been reared and steeped in the cowboy Christianity of New Mexico. As a professor of religious studies, I could not easily hide my religious background from colleagues, no matter how vigorously I may have rejected it or how studiously I may have insisted that I did not teach religion; I taught about it. Even so, I resisted answering their queries, because I wanted to talk about the stories and the character I was struggling to create.

As narratives often do, the Harley stories evoked other stories in response. Most of the ones that colleagues told me that day were more autobiographical (but probably no less fictional) than the ones I had written. There were no women in the department, and some of the men began to tell stories of their adolescence, tales of the struggle for religious identity and of the difficulties of becoming a man. We surprised ourselves with our frankness and intimacy. This was to have been a scholarly colloquium. I remember saying that I had never undergone a *real* initiation. Therefore, I quipped, in the stories I had begun to invent one. But my memory is a tricky and temperamental beast. Later, I remembered that I had, in fact, undergone a formal initiation rite.

Ghostly shapes were lumbering around the huge circle of young men; it was three layers deep. Adolescents and a few adults were perched on logs in the mountain air of the thickening night. Elbows on their knees, some were hunched over trying to keep warm. All were eager, their bellies trembling. They wanted to be chosen; they didn't want to be chosen.

A scream punctuated the smoky silence as one of the ghostly shapes dusted someone with a fog of white powder, slapped an arrow to his chest, and forcibly crossed his arms over the arrow. Then the ghostly ones, clad in generic Indian garb, grabbed the newly tapped-out arrow-bearer with a fierceness that took the boy's breath away. Running, the initiators dragged the initiate to a teepee and rolled him roughly through the half-open flap that was its door.

Senior members of the Order of the Arrow had somberly walked past me several times without stopping in front of me. My heart had already settled down for a night's lodging in my throat when, without warning, the initiating "Indians" whirled on their heels and sprang up frighteningly close to my face. One of the men—surely these were not just painted-up boys—yanked me to my feet. He flung flour in my face, then all over the front of my blue denim, pearl-snap shirt. When my trembling hand finally managed to clench the arrow securely, there was a five-second eternity during which I was able to stand proudly, certain that every other boy could see the glow of my face through the dark.

I didn't mind being yanked this way and that on the way to the teepee. The hands seemed sure enough of their destination, and I rolled easily through the door. The surprise was that the teepee had no back. It was a mere front, a Hollywood set in the southern Rockies.

I had witnessed the tapping-out ceremony before, so I could imagine the awe with which other Scouts were witnessing this one. A few more boys would be chosen. There would be more heavy silence, broken by the ominous tom-tom beat that marked the circumambulation of the initiators. There would be a few more terrifyingly primitive yells to remind us that we the civilized were on the edge of civilization. Then the Great Spirit, whom none of us had ever addressed in church, would be invoked. He (we were sure of his gender) would make his presence known by fire. A great ball of it would fall from the sky onto the apex of the teepee. Only the uninitiated would not know that it was assisted by kerosene-soaked rags and a guy-wire running from a treetop. The campers would gasp, sure their fellow campers had been burned to a crisp. The older ones would have the whole affair rationalized within the hour but would keep the secret from the younger ones. They would tell the younger ones that we initiates were dead.

Before the ceremony we had heard stories. Some guys claimed they had hiked to the sacred grounds on the day before the ceremony. There, just outside the circle, they found kerosene, wire, and a perch in a tree. One or two boasted that they had walked straight across the consecrated circle. Here they were, alive to tell the story. We knew such an act was flagrant desecration, but we hungered after the truths that the violators promised to reveal. We wanted to believe, and didn't want to believe, what they said.

We who had been tapped out were sent into camp to get bedrolls and a match. If we talked to our fellow Scouts, who would be returning about the time we were exiting from camp, we would be expelled from the Order of the Arrow. Certain that silence increased my stature, I said nothing when flogged by questions from my tentmates. Solemnly, I gazed at them. I could now afford to become the strong silent type. The gaze shut them up. In awe, one kid muttered, "Something has happened to him."

"Yeah," another chimed in, "the Great Spirit."

Carrying my sleeping bag to the rendezvous point, I pondered the Great Spirit, this Indian god in whom none of us believed but in awe of whom we undoubtedly were. I pushed the theological problem aside, thinking, "Church camp is one thing; Scout camp, another."

Deftly, senior members of the Order of the Arrow blindfolded the dozen or so of us and then instructed us in walking backward. It began to drizzle as they split us up. Eventually, each boy was led, rear end first, in a different direction. Soon I was a solitary backward-walking initiate accompanied by two anonymous guides. Eventually, I was allowed to turn around. My belly and lower bowels began to shift uneasily at the sound of thunder and the crackle of lightning.

"I must be able to do this, or they wouldn't have picked me," I whispered in a quiet, fatherly voice trying to comfort my fifteen-year-old self. I remembered my sash, which, unfortunately, I didn't have on, or I would have fondled its three long rows of merit badges awarded for camping skills and survival tactics. As a mere Protestant, I had no rosary to clutch, so I tried to envision the silver Eagle medal that would be pinned on my chest in a few months. It would hang there alongside the God and Country Award and the Order of the Arrow medal I was in the process of earning. Mom would be called to stand at my side. She was short. That would make me feel tall, though I had not yet reached five feet, ten inches—Dad's height. Oh well, he was a man; I was a teenager, with pimples. During the ceremony he, my two brothers, and my sister would sit in the pews as I faced them from the sanctuary.

"I am no Tenderfoot. I can do this," I whispered, hoping the guides did not hear.

I had been held off a year. The scoutmaster had insisted that it made no difference that I had satisfied the requirements for Eagle Scout. I was too young. If I got it, he had said, I would just get bored and quit. You need to be sixteen or better, eighteen, he had insisted. I wasn't quite fifteen.

Trudging through the forest in boots now thoroughly wet, I replayed yet another scenario, a summer spent at an aquatic camp for Scouts:

The water safety instructor was impressed with my speed at undressing. I held the camp record: eight seconds. Cowboy boots with no laces, shirts with pearl-button snaps—these were the secret.

The water in the Carlsbad River was impenetrable—so murky that a swimmer couldn't see his own feet. Howard had assured us that he knew we couldn't see but that we were to keep swimming until we touched him. If we came up behind him, that was okay; the drowning man couldn't see us there. But if we were so damned foolish as to come up in front of a drowning man, he warned, we deserved to get drowned ourselves. The thought of a life-or-death struggle terrified us dry-behind-the-ears sons of desert rats.

Howard Brawn, a grown man, was drowning. Ronnie, a mere boy with short legs and short breath, was scheduled to save him. Already in the water, down I went, arms searching. I couldn't find my victim, so, out of breath, I surfaced—in front of him.

Howard was built like Charles Atlas. He sported an expansive bronze chest and long, hairy legs. How I wished to borrow, if not steal, them! With a name like Howard Brawn, why would anyone need saving? Ronnie Grimes—what kind of a name was that?

Howard grabbed my neck, thrashing me up and down until I was crying, spewing, fighting, drowning. When I finally got loose—it never occurred to me that he had let me go—I swam to the dock and refused to go back in the water. I was embarrassed, certain about what all the other guys thought.

What got me back in the river was not Howard's coaxing or threatening but my recollecting the story of Dad's airplane crash. Ever since I was a kid I'd seen the crumbling newspaper picture of him standing beside his trainer plane with what we brothers agreed was a shit-eating grin on his face. Somehow, he had saved a few dollars from farmwork and dishwashing. He'd invested it in a pilot-training course. On his first solo he hung his rear wheel or rudder—I forget which—on a power line, cutting off the electricity to Portales during a report of election results. Milton, the article assured its readers, came down in a big hurry, a ball of fire threatening to roast the underbelly of his plane. His instructor made him go back up immediately in another plane.

In the woods, in the river, I was with Dad. Maybe I was Dad. I was the one blushing at remarks overheard in Portales about attempted election sabotage. I was the one not allowed to hesitate. I had to go back up.

Coaxed and cajoled, I jumped back into the river to rescue Howard, wishing that he were my father or that I were he and he, me. A few feet away from his thrashing and drowning histrionics, I dived beneath the murk. My lungs were ready to burst, but I found his ankles and turned him so I could slither up his backside, get my arm across his shoulder, and set a grip on his pectoral muscle. I was a pair of vice-grips borrowed from a tractor's toolbox. Howard rolled and flailed and carried on, but I dragged the son of a bitch back to shore. When he stood up, smiling on my behalf, blood was running down his armpit.

The "Indians" kept muttering as if to one another, "What was that sound? There are reports of bears and wousers in this neck of the woods. Wousers come out during thunderstorms, don't they?" Surely they didn't think I still believed that shit about wousers—half lion, half bear.

Eventually, they abandoned me, leaving only my match and wet sleeping bag for company. "Find a snag," they had said, as if I were a novice. I noticed that they had posted me near the required lightning trap. This tall dead tree, worthy of a gothic novel, was supposed to save my life by drawing lighting to itself, but its creakiness only added to the terror of the ordeal. All night I heard a jungle of

Eagle Scout, with pimples

sounds—owls, bears, lions, wousers in which I did not believe. I felt snakes and worms slithering in my bed, spiders too. I had no visions. I felt no calm—the assumed result of my competence in the wilderness. I just endured, scared.

The next afternoon I found my way back to camp and entered as I was supposed to, ass first, backing into the dining hall, where I was cheered as a survivor and newly made mentor.

This is the only story I can tell of a real initiation rite. Does "real" belong in quotation marks? It must have been successful, because it happened in the woods. It must have been real, because I soon received an invitation from the governor of New Mexico. He sent his private plane from Santa Fe to Clovis, from the *axis mundi* to the *anus mundi* of the southwestern universe. The plane picked me up for dinner at Bishop's Lodge back in Santa Fe. I had never been to the state capital and had never flown in an airplane. In the photo Governor Burroughs is shaking my hand. Not only does a white sash bearing a flame-red arrow cross my chest, but an Eagle medal also hangs above my pocket.

Some would say that I underwent a successful initiation. But did I really? Forgotten, the event could have exercised formative force. But did it? I will never know. It makes a good story, but did it make a man? If it did operate as a paradigm, why did I need the Lash LaRue story many years later? What was I initiated into? Manhood? The upper echelon of Explorer Scouts? Indianhood? Outdoorsiness?

No sooner did I achieve the rank of Eagle than I gave up Scouting. The scoutmaster had been right. As soon as I achieved what there was to achieve, I was out and gone. I had an additional impetus. Not long after my initiation into the Order of the Arrow, Explorer Scout headquarters announced that it was retiring our forest green uniforms. It proposed to dress us in blue blazers with brass buttons. The emphasis was going to become more social, the post adviser said, less outdoorsy. We were going to learn about dating decorum and sex, he said. As if we didn't already know, we retorted.

Besides the story itself, all that consciously remains of my initiation is that I am not afraid of the dark, I can still tie knots, and I frighten Bryn and Caleigh with ghost stories. When I read *The Ghost-Eye Tree*, little do they know that the old oak of their book is the snag of my ordeal.

Whether or not the event was effective, it now seems in retrospect to be an instance of ritual exploitation enacted at a time before scholars invented the label "cultural appropriation." Many years after my initiation into the Order of the Arrow, I recalled the event after buying some Iroquois masks. Tags hung from Broken Nose and Wind Blower. Each note asked the purchaser to respect these sacred masks and to refrain from using them in pseudo-Indian ceremonies. In my Indigenous Religions course we talked about the masks and discussed the problems with white appropriation of Native spirituality. I counseled students against "Indian" initiations and vision quests.

The hunger for initiation in white North America is deep and dangerous. One only has to read *Shaman's Drum* or other such magazines to witness the lengths to which we European Americans will go in imitating Native Americans. We raid other people's cultures for symbols with which to stud our initiations. Rites of Passage, Inc., for instance, initiates hundreds of teenagers a year and not just in California. In class I say critical things about the *Shaman's Drum* ethos, but my initiation into the Order of the Arrow leaves me no very solid ground to stand on as I launch my polemics. My only defense is that the initiation was in the past and that I now try to adhere to some basic ethical criteria. I condense them into proverbs that would-be ritualizers can memorize and, with luck, remember: Trading, not raiding. Borrowing implies the consent of the owner. Dancing with wolves is dangerous if one is not a wolf. Respect ceremonial privacy with the same zeal that one exercises in locking the bathroom door.

Even those who are not initiated into quasi-Indian groups sometimes long for them, filling their heads with initiatory fervor and the hot desire for vision questing. Robert Moore and Douglas Gillette in *King, Warrior, Magician, Lover*[3] argue that men can become men (and thus be relieved of the necessity to oppress others) only by being initiated. There is considerable truth to this claim, but what do they take as their model of initiation? The movie *The Emerald Forest,* an initiatory fantasy that is as ethnocentric and sexist as any I know. In it a fair-skinned, blond boy is taken by some Latin American natives. There are the predictable face paint and the predictable love interest. She is a girl who looks less native than the rest. Like *Dances with Wolves* and *Black Robe,* the movie is a white man's (actually, boy's) fantasy enacted in a manner that confirms centuries-old stereotypes. I am not opposed to ritual fantasy, but without a sustained critique of ritual, such imagining becomes a license for interethnic and cross-cultural imperialism.

The question remains: Where does one—in my case, a white, middle-class male—find elders? The search for initiation is often a search for power, which is why it is dangerous. It should be a search for wisdom and wise uses of power. Men think they need ordeals, tests, and the outdoors. There is nothing natural about the need; it is culturally generated. But this origin in culture, rather than nature, does not make the scenario any less compelling.

We ride the horns of a dilemma. If we can't *really* be initiated with *real* initiation rites, then initiatory scenarios spring up unbidden everywhere—the return of what was repressed by the Enlightenment and Reformation. And even if we have been initiated into adulthood, the bewildering complexity of contemporary adult life would likely require periodic reinitiation.

2

GOOD GUYS
AND THE WILES
OF PERFECTION

*H*arley was going to be a cowboy when he grew up. Or a preacher. They were the
two biggest guys he knew. One he saw on Saturdays at the picture show, his hands
busy with popcorn and a spare buffalo nickel that turned his sweating hand
green. The other he heard shouting and pleading on Sundays. In church Harley
passed the dreary hour laden with creeds, prayers, and responsive readings by filling out blank checks—always in the amount of a million dollars, always made
out to himself. They should have been on their way from the Citizen's Bank to
God. As he filled out dates on generic checks, he remembered how glad he had
been when finally he could write 50 instead of 49 after the preprinted 19.

Harley was a Methodist and he went to Trinity Methodist Church, because John
Wesley and Francis Asbury used methods like reading their Bibles while riding
horses to spread the word. They were the first cowboy Christians, so ever since,
Christian cowboys—probably even John Wayne and Gary Cooper but for sure Roy
Rogers and Hopalong Cassidy and Gene Autry—have all been Methodists or Bap-
tists. Harley declared it so.

He had heehawed when Miss Agatha, his Sunday School teacher, said the
Wesley brothers were taunted with the labels "Bible moth" and "Methodist." He
knew what it was like to be teased about being a sissy, a goody-two-shoes Christian, or a suck. Each name bore its own special pain.

The Methodist Church was the right place all right, because Uma, Harley's
grandma, had said Peter Cartwright was an old-time Methodist who had
pounded the Gospel into some rowdies at a camp meeting in Kentucky. Peter
Cartwright must have been a cowboy Christian too. Big Papa and Uma had come

in a wagon to New Mexico before it was a state, so they ought to know. They were cowboys, too.

During revivals Brother Boomershine would smash his fist into the Bible. The sound made Harley think of Peter Cartwright. Later, at home, Harley would punch his little New Testament, hoping for the same sound. Brother Boomershine wore gigantic black shoes with laces; they were not boots. The absence of boots bothered Harley, but the preacher's thundering voice and massive hands more than made up for the defect.

Harley daydreamed of being a cowboy preacher, but he didn't know any. He knew preachers, and he knew cowboys, but no cowboy preachers. One preacher he liked wore a silver belt buckle, but never on Sunday to church. Brother Boomershine was as close as anybody had come to being a Christian cowboy. But he couldn't have ridden a horse if he had to. Still, he could drive a pick-up like a Texas Ranger. That was pretty close.

Harley wanted to be a Good Guy when he grew up. He wanted to be a hero who helped women in distress and black people like Samaritans who fell in the ditch. He would be a friend to poor people whom the Scribes and Pharisees wouldn't touch but would walk away from to the other side of the road.

To be a Good Guy you had to kill only Bad Guys, so you had to know how to shoot straight and hit just what you wanted to hit. You had to have strong hands but be able to touch babies without hurting or bruising them. Babies are delicate. A Good Guy doesn't let bullies push around people that Jesus likes. He likes people who don't have any power or much money.

Harley wanted to build muscles big enough to protect and defend people who suffered. He wanted to be able to protect his mom, because she cried. Jesus loves those who cry out for justice. But Dad didn't cry, so Jesus must love Mom more.

Harley didn't cry much either. He was going to be a man and help people who cried. He was going to be a blessed peacemaker, a sheriff for the Lord. When he felt like crying, he usually got mad instead. That's what Good Guys do. They get mad at the Bad Guys who make people cry.

One day Mom was crying. Harley found her hiding in the chicken house. He didn't know what to do with her. Or himself. He guessed he had made her cry, because she wouldn't say why she was doing it. He didn't see any Bad Guys around— no priests or Levites or outlaws. And Dad was a good guy, so Mom's tears couldn't be his fault. Harley began to worry that he himself was the Bad Guy. But he hadn't done anything, so he got mad without having anybody to be mad at.

Later that afternoon Harley recovered an old picture of Jesus from the basement. The savior had long hair like a woman, and he was knocking at the heart's thorn-covered door. Harley sneaked into the garage and drove his fist through the dusty old print. His action made him feel bad. He consoled himself by remembering that when he became a cowboy preacher, he would be filled with wisdom and power and the Holy Ghost. Then he would know what makes moms cry and why the rich oppress the poor.

Without imagination, ritual suffers. The dramatic imagination is not always so personal and violent as Harley's, but induction into manhood without the social drama of interpersonal conflict is virtually unheard of. Harley both resists and is complicit with the fictive and literal violence of the American Southwest. His cowboy Christianity is morally torn, split between the "turn the other cheek" ethic of Sunday school and the "punch 'em out" morality of Saturday movies. Harley shoots to kill but only at Bad Guys—those who start the trouble, threaten the weak, or fail to respect girls and their mothers. Sometimes he loses track of who is good and who is evil. Then he shoots himself in the foot.

Writing the Harley stories forced me to reflect on the relation of performance to ritual and of ritual to experience and memory. Ritual performance is ritual as actually done and witnessed. But even when ritual is performed by a group, it is experienced differently by different individuals. One person is ecstatic about a celebration; another is bored by it. This person thinks it means one thing; that one thinks it means something else. To the elders it means this; to young initiates, that. So ritual experience—what one takes away from, or gets out of, a rite—is not the same as ritual performance. Most accounts of ritual are of ritual texts or of ritual performance. Very few are accounts of experience.

After an experience we are left with the residue of its memory. Ritual memory further filters and shapes ritual experience. Like performance of any sort—for example, that encountered in theater—ritual performance is momentary. Elaborate preparation may lead up to it, and it may taper out ever so slowly. But one day the dancers quit dancing and the drummers quit drumming, and ritualists are left with their memories. They may forget entire portions of a rite or even the whole thing, just as I forgot my initiation. They may misremember a ceremony, not merely leaving things out but even getting it all wrong. Someone who was there dancing alongside the ritualists corrects them. Ritual recalled is not identical with ritual performed, ritual experienced, or ritual as prescribed in a ritual text.

Once I participated in a project run by several prominent Catholic liturgy centers. Interested in the effectiveness of the post–Vatican II mass, interviewers asked parishioners who had just come from a worship service what they remembered. Researchers were surprised at what participants could not remember. The interviewers wondered, Does this failure to recall details mean that the liturgy is meaningless? I thought not. Perhaps worshipers' tongues and spines remember when their mouths (with which to recount) and their hands (with which to write) do not. Ritual memory is not always accessible to that part of the brain that verbalizes. One remembers in all sorts of ways. I remember how to find a wonderful Greek restaurant in Toronto; I can drive there. But I cannot tell my friends how to find it; I don't remember the names of the streets. I can make a good Chinese dish, but each time someone asks for the recipe, I am unable to provide it. My hands remember. My tasting tongue remembers, but my speaking tongue does not. To be effective, initiations need to be memorable, but minds are not the only parts of human beings that do the remembering. Bodies, too, remember; they remember what has been dismembered.

Early in the summer of 1961, having just graduated from high school, I knew that I was about to become a man. The hood ornament of a new-to-me black '54 Mercury was aimed in the direction of Sacramento, New Mexico. I was ecstatic to be departing the great sandbox that the maps call the Llano Estacado, the "staked [high] plains" of eastern New Mexico and the Texas panhandle. Dad had surprised me by sneaking the Merc up to the loading dock at Sears, where he found me soaked with sweat, unloading line-haul trucks. I was speechless. The gift was his way of recognizing that I was on the threshold of manhood and of mending fences torn asunder by my adolescence. Most of our man-to-man conversations had either been about or under cars. He left sex talk to Mom, and she had done that when I was eight.

One of Dad's favorite weekend pastimes was to cruise local car lots, test-driving used cars. This was his recreation, also his form of sociability. "Gabbing," Mom called it. The salesmen knew him and liked chewing the fat with him, though they considered him a cheap old buzzard because he seldom traded cars. Or if he did, he doggedly haggled away their profit margins. Mom insisted that he traded cars like her dad had traded cows: too often with too little consultation.

A few days after getting the black Mercury, mythologized as Ghost Rider in the sky, I received a call from Sacramento Methodist Assembly, a church camp not far from the Scout camp where I had been initiated into the Order of the Arrow. I was to be on the staff and report to work in a week. Landing such a job evoked great expectations. Everyone knew that girls longed to date males on staff. Staff were older men. It made no difference that my new job consisted of washing dishes or that I was only eighteen. I had graduated. I was employed. I was an older man.

Folks at Trinity—Grandma chief among them—were proud of me. I carried the flag of *real* Methodism, the fierce frontier stuff of Peter Cartwright, not the namby-pamby liberal intellectualism of SMU-educated ministers who read their sermons and prayers. I had a calling; they merely had a profession. At Grandma's instigation the pastor had consented to my preaching a farewell sermon to the congregation at Trinity Methodist Church. I don't remember what I said, only that I wore red socks, black pants, and black shoes with a white streak of lightning down the sides. Darrell, my brother, still teases me about them. I accuse him of envy. My dress was a matter of some minor controversy, but the congregation tolerated it. The faithful wanted to hear a few parting words from its would-be evangelist. I had recently been licensed to preach in Fort Sumner, where Billy the Kid is buried and where the Navajos were incarcerated by Kit Carson at the end of their infamous Long Walk. Thirty years later the irony of being made a minor clergyman at such a site would dawn on me. I ended the sermon with a fundamentalist's defiant invitation: "Would anyone who believes there is an error in the Bible show it to me after the service?" No one came to take up the gauntlet. I had not yet heard the phrase "preaching to the converted."

What a sound! The dual exhausts blubbered through their deeply resonant glass-packed mufflers as I shifted down into first to keep my new Merc from becoming a runaway horse in one of the canyons approaching Sacramento. Who can know what it means when a boy's dad not only allows him to sport glass packs but actually buys him a car with such trumpets attached! I was exiting from Clovis in glory. I would work the summer at church camp and then drive east to Kentucky, where, among horses munching green grass and girls wearing long dresses, I would start college and thus begin the long trek to ordination.

On the way to camp I had plenty of time to replay the summer weeks spent there in previous years. Each was connected with a girl's name: the summer of Kathie K., the summer of Judy J. The list was long. Every day at church camp replayed itself. Each was an endless date with the right girl. Each came to a heart-warming, sunset-blessed close around a bonfire surrounded by hundreds of hand-holders singing, "Kumbayah,"—"Come by here, Lord, come by here." Camp counselors never taught us to spell or translate these words. My old Nazarene buddy Loren used to say, "With God behind you and your girl beside you, what can go wrong?" Back then the question was rhetorical. Today I could answer it.

There was the summer of Kathie K. She endured the longest. The relationship (a word that did not exist then) continued for two years. She was from Kermit, Texas, and from a broken home. I associated the phrase with foster homes, homes for the elderly, and funeral homes. My home wasn't broken. I could promise her what she had not had since she was three, a real family. Kermit was near Abilene, a town famous in cowboy songs. I had been tempted to apply for admission to McMurry College just to be close to her, but prayer and holy roulette with college catalogs dictated otherwise. Texas may have had beautiful women—hair all sprayed and pouffed—but spiritually it was decadent. For us poor-but-pious Protestant New Mexicans, Texas was Babylon. I was headed for Kentucky, Peter Cartwright country and the home of Davey Crockett. I longed to live where trees were green, religion real, and horses fast.

I drove into church camp with the cameras rolling in my head. They were recording my biography, the inspirational power of which would rival that of Peter Marshall's *A Man Called Peter.* The fact that my horse was black rather than white, metal rather than flesh, did not trouble me; I had met Lash LaRue face to face. I hung my elbow out the window keenly aware of what a figure I was cutting. My profile was framed through the window of a two-door hardtop. Surely the girls, when they arrived in a week, could hardly help noticing my new status. Following Saint Paul's counsel, I had given up childish things like bicycles and motorcycles. A car owner, I had even sacrificed the black motorcycle jacket with my name splashed across the back. It had been an accessory that stirred ambivalence in everyone—parents, employer, girlfriends, churchfolk. This car could evoke only one response. In case it didn't, surely my position on the staff would. I drove into camp a man.

The camp director, Dr. Bolen, was a retired district superintendent, a DS who had locked horns with Grandma, so I was surprised that he had hired me. Perhaps he had not made the connection between her and me. She was a Williams; I, a Grimes. He led me to the dining hall as if I didn't know where it was. He gave me personal dishwashing lessons, as if my mother hadn't.

"You don't just dip a washed dish in hot rinse water," he instructed. "You let it steep. That way it will dry itself quickly when it comes out."

I had to admit that his way was superior to Mom's. I was excited by learning something new, trivial though it was. The old man was going to teach me. I was the sorcerer's apprentice.

In preparation for the coming week, which promised the arrival of campers, we scrubbed and raked. I washed, swept, hauled lumber, dutifully carrying out the orders of the director and senior staff. I was as obedient as a lamb. "Happy as a pig in shit," Mom had chuckled on the phone. (There was a liberal streak to her Methodism.) On the fifth day it became evident that the good doctor—it was an honorary degree—was including Sunday in the work schedule that he had posted on a log pillar in the dining hall. Although I had delivered newspapers at 2:00 A.M. on Sunday mornings for several years, I had recently been convinced by Grandma that labor and commerce on Sundays were a sin. She even urged me to give up Sunday recreation if it cost money and thereby caused other people to work. Eventually, I weaned myself from all Sunday work—except, of course, "when the ox was in the ditch." Wife of a cattleman, she had to allow the one Biblical exception and its modern-day metaphoric extensions.

I went to the district superintendent (he will always remain the DS, since the title evokes marines and drill sergeants) and told him of my dilemma. "I will work overtime on Saturday," I said. "If the ox is really in the ditch, I will work on Sunday afternoon and evening if you will allow me, please, to go down the mountain to the village church on Sunday morning." I was unusually courteous and resisted saying how surprised I was that he himself was not conducting Sunday services for the dozen or so of us on staff.

"No," he said, "you will work all day Sunday."

"That's really necessary?" I queried.

He clearly considered the question insubordinate but simply said yes without further qualification.

Grudgingly, I said okay and left. We worked three hours Sunday morning and were finished an hour or so after church would have ended down in the valley. I was furious. Late Sunday afternoon I went to see Dr. Bolen and pointed out the obvious. It was his turn to be furious. The inquisition that followed must have lasted a quarter of an hour.

"Who do you think you are?" (I would be asked this question numerous times in the coming years, almost always by the heads of institutions. The last question I would be asked during my doctoral examination was, "Who do you think you are? You are here for us to question; we are not here for you to question!")

"You know who I am. I am the employee who wanted to go to church this morning, like I do every Sunday."

"Where are you going to college, boy?" he queried, changing the subject.

"Why do you ask?" I swelled at being called boy.

"Don't be smart. Answer the question."

"Kentucky Wesleyan."

"Kentucky Wesleyan? Why aren't you going to Texas Wesleyan or McMurry or SMU?"

"Because I am tired of sand, and I like grass. Besides, most of the ministers who come from those places don't know how to preach."

He had graduated from Texas Wesleyan, and he countered in a devious way, "Years ago Kentucky Wesleyan offered me a football scholarship, and I turned them down."

I didn't tell him that Kentucky Wesleyan did not have a football team and that I knew he was bullshitting.

"If you go there, you had better keep your hand on your wallet. All they want is your money."

"What is that supposed to mean?" I was genuinely puzzled.

"It means that if you go there, don't bother to come back to the New Mexico Conference of the Methodist Church."

The logic escaped me. All I could say was, "Don't worry. I won't." Then I decided to push back, "What if they do only want my money? What does that have to do with not coming back here?"

He leaned toward me and hissed, "You're from Trinity, aren't you? You're just like that whole bunch there, always raising hell about something, never satisfied with anything. Who the hell do you people think you are? And your grandmother, she is the worst of the lot, always ranting and raving about alcohol, poor preaching, or some other crap. Why can't you people act like normal Methodists?"

I wasn't shocked to hear the word "hell." Mom and Dad used it often enough. But I was shocked to hear a Methodist DS using such language. At me. At church camp. On Sunday.

"Because normal Methodist churches are indifferent and you know what God says he will do with the indifferent."

"Do you want your check now?"

"What?"

"I think you should consider quitting your job and going home. I will not tolerate insubordination. It is clear that we'll not get along for an entire summer."

"I don't want to quit. I came here to work." I was enraged and a man, but I could feel my bottom lip quiver.

"If it is necessary again to work on Sundays, will you do it?" he asked, testing me. I knew I had to be as wise as a serpent and as harmless as a dove.

"Do you mean, will I do it if only three hours of work are necessary—three hours I could put in on Saturday or Sunday afternoon?"

"That's what I mean."

"You mean, will I obey your commands regardless of what I believe to be right?" I was visibly red.

"That's what I mean."

"I'll think about it," I said in a voice that was beginning to crack.

"You do that. Think about it and come see me in my office after supper."

I was devastated. I climbed "Kumbayah" Mountain crying, swearing, and avoiding the use of God's name in vain but invoking all the other sacred and profane vocabulary I had at my disposal. When I ran out of words in English, I switched to the Spanish expressions I had learned from Art Griego.

Back in my cabin I played Bible roulette, randomly opening the Good Book, searching for divinatory advice. Whatever appeared, it was not memorable. The Heavenly Father remained silent, so I called Dad. I recounted the story to him. He was magnificently angry. I had grown up knowing that however much racket he and I made butting heads, he would always come through when the shit hit the fan. "Tell that son of a bitch to go to hell. You come on home if you want to. I saw Les the other day, and he said they'd like to have you back at Sears." Piety restrained Dad's anger less then than it would in his later years. He still had the vocabulary with which to rise to considerable rhetorical heights on such an occasion. He sensed my shame and encouraged me not to give returning a second thought. I could hardly bear the thought of arriving back in Clovis after having been fired from church camp. No one in its history had ever been fired. I was sure of it.

After supper I went to the DS's office, ready to resign. He didn't give me a chance. The check was already written out. He handed it to me in silence. I received it in silence.

The next morning I gunned Ghost Rider, black, into the rising, blinding sun. I was burning. So was it.

Sears Shipping and Receiving was in fact glad to have me back. I was a worker, Les assured me. After a couple of weeks I was able to untuck my tail from between my legs. Dad helped by being so unabashedly outraged on my behalf. After a month Mom gently suggested that I might try seeing the humor in the story.

"If you don't develop a sense of humor," she advised, "you are going to have a hard life." She was right.

The summer's work was boring, but Les, my supervisor, was himself full of stories and jokes. He teased me until the day I headed east for college.

"You should have been a camp director," I told him.

"Why are you going to Kentucky Wesleyan?" he would mock, trying to sound like the DS.

"I am taking a golden hatchet," I would tease, "to smash up all those whisky bottles." I knew how to hit him where it hurt.

"Oh, God! Oh, God!" he would howl. "All that wonderful whisky, you crazy kid. When are you gonna learn that God gave those Kentuckians a gift? They were meant to share it with the world—with all of us desert rats here in Curry County, which is dry as a bone thanks to your grandma. Have you no compassion on poor suffering mankind?" Then he would pause, "Hey, Grimes, bring me back some at Christmas, eh?"

Every second Friday Les would reenact my church camp dismissal: "Here's your check," he would intone with great solemnity. "Don't spend it all in the collection plate on that bunch of hell-raisers at Trinity," he would howl. I marveled that a drinker could know so much more than an abstainer about human nature.

By the time I would taste my first spirituous substance (by accident of ignorance during a Lutheran communion service at seminary), Les had retired. I couldn't find him to tell him the story. I knew he would have taken perverse delight at the thought of my liturgical entrapment. He would have enjoyed the story of my first intoxication too. I was twenty-five and walking down a cobblestone street in southern France when I discovered that I was drunk. I had to infer it from the sounds of the uncontrolled mirth escaping my lips. I doubt that I could have convinced Mom that Methodists sometimes need a little help in developing a sense of humor. Les would have understood.

Arnold van Gennep, the grand old man and senior elder of rites-of-passage theory, distinguished two kinds of initiation—one into adulthood, the other into secret societies, brotherhoods, professions, and the like. Ordinations are of the second sort. They lead not to manhood but to clerical authority. Social scientists call the second kind of initiation "status enhancement." Having devoured Ralph Waldo Emerson's essays on nonconformity while in high school, I would have considered it a vicious accusation if someone had suggested that my desire for ordination was a craving for status. To be identified with Jesus was to assume a place outside the status system. I was critical of the ecclesiastical status system and hoped to avoid those features of the church that made it resemble a country club.

When the district superintendent called me to his office in 1963, at the beginning of my senior year in college, it was difficult not to identify him with the camp director back in New Mexico. Both were DSs. Both were elderly men shrouded in soft, translucent skin that had known little manual labor. I longed for a kind, grandfatherly mentor with the gnarled hands of a logger. Fate, I was sure, kept dealing me soft curmudgeons instead. As it turned out, I was wrong about this elder.

"Sit down," Dr. Munday said. "Unlike your preministerial classmates," he drawled slowly, "you've not taken a student charge while you've been here. Why's that?"

"I have had three jobs in addition to my schoolwork. I couldn't manage another," I replied.

"You could have had just one job: pastoring a church. You could have been making more money than you do by stocking Gerber's baby food and working with those two old ladies and their street kids."

"Well, to be honest, Dr. Munday, I have heard nothing but bad reports from my fellow students who are part-time preachers. They all seem to become discouraged with the ministry after they hold such positions. I doubt that at nineteen or twenty we are mature enough to be in charge of churches," I said with uncharacteristic humility.

"There have been some bad experiences in these little churches—I admit that," he replied, "but there have been some good ones too." Then he changed pace, swiftly coming to the point. "I want you to take Possum Hollow Charge," he announced.

"Possum Hollow? Bobby James is there."

"He's leaving. In fact, he's gone, and I'd like you to replace him."

"He's gone?" I was stunned. Bobby had said nothing to me about leaving. "I don't know. I hadn't planned to," I replied, groping for words.

"The people need you. I need you. The church needs you."

I waited for him to say, "God needs you," but he stopped short.

"What happened?" I asked, not expecting him to tell me.

"This is confidential," he said. "There is a sordid affair going on—an older couple, close to sixty. A husband in one family is sleeping with a wife in another."

I was shocked. "That sounds bad, but not bad enough to leave," I said.

"There's more. One Sunday when Brother Bobby gave the communion invitation: 'All ye who are in love and charity with your neighbor'—you know the passage—one of the women, watching the 'other' woman stand up and start toward the altar, leaped to her feet and started screaming, 'You are committing adultery with my husband! How dare you!' Possum Hollow has become the scandal of the whole district."

He continued, "A few Sundays later Brother Bobby made a serious mistake. He took sides and preached on adultery. He aimed his words at an individual in the congregation, and that man has now threatened Bobby's life with a shotgun. The situation sounds like a movie version of a hillbilly feud. Even the names sound like those in the movies."

I am sure I gulped visibly. "You want me to go into that lion's den?"

"Don't flatter yourself," he chided gently. "Those lions can still bite, and you are not Daniel. Yes, I want you to go there. There is no one else who can do it."

"I am nineteen," I protested, "and a virgin, and I don't have any training in family counseling."

"I have no interest in your virginity, and I have heard you are a good preacher. Your professors say that even though you are a little rebellious, you have exceptionally good judgment, and you are a skilled public speaker."

Flattered, I countered badly, "I think I have decided to become a teacher."

"You are licensed to preach, Brother Grimes, and you plan to be ordained, don't you? You're going to Emory for theology school, aren't you?"

"Yes." He seemed to know a lot about my life and plans.

"Will you do it?"

I was as stunned by my agreement as I was by the story I'd just heard.

"I'll authorize you to marry and bury; the bishop will have to give you special dispensation to baptize and commune. I have only one piece of advice: Don't become anybody's messenger boy. I can't imagine that you would, but don't. Don't take sides. Try to love them all, though God knows, some of them aren't all that lovable."

A few days later as my off-white Volkswagen beetle snaked through the hills between Wesleyan and Possum Hollow Methodist Church, I replayed my drive to church camp in New Mexico. I hoped to heaven that I would not have a similarly disgraced, tail-tucked return. No cameras were rolling in my head, because I was worried that they might record events best kept private.

The second Sunday that I drove the forty miles to Possum Hollow, Sally met me in the parking lot. Yellow dress flying, the little girl charged out from the middle of a circle of men. They were standing in front of the church smoking. (Methodist proscriptions notwithstanding, Possum Hollow families both grew and smoked tobacco.) Out of the corner of my eye I saw the huddle of males turn, grinning. "Brother Grimes," she squealed, "everybody wants to know if you had to get a special permit to drive all the way out here." At first I missed the joke.

"Permit?" I asked.

"You know, a driver's permit—you look so young and all," she roared.

The men howled. I even managed a smile. "Humor, son, humor," whispered Mom across a thousand miles.

For the year of my appointment I played the assigned role. I was their boy preacher, barely twenty, advising adulterous retirees. What could be more divinely foolish than that?

Church members initiated me, mostly with food. "You're going to be a preacher? Well, you have to learn to eat. Here, have some more." I would stuff my belly until my eyeballs bugged and then feel vaguely guilty for the rest of the afternoon, because I could hardly stay awake during visits to church members' homes.

There was lavish affection between them and me. I was everyone's son or grandson. I didn't have much authority and didn't care much that I didn't. Eventually, I baptized Sally, the girl in the yellow dress. It floated up around her armpits as we waded into the murky pond. I was as badly prepared for Sally as for Howard Brawn, my aquatics instructor. Just before I dunked her (she had a Baptist background) she quipped, "Brother Grimes, what would you do if a turtle bit your toe?" She was laughing so hard at her own joke that she swallowed a mouthful of water, despite the white handkerchief I held over her face.

In 1967 near the end of my seminary training at Emory University in Atlanta, a psychiatrist was hired to administer a battery of personality tests to the graduating class. Afterward, he counseled me, "You have a most unusual profile for a seminarian."

"What do you mean?" I asked.

"Well, you have a low need to feel guilt. Most seminarians have a high need. However, when you feel guilt, you get really hooked by it."

"Is that bad?"

"Neither bad nor good, just unusual, interesting. The other thing is that you have a problem with authority."

"You are going to tell the bishop I am rebellious, right?"

"No. That's not a big problem, although you obviously are. As long as he gives you plenty of room, you will do fine. No, the problem will come when you *have* authority. You believe all that Christian crap about the poor and the powerless. You think they are automatically right and that anybody with power is wrong. But someday you'll have power and authority—you're the type—and then what will you think of yourself?"

Upon graduation I knew better than to petition the New Mexico Conference for ordination. And I had been advised to avoid the North Georgia Conference, where I was in seminary. My name was on a blacklist because of involvement in civil rights activities. I never saw the list, and the pun escaped no one. Word of its existence was leaked to me, and I did not doubt the rumor.

While a seminarian, I had served as a minister to youth in an all-white, suburban Atlanta church with the whitest of Georgian columns gracing its front entrance. On a summer retreat to the Okefenokee Swamp, I took my wards to a swimming pool that happened to be full of black Baptist kids. Worse still, I facilitated the formation of an integrated prayer group. The senior minister was father of two of the teenagers in the group. I disagreed when he insisted that the congregation was not ready for integration, and I retorted that it was the senior minister who was not ready. The remark almost cost me my job, and the incident made me suspect as a candidate for ordination.

Eventually, the Florida Conference of the Methodist Church began my initiation into the clerical hierarchy. I visited the state twice, once on my honeymoon and once at ordination. It is not that sunny state's fault that it is now one of my prime symbols for infelicitous ritual beginnings. Ceremonially, the church laid its collective hands on my head in Lakeland, rendering me a deacon and recognizing my right to preach, marry, and bury. A final ritual step remained: taking elder's orders, which would confer full ordination and the right to commune and baptize. I would no longer require special dispensation from a bishop to perform these ritual functions.

Eventually, however, the Florida Conference balked on conferring elder's orders, arguing that I needed experience in a Methodist institution. I reminded members of the board that they regularly ordained chaplains to serve in the U.S. Army, hardly a Methodist institution. They were unimpressed by my argument.

Later a bishop in the Wisconsin Conference offered to ordain me. "Ah, those southerners," he said with an obvious air of superiority, "they have hang-ups with race—none of that up here. Sure, we'll ordain you."

"I'd like to ask you some questions about the vows," I replied.

"Sure. Shoot."

"Well, we're asked not to drink wine or spirituous liquors. Yet we are encouraged to take communion with other traditions that use wine, the Lutherans, for example."

"No problem. The General Conference will soon do away with that vow. Some folks have pointed out the contradiction and petitioned for a release from it."

"I know. I helped start the petition."

"Oh, really? Well, fine. Good for you. Wisconsin Methodists have never been keen on abstinence, you know. We drink more beer per capita than any other state in the Union. The fruit of the vine is a gift from God, you know—provided you don't abuse it."

"I used to have a boss who said the same thing," I offered, unsuccessfully trying to rouse his interest in the rest of the story. "Anyway, another problem I have is with the question that asks whether I am going on to perfection."

The bishop laughed. "Yes, everybody has trouble with that one. It doesn't mean moral perfection—you know, perfection in behavior. It only means perfection in intention, perfection in love."

"I doubt that I will ever be perfect in either love or in intention."

"Surely you would like to become perfect?"

"Maybe, but I think I'd rather be whole." (My college and seminary education had initiated me into ritual combat with words.)

"What's that?"

"Never mind, just something C. G. Jung said. Another question: You will be asking me if I will work diligently and not trifle away time. I never waste time. You should make me take a vow to play or tell jokes or loaf or laugh. Work isn't the only value. How about humor?"

"We can't make up new vows for every individual."

"I guess not," I replied noncommittally. "What about the vow not to smoke or wear gold and costly apparel? I see you have on a gold watch and ring and that you smoke. Occasionally, I smoke a pipe too, and my folks just bought me a gorgeous new doctoral robe for my graduation from Columbia. It cost them a pretty penny, and I would like to be able to wear it in academic processions—bird feathers, you know." He didn't laugh.

"No problem. Nobody really cares. You can wear whatever you want. Those are just historical questions asked of every Methodist minister since John Wesley."

"Then maybe you should put them in the historical section of *The Discipline* rather than ask them to people whom they force to lie in order to be ordained."

The bishop was growing agitated. Up to this point he had been magnanimous. "Grimes, you talk like a fundamentalist. Don't be such a literalist."

"I am just disturbed at having to be ordained into the ministry with a ceremonial lie."

"What the hell do you think we should do—make a special exception just for you?" He began stretching the gold expansion band of his watch with such force that I feared he would pluck a wad of black hairs out of his arm.

"No, sir, not just for me—for everyone. *The Discipline,* after all, just says we have to give 'satisfactory' answers to the questions. It doesn't say that 'yes' equals 'satisfactory.' You could be satisfied with 'no.' I wouldn't even say no loudly. No one would hear me, because there would be others answering the questions at the same time."

"If you really want to be ordained, you'll quit all this quibbling and just agree to answer the questions in the accepted manner."

"I've wanted to be a preacher since I was six. Even after I gave up the idea of pastoring and preaching in a local church, I still wanted to be ordained—to serve people, you know, the poor, the church, and my students here at Lawrence. When I decided I was called to be a professor rather than an evangelist or pastor, I still wanted to serve them. I wanted to commune them and marry them in the same way my New Testament professor married me to my wife. But I suspect that you are implying the church and I are incompatible. Perhaps I expect too much of it. At least you've helped me clarify my intentions, Bishop. I will write you a letter confirming my decision to return my deacon's orders."

A few days later I wrote the letter that terminated a vision that had guided me for twenty years. I would never be an ordained elder. Though my name is no longer on the church roll, I still have the piece of paper that conferred my deacon's orders. I forgot to include it with my letter. Probably I still longed to be one of God's lieutenants even though I had formally given up the battle.

Not so many years ago I wrote a chapter on ritual failure.[4] Since the chapter was mainly theoretical, I did not say that the motive (as opposed to the reason) for writing it was that I had experienced more failed than successful rites. Who failed in the case of my aborted ordination? From the point of view of the church, the failure was mine, not that of the institution or the ordination rite. From the ecclesiastical point of view, the rite succeeded in weeding out one not well suited to the vocation. In retrospect, I am grateful that I was plucked early. However, no amount of retroactive rationalizing solves the problem of the ceremonial lie. Though, as the bishop accused, I may have had fundamentalist tendencies then, I remain unwilling to sweep such discrepancies under the rug. I still would not want to compromise the ethical issue for the sake of the ritual act.

A friend and scholar who knows my work well once tried to coach me into a more tolerant perspective by using my own ideas about ritual against me. He suggested that I view vow-taking as an example of "ritual subjunctivity" instead of treating it as an ethical issue. Then, he assured me, I would have had no problem. Treated subjunctively, vows could be affirmed playfully, in an "as-if" mode. Alas, I am unable to stretch the definition of play this far. Stubbornly, I continue to suspect that initiation rites trap initiates into ceremonially blessed deception. Sometimes the lying deceives others—witnesses to an ordination ceremony, for instance. At other times the lie takes the more insidious form of self-deception, in which case initiates hide recognition of it from themselves. The rite proclaims one thing (I am going on to perfection), while the initiate proclaims another (I will always fail, even in aspiring to perfection).

My preoccupation with ritual failure—or "ritual infelicity," as the British philosopher J. L. Austin more kindly understates it—is partly a consequence of botched initiations into manhood and into priesthood. But a larger question remains: When there is initiatory failure, who or what fails? The elders (bishops, district superintendents, Scout leaders, parents)? The initiate? The rite itself? The social system that the rite expresses and reinforces? Probably all of these. As a ritual theorist, I am less interested in personal failure (for instance, that of specific elders and specific initiates) than in failure of the system. But the system is immense, so I prefer to concentrate on the rite. Not only is a rite more manageable in scope; it is also a prism refracting much larger social forces and cultural contradictions. So when I say of my stint in the Methodist ministry, "Initiation failed me," the complaint does not preclude my own failure or that of ecclesiastical or other social institutions. It simply means that I understand an initiation rite to be a mediating agent between an individual and a society and that failure can implicate any one or all three.

3

GUARDIAN OF THE THRESHOLDS

If the church with its baptism and ordination rites failed to initiate me, the university did not. My alma maters caught and cradled me when the bough of fundamentalism broke. They relieved me of the burdens of clerical faith and suckled me with the sweet milk of truth. They enabled me to trade declaration for query and the interpretation of texts for the recitation of creeds. Baptized by exam and ordained by degree into its fold, my life cycles to the rhythm of the academic year. Outfitted with gold-tassled cap and emblazoned gown, I am a guardian of the thresholds of academe. I cling to its ivory towers with tenure. So decisively am I married to it, that it can divorce me only for incompetence or moral turpitude.

My commitment notwithstanding, I am no less ambivalent about the university than about the church. Insofar as it is the theater in which I play the shepherd of young minds and the sanctuary that coddles me with pension plans and insurance, I am one of its priests no matter how much I complain about it.

I should not complain. There have been mentors aplenty:

Tom Rogers
Ed Beavin
Bill Mallard
Manfred Hoffman
Hendrik Boers
Ted Runyon
Tom Driver
Theodor Gaster
Walter Wink
Ann Ulanov

Some nurtured me; others badgered me. Some accompanied me; others left me alone. Some overworked me; others taught me to play and dream. Some believed too much of what I said; others believed nothing I said. My genealogy obligates me. I am a tradition-bearer, and I owe it to my academic fathers (and mother) to make unto them ancestral offerings.

Near the end of the academic year 1960–1961, members of my high school class asked me to deliver a commencement address. That year I had been elected Mr. Citizen of Clovis High. But I had also lost the local competition for the National Oratorical contest to an old girlfriend. I suppose I should have been grateful for the honor; they could have picked her. I did not expound the civic or academic virtues, as is proper on such occasions. Instead, I preached a sermon. Even then, before ritual criticism was a phrase that had ever passed my lips, I tried to transform the pablum of high school graduation into an event of cosmic significance. I am sure I failed. No one else remembers what I said. I certainly don't.

I graduated in absentia from college, having preached my last sermon at Possum Hollow, gotten married, and turned twenty-one within the same week. Only when I returned to Kentucky Wesleyan twenty years later to receive an honorary doctorate did it occur to me that graduations were for teachers too, not just for students and parents. When I read the letter declaring that the faculty of my alma mater had nominated me for a Doctor of Humane Letters degree, I could hardly stop laughing. Although I was flattered, my first impulse was to turn it down with a scathing letter in which I declared that neither my wallet nor my belly was big enough to warrant such an "honor." By force of argument I would cut the honorary doctorate to shreds, reminding the college president how such degrees were originally intended as rewards for creative accomplishment or scholarly achievement outside the system of higher education. I would complain how instead they were usually given to potential donors or persons whose association with the college would garner prestige. So, no, I would have none of it.

Then I talked with Dr. Rogers, who for the past several years had been insisting that I call him Tom. Like him, I had become a teacher, and he was—is—my first intellectual father. He was probably my intellectual mother, too. With characteristic wisdom and gentleness, he, my first teacher in religious studies, had offered me a hammer with which to crack my fundamentalist foundation. He had taught me to compare Matthew with Mark and Luke with John and all four with Greek and German philosophers. He had insisted that I argue with Kant, Hegel, and Augustine. This sort of wrestling would eventually become a ceremonial skill, the content of which Grandma, my primordial tutor in piety, would have despised, the form of which she had been a master.

Now Tom had nominated me. The faculty, he said, was tired of giving honorary degrees to retired bishops and district superintendents. For a change they wanted to use the degree to recognize scholarly achievement. He flattered me as he always had. Even though I believed his opinion of me to be inflated, it was obvious that my return to Kentucky Wesleyan to receive the degree was important to him.

Standing in line with the other honorary degree candidates, I was out of my element. The bishop in front of me, who was about to deliver the commencement address, boasted that he had just returned from General Conference, where he had cast his vote to keep "them, you know, the homos," in their place.

After the ceremony Tom drove me to his home, where he invited me to his study, rich with the perfume of old books in Greek. Ceremoniously, he presented me with a gold ring bearing the mien of a Roman soldier. It meant more than the degree (regardless of my attitude toward soldiering and Latin). And the words he uttered meant more than the ring: "Ron, no matter how many students attend your classes, you only teach a few students in a lifetime, maybe only two or three. You are one of those for me."

Teachers and students constitute a lineage. Though academic paternity is even more questionable than biological paternity, it is nevertheless a powerful, sometimes nurturing force. In passing through the hallowed halls of academe, one gains fathers, mothers, children, sisters, and brothers. The brotherhood is not always kind.

A huddle of male graduate students was cramped into a creaking elevator in Lowe Library at Columbia University. We had just come out of a history of religions course in which rites of passage were the topic for the day. A fellow student asked another, "Hey, did you become a man today?"

"What?" queried the second.

"You know, your rite of passage," joked the first, "did you pass it?"

"Oh, the German exam, you mean. Sure, I passed it." Pause. "Why? Wanna check out my manhood?"

All but two of us laughed. Varner, a friend and fellow doctoral candidate, had not passed the exam, even though he was probably the brightest man in the elevator. Devastated by the jest, he contemplated the descending floor in silence. By the end of the semester Varner was depressed and suicidal. After a few rounds in the psychiatric ward of St. Luke's Hospital, he dropped out of the program in order to negotiate a more stringent ceremonial ordeal, shock therapy in a southern mental institution. Although the jest in the elevator did not cause Varner's psychosis, it surely left a barb in a tender psyche. Each time I quip to a struggling graduate student about to face a thesis defense that it is the last bit of hazing before the completion of her or his rite of academic passage, Varner's ghost shudders somewhere in the back of my memory.

The educational process constitutes a ritualization of passage. Academic passage generates ancestors, spawns progeny, and consolidates cohorts. It constellates power and defines outsiders. So we do well not to minimize the impact of academic ritual in either its admirable or its contemptible forms.

Graduations are the most elaborate and public academic rites. On a few rare occasions they actually succeed in becoming the culminating moment of a student's passage into adulthood. More often they are not. Instead, they are usually unimaginative, pseudotraditional routines with little capacity either to dramatize or evoke the values to which universities aspire. The imagination, skill, and sensitivity to tradition with which typical convocations are executed are negligible.

At the university where I teach, honored guests make hortatory speeches to a sea of blank faces. Seminary faculty intone innocuous prayers over bowed graduating heads. The entire population of the hockey arena—Buddhists, Jews, atheists, Christians, and none-of-the-above—are dragooned into lifting sexist hymns to heaven: "Great Father of glory, pure Father of light ... 'Tis only the splendor of light hideth thee." We are trapped into mouthing these vacuous paternal metaphors, failing to recognize how such supposedly divine light has blinded us to the darkness masked by androcentric pomp. Like other typical graduation rites, this infelicitous enactment does not do what it purports to do. Its rhetoric masks, rather than facilitates, its real purpose.

Once I graduated without embarrassment. In 1970 I finished a Ph.D. Since I was in a joint program, I graduated twice—once at Columbia University and again at Union Theological Seminary. At Columbia, where the hoods had degenerated into mere flaps so lacking in folds that they would never have covered our poor scholars' brains in a rainstorm, we rose to our feet, whereupon we were given our Ph.D.s en masse. No one hooded us. No one formally handed us degrees or ceremonially shook our hands. The famous filmmaker who had been invited to address the graduates and receive an honorary degree failed to show up—in protest, some said. It was an era of much protesting.

At Union—smaller, more intimate, and better attuned to ritualized protest—I underwent a second doctoral graduation, this one staged in the massive belly of Riverside Church. Cambodia had just been invaded, disrupting classes and my dissertation defense beneath the portrait of John Dewey. Students debated whether we should boycott graduation or participate in it. We decided to participate after being given the power to design the ceremony. Participants devised several ways of dramatizing protest: not attending, wearing no academic colors, wearing black, wearing black armbands.

The entrance procession was led by a giant of a seminarian carrying a cross fashioned from a tree trunk. When he reached the altar, he hoisted the cross aloft, grunting like a Sumo wrestler and then slamming it into place. Simultaneously, the organist, who had literally pulled out all the stops, laid across the organ. The din was enormous. Gradually, it transformed itself into music, and we graduates began to sing Simon and Garfunkle's "Sound of Silence." Garfunkle, someone whispered across the choir stall, was a student across the street in Teacher's College.

Once again I was drafted into speaking to and for a graduating class. Unlike fellow students at Clovis High, those at Union Theological laid down a law: I had five minutes. We recognized one another's homiletical proclivities. The result was an attempt at prophetic utterance decrying the evils of America, the Babylon of the New World:

TO A COMMENCING CONGREGATION

> *When factory wheels consort*
> *in secret corners*
> *with military bayonets*
> *and the progeny of arrogance*
> *bulldoze clods of false salvation*
> *over Asian eyes,*
> *when the blind lady's scales*
> *are stuck*
> *with equal portions of injustice*
> *and canisters of tears*
> *chase chunks of lead*
> *into innocent flesh,*
> *when the Guardian of Memphis*
> *and the Angel of Dallas plummet,*
> *shot like ducks to the ground*
> *and the limp souls of Jackson*
> *are dumped*
> *on the stiff corpses of Kent,*
>
> *men drape themselves in mother-clothes.*
> *They don the rags of black.*
> *Swimming in an ocean of black robes,*
> *fishy words are drowned in a sea of hush.*
>
> *Listen.*
> *The Sound of Silence girds itself to diffuse like*
> *sacrificial smoke into the Silent Majority.*
>
> *We bear the mark of the fish.*
> *But the moby white whale has gulped*
> *our Jonah-voice down*

and hasn't the stomach to vomit a prophet-word
     on the American shore.
We bear the mark of the fish.
But the fish-become-Word is become bait
     for words-become-fishy,
and only the Silence-become-deed can rescue
     the Word-reduced-to-words.
We bear the mark of the fish.
But his resurrection-white is stained
     with black and yellow blood,
and the hue of purity, so self-proclaimed,
     is but the bestial mark
of the white collar of servitude
     and the Whited House of doom.

The time has come.
Now has arrived.

"Behold I make all things new!" saith the Lord.
"Thy sign, no more the fish but the sea.
Thy mark, no longer noisy word but silent deed,
Thy color, no more pretentious white
     but portentous black.
Go. Die the death of the dark robe.
With pitch draped to your knees
and the skirts of death about your loins,
proceed down the narrow aisle
     to the cave of three days.
He will be cast out
who wears the bleached collar of easy resurrection
to wander in restless guilt,
a ghostly shade who cannot be raised
because he will not die,
and cannot die because he has not lived.
But to those wrapped in harbinger black
is given a sign of apocalyptic surprise—
a sign buried deep in the furls
     of the dark death-skirt:
to those who persevere will be given to die.
Whose body is on the line of the grave
is given a soul which refuses to part,
and on that day
only the body with soul intact will rise."
               Thus saith the Lord.

You who thunder in silence
       and die in white whale-belly tombs,
hear us.
You who made for our ancestors a portent-sign
       of a prophet-eating fish,
show us.
You whose darkness is light but whose pale children
                     are now shrouded in black,
color us.
You whose sons of the third-day hue promise to save
                     the yellow world from red peril,
take pity on us; do not laugh.
Save us from our own salvation.
You
who surprise us from Egyptian fleshpots
              and Alabaman shacks
surprise us once more
from Capitol Hill and middle USA.
Come
Lord   Come blow your horn.
Come
              Come do your thing.
                Amen

If I could put the words spoken at Clovis High in 1961 alongside these from 1970, I would likely find that I had said the same thing from two different angles. Things don't change all that much; human beings progress in circles. In 1961 I shot from the right. In 1970 I shot from the left. Now, of course, I shoot from dead center. (I still would not want to shoot Lash LaRue.)

This homiletical poem ended my formal career as a graduate student. I had passed the institution's exams and so was passed through, passed on. Crossing the finish line faster than most, my rite of academic passage through "higher" education was finished after nine years. I became a "doctor" with the same tim-ing that I exercised in becoming an Eagle Scout: early. "Compulsive achiever," joshed a compatriot who took the usual twelve years.

Though I had never suffered a course in teaching or been instructed how to write, at twenty-six I became a professor. Now I was qualified to instruct the young and to shape their inquisitive minds. (In those days good students were "good minds." They did not have bodies.) A major theme in my life seems to be that of teaching things about which I am ignorant and of initiating people when I myself have not been adequately initiated. The pattern gives one pause.

Some of us spend so many years in educational institutions that we have little sense of education as an event, as a performance, therefore as a rite of passage. But when functionally considered, it is. Whether it is a good one or the best one

Doctored at twenty-six (photo by Roy Amore)

is another question. Education is our society's most sustained effort at initiation—far more serious in this respect than the energies that most churches, synagogues, and temples invest in initiation. Much that is considered essential to traditional initiation rites is missing from education. For example, most universities now forbid hazing. Orientations have become exercises in personal, vocational, and academic counseling. The models are largely therapeutic and social, not initiatory. I am no advocate of initiatory hazing. As a victim of some of its most violent forms while in high school, I detest it. Nevertheless, educational institutions need to recognize that socialization, counseling, and information transfer alone do not make adolescents into adults. Educators would do well to recognize the initiatory remnants, both oppressive and liberating, that remain. A friend tells me that over the entrance to her prep school was this motto—in Latin, of course: "Come hither, boys, that you may become men." For better or worse, schools are initiatory preserves, set-aside places laden with ceremony not labeled as such. Students still speak of leaving universities to go out into the real world. Insofar as school is a liminal place, a threshold zone, it is a place of initiation. Schools, colleges, and universities are not the only places where our culture is transmitted and our values perpetuated, but they are one of the major institutions doing so with deliberation and on a large scale.

As a professor of anything I would have eventually become an initiating elder, though not necessarily aware of the office's title. I began to be cognizant of the

ritual nature of my position at the hands of my students; they were my first in-
structors in ritual pedagogy. In 1972 a small group of them at Lawrence University in Appleton, Wisconsin, came to me with a proposal. They wanted to know if
I would supervise a student-designed course on myth and ritual. It was the early
1970s, and the times demanded workshops. These students wanted to invent
their own myths and rituals. They wanted to initiate and be initiated. They
wanted to play at marrying and burying as well. (In northern Wisconsin birthing
was not yet in vogue as an occasion for ritualizing.) They wanted to tell stories as
a way of thinking about, and playing at, religion, which, they were sure, knew no
cultural or ethnic bounds.

I agreed, joking that I could learn as much from supervising a failure as a success. The word *ritual* was hardly in my vocabulary then. I already knew about
the so-called myth and ritual school, but the ritual half of the pair was as far removed from consciousness as an uncle lost at sea. If ritual meant anything to
me, it connoted either boring routine or simply the acting out of myth. I had not
knowingly participated in much of it, nor had I studied it with any degree of seriousness. I consented to lead even though I was intellectually blind.

The myth half of the course went well enough. We read, wrote, and told stories—not well, but well enough. We had animated discussions about them, and
they satisfied us. The ritual half was a disaster, or almost so. We could find little
to read that enlightened us. Accounts of ritual were either cursory or compul-
sively detailed and lacking in insightful interpretation. So we quit reading and
went to acting. We enacted a funeral. Not long after I was called on the carpet by
the department chair, who had been called on a longer carpet by the university
president. The president had been disturbed at hearing that students were floating corpses down the Fox River. "What's the problem?" I teased. "The Fox River is
one of the most polluted in North America. Surely the president can't be worried
about one more dead thing in it." When I explained our rationale and then assured the chair that the corpse was cardboard, not a chicken, goat, or student,
he was satisfied. The president issued a vague caution and backed off.

The class enacted a wedding. Later the couple who acted it out actually married. Then divorced.

One night a handful of black students who had heard about the course asked
if I knew anything about exorcism. "A little," I said, exaggerating terribly. They
confessed that they believed the Black Culture Center to be haunted. Would I
consider exorcising the ghost? They assumed the haunter was a white man and
that it would likely take one to expel one. To this day I do not know how literally
they took either the presence of the ghost or the exorcism. I didn't take it very literally; there was a bemused silence among us. But no one asked whether we believed or didn't. It just seemed like a good idea to purge the newly acquired center of whatever maleficent forces might be hanging out in its rafters. Like kids
delighting in ghost stories, we thoroughly frightened ourselves. Some of the
fright was subjunctive; some of it probably was not. Whatever the sage, bells,

candles, chains, and chants did to whatever ghosts there were, the exorcism rite animated some of the most spirited black-white dialogue on campus that year. Once again the president was disturbed by what he heard.

At the end of that academic year I took a leave of absence to study ritual, not knowing I was about to be initiated into fieldwork by Victor Turner. He, with the encouragement of Saul Bellow, invited me to the University of Chicago as a guest of the Committee on Social Thought. Vic quickly sent me beyond the safe confines of the campus into the field, declaring, "You aren't ever going to understand ritual until you go out and participate in some of it. So go do some fieldwork, and then come back and write about it."

Anthropologists quip that fieldwork is the rite of passage into their guild. They mean it. As North American academics do fieldwork, no one goes with them except spouses and offspring. They suffer through it. But no elder goes along to encourage and supervise. The ceremonial ordeal requires a lone, heroic quest for what we are now calling "the other." Fieldworkers go to a faraway place in order to come home with a new perspective and a lifetime of stories.

I did fieldwork backward. By going to Santa Fe, I was in some sense going home in order to come back to exotic Chicago with treasures mined in the field. When Vic put *Symbol and Conquest*[5] in his Symbol, Myth, and Ritual Series, the volume was a badge certifying my initiation. Now I knew something about ritual, and I in turn was expected to initiate others into its study.

Fieldworked, I went to Wilfrid Laurier University, where in 1975 I established the Ritual Studies Laboratory.[6] It continued in a more formal way what the students had taught me informally at Lawrence. The Lab has survived for almost twenty years, so it is more than an experiment. Though the university still likes to claim the Lab as one of its experimental centers, the administration has demolished every house the Lab has ever occupied. The Lab is always edging away from some creeping abyss. Inhabiting perpetually temporary quarters at the edge of campus symbolizes its status well.

Since the major aim of the Lab is the study and assessment of ritual processes, it resembles an art or dance studio more than an archaeology laboratory. As in any studio course, one of the chief aims is practical. Students are expected to absorb the attitudes and skills necessary to the construction of effective rites. And like a lab in any discipline, its aim is to test and evaluate various ways of engaging in ritual practice; this is its primary academic function.

Students say that I am a different person in the Lab.

"How so?" I ask.

"You are a mama eagle there," they observe, "attentive, fierce, nurturing, territorial, caring, hovering."

Like the Archaeology Lab, which originally had its quarters in the same building, the Ritual Studies Lab is intimately linked to teaching. But unlike the Archaeology Lab, its purpose is not formally scientific. Its purpose is to foster in an embodied way the creative and critical study of ritual.

In the Lab students work on ritual skills: music, chant, spatial design, bodily movement, object-making, and so on. To the students it appears that I teach these skills. They imagine that I proceed from knowledge, and they often persist in their blind faith that this is the case even when I tell them otherwise. They have no idea how musically illiterate I am, how little artistic skill I really possess, how much I teach out of ignorance. I enjoy the groping, which sometimes creates the illusion of knowledge.

We study different sorts of rites—initiations, marriages, funerals, graduations, divorces, birthing. We work with gestures, motifs, and the other basic factors out of which rites are constructed. We do not *do* rituals; we experiment with the process of ritualizing.

Lectures in the Lab are short; often they are printed and distributed. Sometimes they border on poetry. The readings and written assignments, in contrast, are lengthy, and discussions are usually confined to the ends of class periods.

Much class time is spent either in maintaining silence or in using nonverbal means of communication. The spirit of silence is valued, so the tone of a Lab class is different from other university courses. I talk less, but my few words mean more. Sometimes I exercise more control; sometimes, less.

Rites of Passage, one of the thirteen-week undergraduate courses taught in the Lab, is itself a simulated rite of passage. I compare it with mock parliaments in political science or stock-market games in business and economics. It follows the three phases outlined by Arnold van Gennep's *Rites of Passage:* separation, transition, incorporation. The pattern is repeated in some fashion at every class meeting and then intensified during a weekend retreat simply called Journey, during which a dying-rising motif serves as an axis around which this threefold process is structured.

During the first few sessions, ordinary activities receive special treatment: pouring tea, taking off shoes, greeting, saying good-bye, entering a room, walking, sitting down, breathing. I say nothing about my training in Zen. We avoid the exotic in order to make the essential point that rites are constructed out of the most mundane stuff imaginable. We cultivate an attitude that is attentive, though diffuse rather than focused. I teach students actions I have only imagined, gestures I wish someone had taught me. For instance, they learn eye comportment. They are not to stare. They are to see with the eye of a fish—with circular, rather than focal, attention. They learn to move like a school of fish or a flock of Canada geese, that is, with flowing, rather than rigid, form. They learn to respond bodily to what they see and hear as long as they can do so without violation of another. Sometimes I am active—visibly and unquestionably leading. At other times I recede, following inconspicuously in the wake of student initiative. Participants attend to the feel of the floor, the texture of the walls, the turgor of the cushions. They notice the smells of food and sweating bodies. They are encouraged to attend to their senses without becoming sentimental about, or attached to, things that stimulate them. They pause in the doorway, hands on its oak framing, and they chant—occasionally with considerable attentiveness, often with considerable hyperbole and humor—"Separation, transition, incorporation, separation, transition, incorporation."

Each three-hour class consists of three or four related activities. One, for example, consists of passing a wooden egg around the circle. Its meaning is never explained, even when students inquire. Some do not even see it as an egg. This egg-passing is the most repeated action in the course. Each time it varies. The egg is dipped in water and passed. It is wrapped in cloth and passed. It is bound in gauze and passed. And so on. Because of the persistence of the action, students alternately despair at its meaninglessness and marvel at how meaningful it becomes. Some decide to look up eggs in symbol dictionaries; they do Jungian numbers on their classmates. Most eventually give up any attempt to decode the thing. "Maybe decoding is not how these things work," one student concludes.

When participants try to extract from me what the egg means so they can appropriate this authoritative meaning for themselves, I am silent. I do not tell them stories about childhood fears on the farm. I do not talk about the assigned daily chore of slipping my hand under motley hens who would sometimes greet my intrusion with a sharp peck delivered with penetrating ferocity. Nor do I tell them how much I feared the occasional bullsnake lying curled and cool in a dark chicken's nest while it sucked slick protein through a freshly cracked shell.

By the end of the course the egg-passing is less like a cipher one decodes than a thread stitching together a patchwork of meanings contributed in silence by participants. When this becomes a widespread perception, they learn about Lévi-Strauss's image, the bricolage, and discover the power of form over content. The egg-passing is an exercise in meaning-making that sticks in students' memories, because it is predicated on the notion that memory is not merely in the brain but also in the hands.

Two-thirds of the way through the course, class members bring pieces of old clothing to build an effigy affectionately named OD (Old Death). He/she sits silently in the corner after being built of bailing wire, old ties, tattered underwear, and other bits and pieces from each student's wardrobe. OD is the traditional name, but the class usually cannot resist amplifying it into something like Odee Melodee Barnswallow III. Unlike most of the preceding exercises, building Old Death is a onetime activity. Because of the shift from repetitive to onetime actions, class members sense that they are finally headed somewhere. But where?

The Lab assistant and I begin to tease and tantalize the students. The atmosphere is like that of Halloween or Christmas. Secrets are in the air. Participants have known from the beginning that they must keep one special weekend free, so they surmise that the change of pace has something to do with Journey, about which they have heard vague rumors.

Journey occurs either in late November or in March, the dead of winter in southern Ontario. The overriding ethos is what one might call subjunctive fear, the tremor that kids drum up in themselves by reading ghost stories.

Participants are blindfolded and taken in vans to an unspecified site. From Friday afternoon through Sunday afternoon they meet their deaths. They write wills, make death masks of their own faces, and hear stories about dying and rising deities. They fast and shiver in the cold. They huddle close to one another and wonder what is happening next.

Saturday night is the culmination, as they sit around a fire making music. When Death arrives in a white mask, and Life, clothed in red, does battle with Death, students know they are watching their professor and lab assistant in costume. Nevertheless, many are afraid when their time is up. When Death comes— as it must for each—the students' teeth chatter. "Just the cold," they say to each other. When they are taken outside alone and buried at the cemetery in a white sheet to the sound of a high-pitched flute, they sometimes cry, moan, or remember things long forgotten. Death does not comfort them with autobiographical stories.

When Death finishes with each person, Life takes over. She and the chosen participant make their way to the birth cave, stumbling in the deep snow. Students later swear they heard someone else following behind. Together in the cave the neophytes squat or sit, sometimes for two or three hours. Life gives them hot cider and new, blank-faced dolls, which they can name and keep. They are given blackstick and red lipstick with which to give it a face.

These poor, huddling souls have been through a great trial. So Life rewards them. After the last soul makes its way from fire to graveyard to birth cave, she leads them on a screaming chase after Death, whom they pummel, unmask, and drag back to the fireplace indoors. Afterward, there is food and champagne as OD's body parts are fed to the fire.

The next morning is Sunday. The cemetery—built on Friday of sticks, stones, bones, and found junk—is dismantled. Kites and balloons are hoisted aloft. The newborns get to see the cave in the daylight.

The drive into town is followed by a huge breakfast of eggs and pancakes.

The last act of the weekend is a silent foot-washing back at the Lab to remove the dust of the journey. Most are surprised by the sensuality of the act.

This is the climax, but not the end, of the course. After any retreat there are re-integration problems. People are high for weeks, and their mates do not know what to make of them. Why can't it always be like this? Why can't the course go on forever? The remaining weeks are spent demystifying the experience. Everything is turned wrong side out. All the glitches are pointed out and the seams, analyzed. The script for the weekend, which is several pages long and indicates every planning detail, is passed out and dissected. And finally, in whiteface, the whole event is shamelessly mocked and inverted. It takes hours to clean up the

Lab afterward, and the scouring reminds students of the ceremonial house-cleaning on the first day of class.

When the course ends, I am sad, because it exercises parts of me that lie dormant in other courses. It resurrects the imagination, stretches the muscles of the soul. Yet I am always reluctant to offer the course again. I hang back, dragging my feet. The course is emotionally draining, sometimes threatening, always unpredictable. I fantasize that last year's class was excellent beyond compare and that next year's must surely pale by comparison.

The Rites of Passage course precipitates serious questions about ritual and authority. Who am I to be putting students through such an ordeal? Does this sort of teaching confirm or undermine my credibility as a ritual studies scholar? Does this kind of course really belong in a university curriculum? What does the structure of the course imply about gender relations, class distinctions, and ethnicity? What is its ethic regarding the appropriation of symbols from other cultures and religious traditions? I ask myself such questions. Other people ask them too.

Because of my twenty-year directorship of the Ritual Studies Lab, some attribute ritual authority to me. But for me the Lab itself is one of the most persistent reminders that such authority is made up. It can just as easily be unmade, seen through, demystified, or destroyed. A recurrent fantasy is that each time I play Old Death during Journey I subtract a year from my life.

During the course I sometimes get as enchanted as the students do, but the ritual inversions that demystify Journey for them do not work for me. I require the homegrown stuff of domestic ritual to demystify the academic ritual. I play at countermagic by wearing parts of my Death costume on Halloween, when Caleigh, Bryn, and I go trick-or-treating. Students who have taken Lab courses would likely consider my behavior a sacrilege, since they become territorial about everything connected with the Lab. But for me, wearing the Death mask while being accompanied by my kids helps demystify it. They are less fooled by the costume than the students are, because they have their own costumes, live with me, and see me put on Death's big white head and take it off again. They get to punch on the tape recorder that projects the sound of the north wind from Death's chest on Halloween.

The rites-of-passage model that shapes the course depends on mystification of authority. A rite of passage has a dramatic quality that is missing from more ordinary and repetitive ritual forms such as worship and meditation. And one cannot depend on Halloween and Christmas excitement in designing weddings and funerals. So the liminally heavy, rite-of-passage model needs to be questioned. In the Lab we regularly, sometimes severely, question what we do. We try to avoid developing a success ethic. And we subject much of what we do to overt, ritualized iconoclasm. Several times in the course, especially after returning from Journey, I am mocked and pummeled. The ultimate demystification is doing what I am doing now: writing publicly about Journey. Since its structure is now an open secret, its revelations will no longer reveal.

Someone inevitably poses the question, "What are these students being initiated into?" My answer is usually that they are being initiated into the tradition of this class and thereby the study of ritual. Certainly, the process is not the same as being initiated into a religion or secret society. The class has a limited life span, and it offers no ongoing community. Part of the message of the course is that ritualizing is predicated on the fact that all things, including traditions and courses, die.

One concern is whether such a course raises unfillable expectations and whether it plays into the decadence of late-twentieth-century workshop-circuit spirituality. Students who take the course are sometimes tempted to try continuing the experience in other contexts. No matter how solid, responsible, or academic such an experience is, it still suffers from what the Protestants in the course call the church camp syndrome. After climbing to the mountaintop, everything else seems downhill.

Once several ex-Lab students organized a ritual group. For some, this group was merely an exercise in nostalgia in which they attempted to re-create the experience they remembered. For others, it went beyond their experience in the Lab. The predictable problems arose. Some wanted the group to provide support for therapy. With no designated leader, no grades, and no hierarchy, discipline was hard to maintain. People began to skip the sessions. Some shirked their responsibilities. There were ongoing debates: What was the group's real purpose— to study ritual, to be a community, to serve as a group of consultants for other people's rites, to have periodic celebrations? What would motivate attendance and participation when people were busy, tired, or on holiday? Which of the various ideologies should be determinative—feminist, artistic, therapeutic, scholarly? Which subgroup (ex-Lab or non-Lab students) should determine the direction of the group?

Whereas in the Lab the infrastructure was built for the students, in the ritual group they had to create it themselves. The process lost its mystery, and its demands sapped the time the group would have preferred to spend ritualizing. After a few months the group collapsed.

I am not optimistic about the longevity of such groups, but they keep springing up. Years after the Lab's beginning, participants still ritualize on the basis of principles learned there. Some are now teaching ritual studies courses in universities and seminaries, so it is hard to be entirely pessimistic, too.

So far, the Lab assistants have been women. This arrangement was not by design. I chose as assistants former students who most fully embodied the spirit of the course. In addition to the fact that the majority of religious studies students are women, those who excel in experientially oriented courses such as this one are likely to be female. So perhaps I should say that, whatever my intention, the design of the course draws on processes that in our culture are identified with the socialization of women: receptivity, attentiveness, ability to follow respon-

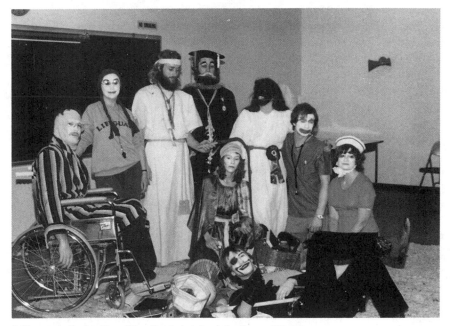

Self-parody in the Ritual Studies Lab (photo by Aarne Siirala)

sively, a trust of emotions, and felt connectedness with birth and death. It is the rare male who is willing to act on the basis of such qualities, if he can locate them within himself at all.

The Lab assistant tends the cave-womb; I stalk the cemetery. She is the guide in the territory between the two zones. That I, a male, play Death, while the Lab assistant, a female, plays Life has continued to seem appropriate both to us and to the students, even though we openly comment on the stereotypes perpetuated by the roles. In the end, Death is overpowered by Life. On one level, life and femininity win. However, on another, death and masculinity triumph, because even after the death of Death, I remain the professor. I tend the gate that opens toward the future that awaits students beyond the hallowed halls of academe.

A former student came to my office. No longer at Laurier, she was at another university in a Ph.D. program. Faculty there saw her as my academic child; she was interested in feminist ritual in North America. "But whose academic progeny am I really?" she asked. Was she my offspring? She felt awkward in coming back to talk about the issue. I had been her thesis adviser. Should she refrain from showing me papers she was writing for other teachers? Should she have cut the cord by now?

Her visit precipitated considerable reflection on the topic of academic progeny, and it led to conversations with other former students. I received a long-distance phone call from a woman who had been active in the Lab over a dozen
years before. She had come into her own as an artist and community leader. Not
prone to kowtow to males, she nevertheless called to ask for some kind of blessing. We both felt awkward. Though capable of generating collaborative authority
among female peers, she still felt the need for an explicit acknowledgment, a formal and public declaration that she was qualified. I balked. Was she? Was I? Did I
have a right to commission her? Did I have a right not to?

For Plato and his school, the student-teacher relation, not the husband-wife
relation, was the model for love. He understood the eros of intellectual engagement. We don't. What are we to make of a process that generates a relationship
as loaded as that of therapy or of marriage? What happens between the teacher
and student who work closely together? Is the relationship best conceived as ordination? As psychoanalytic transference? As dharma transmission (the conferring of legitimacy between a Zen teacher and student)? None of the models is
adequate, but neither is the distanced information-transfer model. If we were to
ritualize the student-teacher bond more effectively, would we hear fewer tales of
sexual harassment between male advisers and female graduate students? No
one discusses this kind of question in commencement addresses.

Lacking good alternatives, we iconoclasts resort to mock ritual. I have a photograph taken after commencement a few years ago. I am decked out in my doctoral bird feathers. Sasha, a graduating student in a black robe, is kneeling in
mock deference before me. I am baptizing him with a pile of red and yellow October leaves, which a friend with a camera caught in midair. Mock ritualizing
and questioning of ritual authority are useful, but they are no substitutes for
good ritual. Even in our ritual ignorance, we elders still have initiatory obligations.

A Nigerian graduate student arrived on campus early. It was late August, and
the university was between terms and therefore sealed tightly. Security found
him on Sunday morning, treated him to a McDonald's breakfast, and drove him
to mass. Meanwhile, they contacted me, since I was the department's graduate
officer. I rescued the young man from an empty dormitory room where he was
shrouded in loneliness, the blank stare of culture shock and jet lag on his face.

Valentine showered me with gifts lugged across the ocean. Among them was a
red, white, and black cap for Igbo men of title. With considerable ceremonious-
ness he began to declare his seriousness about his studies. Then he described
his uncle's respect for me because of the courteous letters I had written when his
nephew was applying for admission. He concluded with a grand and solemn
declaration, "So, prof, my family has sent me here so you will make me a man!"

My family and friends teased me about the cap; it looks like a Canadian winter
toque. It has a tassel designed to be pulled forward rather than thrown back. I
look silly in it, especially if I wear the Nigerian shirt and carry the black drinking

horn that accompanied it. When Susan inquired whether I was, in fact, going to initiate this student, I replied, "He's already performed the ceremony. Henderson the Rain King only drafted himself into rain-making. I've just been drafted into man-making. My new student is the one doing the initiating. He's just initiated me as an initiator."

The student's request was serious, but I was seriously underprepared for the role. My beard, graying rapidly as I pass the half-century mark, may lend me an air of authority, but if I were to shave it off, no one would take me seriously. In what does my authority reside? Does having a Ph.D. qualify anyone to make men? How do I become an elder if there is no one to elder me?

In Nigeria there are traditions for making titled persons, but in North America there are few such ceremonies. It is a strange experience to be regarded as an elder, man of title, or academic uncle when I am looking for an elder, man of title, or enlightened master.

The quandary over intellectual progeny drives me to imagining some parallel rite to commencement for those half-dozen or so students whom I will teach in my lifetime. (I lack the humility of my teacher; he claimed only two or three.) But I get only partway through the imagined ceremony before I paralyze myself with questions: What if I should choose them and they don't choose me? What if they have intellectual mothers or fathers or uncles elsewhere? Or what if they choose me and I don't want to own up to them? Things could get complicated if I were to create counter-rites.

The value of university-sponsored and -designed commencement ceremonies lies in their impersonality, their vaunted objectivity, their claim to represent the judgment, not of one or two individuals, but of a whole faculty. So the rub is that even if I could construct a parallel commencement rite for a select few, it would always lack the power to symbolize the consensus of an official institution.

I have not solved the quandary of intellectual kinship. So I bide my time by recalling my lineage and recollecting my mortality.

November 27, 1992. Yesterday I was about to deliver a paper at the American Academy of Religion. Its annual meeting is a seasonal circus in which I join colleagues in a series of sideshows and displays. Already at the podium awaiting introduction, I was suddenly startled.

An elderly man entered, his face twisted. He recognized me, but for a minute or two I failed to recognize him. As he passed, he pivoted with resolve in my direction. Only as his arms locked around my chest and his half-paralyzed face neared mine did I know the man. He was my teacher, friend, elder brother. My God! He had approached death twice in the past year, and it had rendered him other. I shivered at his aging and at my mortality and then proceeded to deliver the paper as if nothing had happened and no one had noticed.

4

ZEN CLOWN

Five years after I refused to be ordained an elder in the Methodist Church, I scheduled a retreat at a Zen monastery in the Catskills. It would become an initiation of sorts. My intention was to receive serious instruction in Zen practice and to forge an official connection with a Buddhist master. I knew I would spend most of my time doing zazen meditation—just sitting, as Zen Buddhists say. I was not merely curious, nor was I studying ritual or engaging in professional research. My motives were urgently religious, not academic. My son had a terminal illness, and my wife Mary Jane and I were playing in separate playpens. I was consumed with what Buddhists call "monkey mind."

Two nights before I was to leave, anxiety seized me. I began waffling. I remembered the pain and loneliness of the last Zen retreat and was unsure of my commitment, even though I had sat alone, faithfully, for over a year. I had this dream.

I have on the brown meditation robe and black sash that I bought after my introduction to Zen practice. I am standing in a meditation hall and see a woman watching me. She has short hair. I am drawn to her.

I am standing in front of her. She looks quite ordinary, nothing special, yet I am deeply attracted to her. I say, "I want you." She makes no reply, so I repeat, "I want you."

She says calmly, "You can't have me."

I am distraught.

Abruptly, I awaken in the most excruciating emotional pain. I want this woman more than anything in life. I sit up in bed seized by an awful, cloying sensation in my throat. I cannot go on without her.

Eventually, I lie down again and try to do what I had never been able to do, deliberately reenter a dream. I am surprised when I succeed. I am standing in front of her again. I say, "I want you. I must have you."

Silence.

I shout.

She replies, "You can't have me. You don't need to have me. You are me."
I awaken for the second time astounded, gratified, and a little puzzled. I smile as I recognize that Jung and the Zen masters teach me while I flee them.

DESPERATELY SEEKING SOPHIA

I search you out in hay
stuffed in the barns
of other people's dreams.
I ransack the bevies and rifle the broods.
I crawl under pews
to glimpse you chirping,
tiny, on the windowsill.
I find you swinging
from the chandelier,
hiding behind the mantle,
entertaining genii
with the flick of your eyelid.
I hunt you
in empty mailboxes,
peek under the feathers of jays,
check the roots of plants.
I measure the seed of men,
whom you call to silent waiting.
I enter the caverns of my soul,
scratching your name on its orifices,
hoping to conjure you home.

I have not given you my leave,
You, my want, my flight,
my faithful infidelity.

The day after the Zen Woman dream, I left Ontario on a bus headed for the monastery. I did not take a car, plane, or train, because for me bus riding transforms a trip into a journey. On a journey the pain of uncertainty forces questions of ultimacy to the fore.

By the time I reached the station where I would make my final bus transfer, I had ridden most of the day with a severe headache. I kept recalling the dream. I dreaded the Zen master. A drunk sat behind me, reeking of vomit and disturbing the peace that so regularly eluded me.

I trudged from the Greyhound terminal to a smaller one from which I was to catch a regional bus in the morning. I bought my ticket, inquired where the YMCA was, and started down the street. An oddly metallic, strangely amplified female voice from god-knows-where addressed me, "Sir, you are going the wrong way." I was startled and craned my neck like a giraffe. The message was repeated several times before I could discover its source and reorient my walking.

"Zen Woman," I muttered under my breath, thanking the ticket agent and grateful for outdoor speakers on regional bus stations.

I found the Y, felt much too old to be there, and left to get aspirin and supper. It was a Sunday evening, and everything in this southern New York town was closed. I was lonely and feeling a little sorry for myself because of the suffering I was about to undergo. Despite my upset stomach and throbbing head, the sight of so many closed restaurants provoked a ravenous appetite. Then, with a joy that shocked me (because I detest the hamburgers and beckoning arches), I saw a downtown McDonald's and rushed in with a deep sigh of warm recognition— an American cathedral.

When I arrived at the monastery, no Zen Woman greeted me except the dreamed-one who sat on my cushion largely unrecognized. The old Zen master whom I trusted had returned to Japan. The only two things he had said to me the summer before were, "Hmmm, must learn more confidence in the dark," and "Come, my teacher, have tea with me." He had been mocking my authority, and I loved him for it.

I was disappointed that one of the senior monks, a friend, had also departed. This friend was officially and temperamentally of the dramatic Rinzai school of Zen, not the understated, less goal-directed Soto school with which I was affiliated. He was bent on enlightenment, whereas I thought I was doing well to just sit. Later, I would hear that my monk friend had departed to protest the behavior of the Zen master who was now in charge. The story was that he was busy seducing the women under (as they say) his spiritual direction.

The new senior monk should have been in the Marine Corps. While sitting formally, along with other Zen students, in a large meditation hall, my hay fever began acting up. The sniffing elicited a shout. My knees and back began to hurt so badly that I felt I would pass out. Then I discovered what I came to call the center of the pain, a state of mind and body in which I no longer resisted pain. It still hurt, but the hurting made no difference. I had a glimpse of how it might be possible to cut through the Western, romantic courtship with pain. I experienced a tiny crack between two terrible alternatives: on the one hand, fleeing pain as if I had a right to be free of it and, on the other, being drawn to it as if it were the source of salvation.

After I finished my stay at the monastery, I hitchhiked into New York City for a visit. Not until I had arrived and my friend Ferd and I had bought tickets to the theater did we know that a hurricane was tearing its way up the East Coast. We decided that we preferred the glory of dying while seeing *Equus* to the ignominy of expiring at home. So we went downtown to the performance in the middle of the storm.

I cannot forget Dysart, the psychologist in Peter Shaffer's play. He claims that the most harm people can do is to destroy another's capacity for worship. Himself unable to worship, he tries to help Alan, a teenage client incarcerated for gouging out the eyes of several horses. But Dysart fears that therapy may cure the boy of his angels as well as his devils.

Dysart wishes he could take Alan to ancient Greece and England, showing him all the living, local gods, "the geniuses of place and person," and inspiring him to worship as many as he can discover. The psychologist longs to initiate Alan. Spiritually shrunken because of his own spiritual impotence, Dysart collects primitive artifacts and boasts that he is the pagan in his family. But he actually does little more than flip through art books on ancient Greece and spend three weeks in the Peloponnese, every room booked in advance and his meals paid for by vouchers.

One night, Dysart dreams that he is a Greek priest:

> I'm wearing a wide gold mask, all noble and bearded, like the so-called Mask of Agamemnon found at Mycenae. I'm tops as chief priest. It's this unique talent for carving that has got me where I am. The only thing is, unknown to them, I've started to feel distinctly nauseous. And with each victim, it's getting worse. My face is going green behind the mask. Of course, I redouble my efforts to look professional—cutting and snipping for all I'm worth: mainly because I know that if ever those two assistants so much as glimpse my distress—and the implied doubt that this repetitive and smelly work is doing any social good at all—I will be the next across the stone. And then, of course—the damn mask begins to slip. The priests both turn and look at it—it slips some more—they see the green sweat running down my face—their gold pop-eyes suddenly fill up with blood—they tear the knife out of my hand ... and I wake up.[7]

Since I had never been able to see Anthony Perkins apart from his role in Hitchcock's *Psycho*, I dreaded seeing him in the lead. Who wants to watch a psycho try to save a psycho? When the roof over the stage began leaking in the middle of a crucial speech, Perkins, with a style tensed between icy intellectualism and shamanistic chant, simply incorporated the dripping water into his performance. He reached toward heaven to catch it in his palm as if the event had been planned and the cosmos were being dutifully complicit. Perkins was perfect for the part. Having played so effectively the demented murderer in *Psycho*, his cool rationality in *Equus* seemed more dangerous than the boy's rage- and pain-filled flailing. This tension, coupled with the drama of Mother Nature's one-woman, outdoor pageant, left an indelible mark on me. Dysart has become a symbol of the dangers in armchair theorizing about ritual. I attempt to counter them in the only way I know—by getting out of the armchair to do fieldwork or to engage in ritual practice. But that doesn't get me off the hook any more than it did Dysart. He symbolizes the dangerous, contemporary desire to initiate and to be initiated. He has to capitalize on someone else's destitution and neurosis in order to actualize that desire. Dysart, a fictional character, questioned my ritual authority more profoundly than either bishop or Zen master had.

Peter Shaffer and Anthony Perkins dramatized a distinctly contemporary conundrum. I call it Dysart's dilemma. Dysart is a man trapped between two alternatives: Alan's pathological ritualizing and his own sedentary nostalgia for the ritual sensibilities of exotic cultures. He is unable to follow through on either possibility: He can neither go mad nor go native. He can neither *act out* in the psychological sense—which is what Alan is doing—nor can he *enact* sacred ceremonies. This is Dysart's dilemma: the curse of living one's life in a state of ritual disability, unable to escape ritualizing completely and unwilling to enter it fully. The depth of this disability becomes evident to the psychologist only in the process of trying to understand why his client is driven to gouge out horses' eyes. The psychologist needs violence to bring him to the threshold of self-recognition.

Dysart's dream and mine are at once promising and dangerous. They are forms of the return of the repressed that Sigmund Freud did not anticipate. However much dreams may be about sexuality, they also contain much about ritualization, gender, and religious nostalgia. Popularized Freudianism assumes that the traumas pressed deeply into the subconscious are sexual. I believe we hide many other kinds as well.

Ferd and I did not die nobly while watching *Equus*. The play ended with an exuberant standing ovation for Perkins, after which my friend and I went to the men's room to relieve our assorted pressures. And who should be standing at the urinal next to me but my rebellious, shaven-headed Zen monk friend! I was shocked. When I told him where I had been and how much I had missed him, he launched into the story that accounted for his departure. Wading through the aftermath of the storm, we found an open Irish pub and talked long into the night about the dangers of being initiated into spiritual practice and the responsibilities of presuming to initiate anyone else. My Zen friend's wife accompanied us. I never told her how much she looked like the Zen Woman in my dream. And I was unsure how to respond to my monk friend's confession that he wanted to earn his black belt in spirituality. The image stuck, and I later would use it to criticize my own spiritual aspirations.

I tell this story, not because of the long-term fascination that the extraordinary sequence of images and events has held for me, but because it illustrates something essential about initiatory experience. The play of inner and outer realities, planned and chance events, performed and nonperformed actions, is fundamental to understanding the power of passage North American style. The surreal backgrounds of a mountain monastery and a New York stage in a hurricane figure no more prominently than bus stations, headaches, back pain, McDonald's, and chance meetings at the urinal. These miscellaneous settings typify the sacred and not-so-sacred spaces in which American initiations occur. Initiatory settings range from the nitty-gritty to the sublime. And the would-be initiator, such as Dysart or the young Zen master left in charge of the monastery, not only promises enlightenment but also threatens practitioners with frightful possibilities for self-deception and exploitation.

Several years after my stay at the monastery, I found a new Zen master, this one Korean rather than Japanese. He drafted me into a training class for Zen teachers on the pretext of instructing me to play the *moktok*, a small fish- or skull-shaped meditation drum. I was already teaching courses on Zen, he said, so I might as well be qualified to do what I was doing. This, he announced, was to be the first Zen seminary class in Canada. The idea of a Zen seminary was hilarious to me, though apparently not to the other students. After entering the program, I had recurring dreams of myself as a clown, somersaulting, leaping, disrupting. True to form, I was a cheeky student. The other students were younger and quieter.

"Sunim" is a generic title. Like "Roshi," its Japanese equivalent, it simply means "teacher" or "master." Sunim's Korean mystique mystified many of his students. Sometimes it mystified me, too, but often it did not. Occasionally, I wished it did. I asked questions one should not ask—evaluative ones, as well as ones that revealed how much I was thinking instead of responding with my whole being. I was the only student in the Zen teacher-training class who had not taken the precepts that would have made me officially Buddhist. Sunim said he did not care whether I was both Christian and Buddhist, only that I did what was required.

Dream of August 13, 1986: I am watching a bunch of Zen Buddhists, all adolescent males. They are doing a demonstration ordination. Ordination is effected by tying a thin cord over the left shoulder.

Then I notice another group: women who have sashes over their right shoulders. Somehow I know this is the "Christian" or "slave" shoulder. It is inferior, and having a cord over that shoulder does not constitute official ordination. I put a cord over my right shoulder; I already have one over my left. Now I have crossed cords, reminding me of old photographs of Pancho Villa. I hear the words Bandito Buddhisto *and break out laughing. Like the women, I am not a real Buddhist but a bandit Buddhist.*

The young men walk around in a circle with their penises hanging out. The women are shocked. I find the scene funny, as I watch a prepubescent kid try to hide his hairless penis, which is hard because his coat keeps rubbing it.

The women are now walking around, but I can see them only from behind. They are pretending to be boys. They are kissing "the girls" on the cheek.

Suddenly, I leap up, grab a handful of spoons, and begin to clown my way around the circle, playing them like chimes in the ear of each person. When I

come to the Zen master, he is furious. He says I am taking too long with each per-
son; I am clinging (in Zen, a bad thing). I know the real reason for his anger is my
biordination—unauthorized as both ordinations are. But I know my ordinations
are nevertheless real, because I am aware of their fictionality. What a paradox!

The sound of a cold wind awakens me. I can hear the spoon chimes ringing
downstairs in the kite room. I go downstairs, pee, and begin to meditate. A wind
fills the rooms with … what? Spirit. A tiny kite on the door flips over. The night is
full of mystery, comedy, jubilation.

Dream notes, August 14: This seems like my most significant dream since the
first Zen Woman dream. It fills me with gratitude.

The penis display is supposed to be a show of power, a claim of privilege. But for
me, it is amusing, because it reveals how paltry penile power is. In the dream I al-
ready hold male ordination, but I deliberately identify with the women.

The master is angry because he thinks that my taking too long is an expression
of ego. In the dream I know it is not, so I am not worried. I am delighted because
the spoon serenade feels like a refusal to be trapped in the male/female split.

After playing with and working on this dream with every means at my disposal, I felt sure that I should pursue Zen ordination no further. It had become a
temptation to grab power, a quest for the spiritual equivalent of Eagle Scout and
black belt. In addition, the conflict between Zen monastic models and my domestic life as a father had become acute. So I aborted my initiation as a Zen
teacher.

It is tempting to overstate the degree to which we give up what we claim to
have left behind. I gave up a half-completed Christian ordination, and I decided
to pursue Zen ordination no further. Still, I remain inescapably Christian and
Buddhist, though in inverted, often hyperbolic ways. Most of my ethical values
retain a distinctly Christian cast, and my emphasis on the practice of silence,
stillness, and attentiveness is obviously nurtured in Zen. But I am ironic in my
appropriation of Christianity and ludic in my practice of Zen.

We in the West imagine Zen to be anti-authoritarian and iconoclastic and
therefore amenable to American individualism. It is ecologically attuned and
nontheistic and therefore in accord with postmodern science. It is spontaneous
and not laden with ritual or ecclesiastical hierarchy and therefore easily disentangled from the cultural trappings of Japan and Korea. Zen, we imagine, is pure
meditation, pure mysticism.

Each of these assumptions is skewed. Zen is a religion and therefore inextricably entwined in ritual and laden with its own cultural history, which is not easily
distinguished from some assumed universal, noncultural core. It has its own
kind of hierarchy and orthodoxy, authoritarianism and bureaucracy. Thus, the
possibilities for disenchantment among North American converts are considerable.

North American Zen practitioners speak of Zen's Japanese or Korean baggage. We practitioners, like the tradition, have ours, too. But upbringing and culture are more skinlike than baggagelike. We cannot just decide to put the stuff down and walk off from it. We remain whatever we are—Canadian, American, Christian, Jewish, female, male, black, white, married, lesbian, domesticated, militaristic, consumerist. Though we convert, we remain the same. It is easy to exaggerate the degree of transformation wrought by a rite of passage or experienced in converting from one tradition to another. For me, it was a surprise to learn how academic and how Christian my appropriation of Zen was. My academic life, no less than my Christian one, exercised what can only be called religious force. A kind of secular religion, academe exercised power from below; its values unwittingly shaped and inhibited my practice. Only in the midst of that practice was I able to see how successfully academe had inscribed its values, especially those that require critical questioning, in my bones. But neither Christianity nor the university nor Zen prepared me for domestic life. Jesus never married. Buddha is extolled for abandoning his wife and child in order to search for enlightenment. And the academic mind, which transcends bodily fluids and the sticky stuff of the merely interpersonal, neither marries nor is given in marriage.

PART TWO

MARRYING

O wife I'll eat your leavings
I'll be your slave
I'll stay by your bed
I'll fan your cheeks
I'll look at your parted hair.
And if I find it bare
I'll jail your father
And buy you a spangle.

—**Traditional Wedding Song**
from India[8]

I was being accustomed to the idea of the Church: children's toys, devout
books, images of saints, conversations at home, everything converged on
the altar. When we went to Mass, she [the boy's mother] would always
tell me it was to learn to be a priest and that I should watch the padre,
that I should not take my eyes off the padre. At home, I played Mass—
somewhat on the sly, because my mother said that Mass was not a
matter for play. We would arrange an altar, Capitu and I. She acted as
sacristan and we altered the ritual in the sense that we divided the host
between us; the host was always a sweet. During the time that we used
to play this game, it was quite common to hear my little neighbor ask:
"Mass today?" I recognized what that meant, answered in the
affirmative, and went to ask for the host under another name. I would
come back with it, we would arrange the altar, mumble the Latin and
rush through the ceremonies. Dominus non sum. I was supposed to say
that three times but I believe that I actually said it but once, such was
the gluttony of the padre and his sacristan. We drank neither wine nor
water: we did not have the first and the second would have taken away
the savor of the sacrifice.

—**Machado de Asis**[9]

5

MARRYING BY
THE BOOK

By the time I was three, I had a girlfriend. Nancy lived around the corner. For us the barbed-wire fence between ritual and play had not yet been strung tightly by the guardians of boundaries. It was slack, and we easily jumped it to marry our dolls one day, each other the next, and our parents the day after. I have few memories of her. Mostly I draw on stories Mom used to tell, along with a couple of old photographs. In one I have my arm around Nancy's shoulder; I am being the boy and she, the girl. In the other we are both girls—splashed in scarlet lipstick and decked out in dresses and curlers. I recall a third, now-lost photo in which we are pretending to be Hawaiians. We had seen these exotic folks in movies and knew they lived across the Pacific, which hovered just beyond the horizon over which the sun set in San Diego. We are sporting newspaper hula skirts, never once imagining that we are dancing out the national ambition to annex the paradise of the Pacific.

Women are not alone in yearning for marriage and predicating their identities on mate selection. I know men who are determined by that expectation as well, though they typically wrap their marital longings in vocational aspirations. For me, marital and vocational daydreaming emerged early, and they were inseparable. By the time I was six and people were asking me what I wanted to be when I grew up, I was replying, "A preacher or a cowboy." Either way, I needed and wanted a wife. Though the single lifestyle may have been more compatible with both historic and Hollywood cowboy life, a lasting impression was made by Roy Rogers, king of the cowboys, and Dale Evans, his queen. I saw dozens of their movies. Mom and Dad reinforced the myth of the singing cowboy (Roy's other title) by assuring me that Roy and Dale were not only Christians but married in real life. What could be more real than that combination—real on the screen and real in life? The notion planted a serious daydream in my young head. Early on I realized that without a female partner (I still have to work at not saying pardner), my life would be incomplete. I acted out the scenario whenever I could draft a girl, often a cousin, into cooperating. There was no separation between the dramatizing and ritualizing of my aspiration to cowboy coupledom. I not only acted out the role; I also sanctified it.

It didn't take me long to figure out that cowboys existed largely in Hollywood movies, so I grew certain that I was destined to be a preacher. I would preach—that would be the verb. But I would do so cowboy style—that would be the adverb. Preachers needed vivacious wives who played the piano in church, looked after kids, entertained visitors who threatened to disturb prayer or sermonwriting, and kept the poor happy with baked goods. Cowboys had wives only at the end of the story, so I never knew what their domestic lives looked like. Cowboys required women, but when they found them, the tale came to an end. Drawing on the two images of cowboy and preacher, I paved the road to marital bliss with good intentions.

My first wedding went by the book. Mary Jane's father was paying the bill. She reminded me of this incontrovertible fact each time I got cantankerous. I would have made the wedding more Christian; she made it more proper. I would have sung congregational hymns; she wanted room for heartrending solos. Since she was the bride, ultimately she called the shots. I would object but back off, reminding myself in good consumerist fashion, "Her dad's paying for it, after all." The only unorthodox thing we did was to invite our New Testament professor, rather than the local Methodist pastor, to perform the ceremony. This was the only decision about the wedding that I would not live to regret.

We had a receiving line, white cake, and white rice (uncooked, thrown). We did the wedding march, picked china, and went on a honeymoon. It was May 31, 1964. We did what the times required. There were matching dresses, matching bridesmaids, matching best men (in fact, twins), and matched anxieties. Two hands were on the handle of the knife as it sliced the cake, putting asunder what had been sugared together. Family and friends were there; the bride and groom, just barely so. Mary Jane's father had to pry her arm from his in order to "give her away." (Back then we did not put the phrase in quotation marks.) I longed desperately to tell someone that I was making the wrong choice.

On our Nashville honeymoon night, Mary Jane awoke crying in the Howard Johnson's motel. She insisted that the tears were because she missed her mother, not because "it" hurt. I had waited twenty-one, stubbornly virginal years for this? Months later she told me the story about her father's having to pry her hand off his arm. Thirteen years later she would ask herself why she had not heeded that obvious sign. Thirteen years later I would ask myself the same question; only the obvious sign would be different. Driving back to the dormitory from a late date shortly before the wedding, I heard myself utter in a hollow, disembodied voice, "Lord, I am violating your will by getting married to Mary Jane." Though I no longer employ the rhetoric of traditional Christian prayer, I still recognize the sentiment and wish I could lay claim to the excuse that our marriage had started off well and then declined as it aged. Unfortunately, it started off badly and ended that way. Thirteen years was the time it took to admit failure. Another six would be required to burn all the bridges.

Mary Jane exercised her tyranny over the actual wedding ceremony. I exercised mine in the tactics used to prepare her for married life in a Methodist parsonage, even though I was already beginning to question whether I wanted to live in one and spawn a brood of preacher's kids. I harangued her about the pairs of shoes she owned, twenty-six in all, and said that a minister's wife should learn to live with less. I gave her a book by the wife of someone named Blackwood. If I recall correctly, it was simply called *The Pastor's Wife*. Not long after we married, I asked my new bride where it was and if she had read it. She admitted that she had and that she hated it. She had cried in secret and thrown the thing across the room. Its corners were bruised and its cover torn. The poor thing was now hiding beneath her panties in the chest of drawers. Eventually, I would sneak the book off the family bookshelf, where I had temporarily restored it to dignity, and I would toss it in the garbage, but only after it had done its damage.

What held us together for so many years? Love, fear, inertia, hope—the same forces that hold other couples together. Why then did we split? For the same reasons. I have no intention of analyzing our marriage and divorce here. Yes, of course, there were good things about the relationship, but my aim is to reflect on the wedding, not the marriage. And the point of my all-too-compressed summary is this: Had we been able to divine the wedding rightly, we would have seen that it foreshadowed the marriage. Our difficulty in negotiating the ceremony was the same one that we would unsuccessfully negotiate in our marriage: conflicting religious sensibilities.

"Dad? Dad? Hey, dads don't cry."

"This one does."

"How come?"

"Let's go for a walk."

Eventually, Harley and his dad drifted to the sandbox, where they sat making sidewinder trails. Harley named them that. He offered his father a hammer and nails. Dad, strangely silent and compliant with his son's example, pounded a few spikes into the apple tree's tough bark. Harley kept eyeing this man whom he had learned to call sir, even while being cradled in his arms.

"Well?" Harley drawled with unusual intensity.

"Well, what?" asked Dad.

"You know."

"Oh, my crying?"

Harley looked astonishingly grown up and yet terribly young and fearful. The father wondered who this child was, sitting sand covered in front of him. For a moment he fancied they were brothers or even that he was the son and the son, the father.

Then Harley began to probe his dad with his eyes, as fathers sometimes do to their sons. Finally, Dad gave in to the impulse to blurt out the hard truth, "You and your mom and your brother are moving into town to live with Uma."

"I'm not going to Grandma's," Harley retorted without hesitation or surprise.

"Yes, you are."

"No, sir, I am not."

"Yes. I'm sorry. You are."

"Why?" whipped Harley angrily.

Dad took a deep breath, but Harley did not wait: "We can't do that. You will be lonesome, and who will play 'Lonesome Valley' for you on the harmonica like you taught me? Just because Mom cries by the chicken house and you work from day-light 'til dark until your tail is draggin' the ground doesn't mean we have to live half of us in town and half in the country like the busted up wishbone of a chicken. I heard you and Mom arguing the other night about National Geographic *and your foolish dreams and her crying for something that wasn't a vision. And I heard what she said about Watermelon Woman from Elsewhere in your dreams, and I didn't like what she said. I want to be the big brother of the baby in your dream. So I can't go away. Or else you can't stay here by yourself. We'll all move to town together. The Heavenly Father put us together so nobody could put us under. I know how I got made, and you two had to become one—front to front—so you can't turn your back on us now."*

"I am not turning my back on you, damnit," said Dad, wincing at the sting of Harley's attack.

"The Lord says you should not swear, because you are my father and I honor you and my mother."

"Don't sass me with the Bible. I am as sad as you are. But I need to be alone. I have to spend some time … in the desert, you might say."

They sat in silence. Dad wished for a November hailstorm. He imagined the two of them, father and son, sitting up to their waists in leaves that had been hail-stricken to the ground at the height of their color. But neither hail nor leaves fell. Dad got teary-eyed again. The only other time Harley remembered Dad's crying was at Grampa Boaz's funeral.

Harley asked hopefully, "Is Uma lonely? Is that why? Did she lose her faith after Little Billy went to heaven? I heard Uncle Hugo say so."

"She did not lose her faith!"

Harley's eyes quizzed his father carefully. Dad looked the other way.

"Yes, she's lonely. But that's only one reason you are moving. Your mom and I just can't live happily together."

"You are supposed to live happily ever after," announced Harley in a voice carrying the authority of a textbook. *"But if you can't, well, then I'll live here with you then. Randy Joe and Mom can move into town and live with Uma. You are my favorite. You are my hero."*

"We've taught you not to have favorites. And Randy Joe is your brother. He needs you."

"He doesn't need me. He is too big to be my boyfriend or my brother, and his pimples make him grouchy. I want to be with you. We will go to Japan and stay up late and eat watermelons and rent a pet bear together."

"Bears are dangerous. And a child should be with his mother. She carried you and gave you birth."

"I know that! I am almost nine," he shouted. Then he softened, *"I know that, Dad. I don't care. You stuck the seeds in her and made her pooch out like a watermelon. So I get my choice. I know, halfsies, we'll go halfsies,"* Harley exclaimed, surprising himself with the originality of his solution.

Dad was only half listening. *"You don't have to make a choice, son. On weekends, on Saturdays and Sundays, you will be with me here at the farm."*

"Ranch."

"Farm, I said."

"Those are the best days anyway. Popcorn and movie and Welch's grape juice days."

"What?"

"Nothing."

"Uma says she will teach you about the Bible, since you will be living with her. And Big Papa will take you fishing."

"I already know all about the Bible."

"She will teach you more."

"Can we do quick-draw Bible quizzes like the Baptists at Central?"

"I imagine so."

"Goodie."

There was a long silence between them.

"Won't you get lonesome, Dad?"

"Probably."

"Will you get another mother?"

"You mean, another wife?"

"Yeah, another wife."

"I don't know."

"I don't want another one. Maybe you can get a horse instead, like Sissie."

"Who?"

"Sissie, you know, Kittysue's horse."

"Oh. Yeah. Maybe."

"Dad, Uma says we should always walk in Jesus' footsteps. If he walks in the desert, do they blow away?"

"Why on earth do you ask such a thing?"

"You said you had to be in the desert." For a moment Harley lost track of what he was saying, but he continued nevertheless: "I mean, does Jesus or God or the Holy Spirit or the Judge or somebody think you and Mom are bad guys for not walking his path together?"

"They're sad, I guess."

"Are they mad?"

"Sad, I said."

"Is that all?"

"Lord, I hope so."

Harley began to swing on an old tire that Dad had hung from Mr. Tree. For a while Harley seemed almost content. His father sat and watched him. Then Harley began to sob, softly at first and then dramatically. Often he would discover his grief or sadness while swinging from the tire hanging from one of Mr. Tree's muscled arms.

Dad scooped him from the circle of rubber and cradled him. In turn, Harley tried to hold and comfort his dad. After they cried together and milked the cows, Harley asked, "Dad, did I do it?"

"Do what?"

"Make you and Mom mad at me so now I have to live in town?"

"No, Harley," Dad assured him, "You are an honor to your father and mother."

"Which one?"

"Both. You are an honor to both of us."

"No, I mean which father—you or God? Jesus said he didn't have a father except the one in heaven."

"Both. Both, silly beloved son. You have one on earth too. Come on."

Harley rode his dad in a gentle lope to the supper table.

Upon separating, Mary Jane and I vowed not to fight. We had already fought and separated, fought and separated. We weren't going to let lawyers make us adversaries. How little we knew about the law and the inevitability of ritual combat. Of course, we fought. Over and over. I have half a dozen discarded separation agreements to prove it. Each is followed by a new separation (dis)agreement initiated by Mary Jane's lawyer at Mary Jane's request. She was learning to fight, a form of engagement that she claimed never to have witnessed between her parents. The battle was all but compulsory. It was necessary to fill up the three-year waiting period then required by the Province of Ontario. Waiting, and thus mind-changing, was our only choice unless we conspired in an adultery charge, in which case one of "the parties" had to be the fall guy for the other. Neither of us was willing.

When we divided up our belongings, each of us was unprepared for the symbolic freight we had either to carry or to abandon for the sake of the other. I had thought that the pain would be focused on the white wedding china that Davidson's Department Store had set out on a special counter for our wedding guests to buy. Later someone dubbed the design "neo–paper plate." I had hated it ever since and had no difficulty giving it up. When it came time to split the sheets, as my brother insisted on calling it, neither of us was very interested in the china. Eventually, some of the cups made their way to the Ritual Studies Lab. And Susan has since broken most of the remaining plates. She insists that there is nothing symbolic about their breakage: Dish soap is slippery. I insist to the students that there is nothing symbolic about using the chipped, cracked cups for serving tea in the Ritual Studies Lab: They have no idea what the cracks mean.

Prior to our wedding, Mary Jane and I had argued about the glasses. She wanted wine glasses, but I was still as dry as Curry County and argued for water glasses. (Grandma would have been proud.) We selected Mary Jane's favorite china and my favorite water glasses. They were mismatched from the beginning.

I shudder when I recall the melodrama of the divorce rite with which I marked the end of our marriage. Despite the years that intervene, it remains kinesthetically vivid, whereas the wedding has faded into a few paragraphs. My hands can still feel the sharp snap of my white-and-yellow-gold wedding band as the hungry jaws of the blue-handled wire cutters bit through it. The half of the ring with 5/31/64 inscribed on the inside of it is now in the attic, sealed in a box within a box within a box within a box. I opened the series of boxes to listen to whatever the objects might whisper about the writing of this account and to provoke my fading memories. Things I would like to recall I can't recall. Things I'd like to forget I can't forget. One doesn't get to choose which is which.

I acted out the gestures of our severance in the country near the spot where our son Trevor and I had buried Muff. The two-month-old pup had been flattened by a car. Why I went there alone for a divorce ceremony I don't know. Now, every time I drive by the place, I avert my eyes as one might do upon passing the scene of some crime or awful accident. I took no one with me whose witness might have supplemented or corrected mine. Though effective in making the divorce memorable, the ceremony was an exercise in ritual masturbation. Now I wish I had taken a friend along.

Wrapped around the golden half-circle of the wedding band is a slice of brown cloth with the rip of a knife blade through it. I gutted a brown meditation cushion and sent kapok flying across the dry autumn weeds and bushes, bearding the Canadian bush with fuzz. I recall—or imagine I recall—shooting an arrow. It was flaming. The extremity of the gesture, though effective, remains an embarrassment.

Nestled alongside the half-ring and brown cloth is a check made out in my name and signed by Mary Jane. I saved it. I was not that hard up for cash. The check is dated May 16, 1979, and made out for $1.99. I chuckle. It evokes recollection of all the million-dollar checks I used to make out to myself while sitting bored in Trinity Methodist Church in 1949. In the "for" slot of Mary Jane's check is written "lum-sum settlement." Whether she was just nervous or actually heard "lump" as "lum" I don't know. In either case the phrase makes a wonderful chant: lum sum settlement, lumsumsettlement, lumsumsettlement. Lumsum-settlement is the Province of Ontario's idea of symbolic justice: I give her custody, personal financial support, child support, the house, and the car, and she gives me $1.99. Each must give something to the other to ensure a just settlement. The fact of exchange, though not the amount of it, must be mutual. I had a hard time taking the lawyer seriously when he insisted that a check for $1.99 was a legal requirement. For all the things I have deliberately tried to make into ritual objects, the check, which I did not try to make into one, remains one of the most potent. It reminds me that I lost. The winner has to pay. Justice demands it. Custody of Trevor was awarded to his mother, because my lawyer assured me that fathers in Ontario did not win custody of children of tender age unless they could demonstrate that the mothers were unfit. "No matter what the law says," he assured me, "the jurisprudence, most of which is rendered by men, is prejudiced against awarding custody to men."

Probably, I read into our wedding too many obvious portents of divorce; hindsight makes it seem the inevitable conclusion to the story. But there were such signs, and they were evident even—no, especially—on our wedding day. We recognized and named them, but the naming did not empower us to heed them. My desperation to escape loneliness and her desire to achieve suburban normality drove us with astonishing force in a circle. Our marital points of departure predicted our marital end. So it is worth considering the nature of ceremonial beginnings.

With the unconscious forces, family tensions, and social pressures that bear on contemporary marriages, some couples long for weddings that wed, rites with the capacity to divine and shape what is beyond conscious control. But we need a healthy fear of weddings. Søren Kierkegaard, the Danish philosopher and theologian, wrote, "In the marriage ceremony I must take an oath—therefore I do not dare conceal anything. On the other hand there are things I cannot tell her. The fact the divine enters into marriage is my ruin.

"She [his fiancée, Regine] can depend on me absolutely, but it is an unhappy existence. I am dancing upon a volcano and must let her dance along with me as long as it can last. This is why it is more humble of me to remain silent."[10]

After Kierkegaard broke his engagement with Regine Olsen and penned these words in his journal, he was propelled into a lifelong career of reflecting on and acting out what he had done. Initially, he regarded the sacrifice of his fiancée as an act of faith analogous to that of Abraham's binding of Isaac. Before he died at forty-two, Kierkegaard willed all his belongings to Regine, now long married to someone else. He concluded his will with these words: "What I wish to give expression to is that to me an engagement was and is just as binding as a marriage, and that therefore my estate is her due, as if I had been married to her."

Not only would many of us consider this view of engagement pathetic rather than admirable, but couples would also probably have difficulty sharing Kierkegaard's dread that the divine presence at a ceremony might necessitate deep silence. Our view of ritual is depleted. We are entranced with words. We consider the saying of vows a synonym for a marriage rite, implicitly suggesting that the ceremony is reducible to verbal gestures and promissory notes. Participants ignore a wedding ceremony's silences and actions, both of which are wrongly construed as incidental or merely decorative. Fidelity based on promises is essential, but a marriage needs a strong ritual beginning and an ongoing basis in domestic ritual as surely as it requires a moral foundation.

If a wedding rite does not make a couple the way a tribal initiation rite transforms a girl into a woman or a boy into a man, it fails. Since ours is not a tribal society, we need to use the engagement period for building community and embodying symbols that do the work of wedding. The success or failure of a wedding is a major factor in marriage-making. Consequently, engagements should be a time for divining the ritual work that needs doing at a wedding. We do not need more premarital counseling of the psychological or ethical sort but a more profoundly embodied way of ritualizing engagement, wedding, and marriage. No matter how deeply couples share on retreats or learn, under priestly or therapeutic guidance, to talk things through, they are not prepared to be wed until their insights are somatized, made flesh, in ceremony. It is a mistake to assume that couples automatically incarnate their own insights, just as it is courting disaster to relegate the work of embodying to the bedroom.

Since North American society lacks significant domestic rites (having mistakenly imagined that ecclesiastical and legal ones are adequate), the tendency is for men and women to concentrate their ritualization on lovemaking. Both before and after the wedding they typically have few other ritual activities, or if they do, these activities lack the power to engage the couple unconsciously and bodily, which is to say, spiritually. An engagement-wedding is best used as a time for discovering and constructing rites in a manner that keeps sexuality from having to carry all the freight of marriage and that avoids making the wedding ceremony a mere act of piety that duplicates or extends ecclesiastical liturgy.

A wedding is not the only factor determining the longevity or richness of a marriage, but it is an important one, grossly undervalued and regularly misunderstood. Assuming that most of us will not in fact experience weddings that wed, many of us can expect divorces that are as interminable as Kierkegaard's engagement.

6

BLOOD
WEDDING

Whether or not one chooses to end a marriage with a formal divorce rite, ritualization during divorce is all but inevitable. Mary Jane and I were almost as long in ending as we had been in the great, swollen middle of our marriage. With much of the grief work done, the final expulsion from the marital home was nevertheless a surprising jolt even though we had taken years, full of circles and cycles, getting there. Finally, I popped out like a Ping-Pong ball blown from the barrel of one of the Burp guns that Darrell and I used to shoot at each other when we were kids.

On the streets in search of a one-bedroom apartment, dizzy with hard-won freedom, and riddled with guilt, I acted out what Freud calls the death instinct. I rushed toward the darkness of another relationship that promised to give me the punishment I deserved.

When I began doing fieldwork on the ritualized performances of a nearby theater group, I was in the midst of separating. I was taboo but did not know it. Separation had left me with contempt for ordinary suburban life, the primary symbol of which was Mary Jane. She longed to be normal; I, to be mystical and prophetic. I could not have chosen a more appropriate group for field study. Inspired by the "holy theater" of Jerzy Grotowski, a renowned Polish director, the group produced physically furious, psychologically tempestuous plays aimed at expressing the unconscious of the actors, with all the darkness and chaos that such a source can deliver. The group's plays were improvisations on classical works such as García Lorca's *Blood Wedding*, Brecht's *Jewish Wife,* and Dostoyevsky's *The Idiot.*

My entry into the life of this theater group was both an initiation and a wedding. The director required me to spend a night working with the performers. They poured water on me, chased me, teased me, rolled me in a mound of earth, and tried, symbolically and psychologically, to seduce me. The initiatory motifs were strong. In exchange for the right to observe, document, and interpret, I had to agree to train with them and participate in "the work," a form of psychophysical, spiritual exercise that courted the dregs and peaks of unconscious forces. I was eager to do so and did not resist being lured out of my scholar's spectator stance. The process changed my life—in the short run, for the worse, in the long run, for the better.

Working with these actors—who insisted that on stage they were not acting but stripping away pretense and allowing themselves to be publicly witnessed naked—was like dwelling in the vortex of a hurricane. The social, sexual, political, and psychological dynamics were a snake's nest, truly chthonic stuff, and I was more than ready for the plunge. I hoped to be initiated and get academic credit for it. The actors wanted to be publicly appreciated and understood. Since I would interpret their work, I could offer that possibility to them.

So I was initiated. I took notes and interviewed, but I also danced, stayed up late, flailed, whirled, bowed, and wailed. I did what they did—only with a notebook and camera in hand. Eventually, I received an invitation from Poland to work with the master himself. When Grotowski invited me to the Theater of Sources Project on the condition that I not participate *in order to write*, I had no trouble assuring him that my motives were also spiritual, not just academic. I was participating in order to carry on my own quest. I did not say that I seldom did otherwise. My life, religiosity, and intellectual pursuits have always been entangled, for better and for worse.

The work of wedding soon displaced the initiatory process. I became involved with Morag, a performer in the group I was studying. It now seems prophetic that I first saw her in Brecht's *Jewish Wife* and that I watched her rehearse and perform García Lorca's *Blood Wedding* endlessly. Writing about the work of the theater group, I used some very telling metaphors, for instance: "Celebration rises as a bubble in a cauldron of public ritual. Rituals are the lifeblood of culture. They circulate and keep in process what is immensely destructive if spilled into society at large and left exposed to dry. Rituals, like blood, must be contained and must flow or they signify death as surely as they signify life. They float on the surface of crisis and rift. What if the dark chaos unleashed by a group's ritualizing corrodes group integration, precipitates hasty or faithless marriages, or reduces directors to wordless idiots?"[11]

I have ransacked my journals looking for cues that would explain both the beginning and ending of the relationship with Morag. I have rifled through collections of useless objects—keepsakes, junk drawers, paintings, letters, poems, and ramblings scribbled on napkins. But only a few suggestive fragments remain that might help me reconstruct and understand. In a journal entry dated January 7, 1979, there is a brief note scribbled by me in Morag's aftermath. At first I thought it was poetry I had composed. Then I realized that it was merely a list of things left behind when she moved out of the house we tried to share on Mt. Hope Street (which deadends into Eden Street):

- A mattress tied to a tree in the front yard
- A smashed crab shell on the attic floor
- A blue jay's feather jammed into the blades of the blender
- A Buddha propped upside down on a pin cushion
- A note alluding to the children's book *Who Needs Doughnuts?* (The hero, a kid in a cowboy hat, asks, "Who needs doughnuts when you've got love?")
- A Humpty-Dumpty card

I had never hit a woman. Never. I had been trained well. My father had never hit my mother. Christian men defended women, children, and the poor. Christian men respected women. If they didn't, they simply walked away. Under no circumstances did they strike back—not if the provocation came from a woman.

Nothing prepared me for the experience of being physically assaulted by a woman, spat upon, or called names that only men are supposed to blurt into the angry faces of other men who are courting big trouble. When Dad and Mom taught me to defend myself, the would-be attacker was always another male.

Morag was brimming with sorrow and anger. She was a victim. She had been abused. She had given up a child. In her performances she continued to play the victim. In her relationships she also insisted on the part. I was a perfect partner for the psychodrama. Reared a Good Boy, I could not conceive of myself as the Victimizer. But neither had I trained at playing the victim; I was poor at yielding. So I was perfectly suited, and I was ill-suited. At the beginning of our relationship Ken Feit, friend and professional fool, declared to me like a court jester to his mock king that the relationship was a profound mistake. No one thought we were a good match, but I was hungry for chaos and darkness.

When I married Mary Jane, it was a wedding of the day. I was virginal, and the ceremony was official, by the book, legitimate. I wore a white jacket; she, a white dress. Though I did not marry Morag, we nevertheless became what Rilke would have called turbidly fused. This "wedding" of the night, a blood wedding, was wrapped in furtive glances and massively entangled projections. It was jolted by a pregnancy scare. It was as haunted as the edge of a precipice. The contrivance of secrecy continued long after there were good social reasons for such decorum. Something deeper and wilder drove us. Everything we did became part of an elaborate rehearsal for García Lorca's play, in which marrying is a contorted way of burying.

Morag wanted to share, if not own, my car, my house, my son. He was barely mine—just for alternate weekends—and neither the house nor the car was paid for. She had earned more time with him, she insisted, because she had known him for six months. Furthermore, she had lost—no, given away—her only begotten child. I owned my prized possessions, she accused. I was a selfish, controlling bastard unwilling to grant her free access to things she deserved. She called me what no man would call me and be allowed to walk away. She spat and slapped until finally I dragged her to the floor by her long, dark hair. Her already-large blue eyes bulged as I held her, screaming, to the floor. The scene is still there, frozen in time. I carried Morag out the front door and threw her, kicking, off the front porch. I watched her flee down the street, past the detox center at the back of K-W Hospital. Her eyes were wide and white with terror. My nostrils were flaring like those of a maddened bull, and my belly was heaving air like a protective mama bear whose territory has been invaded.

This was not the only time we behaved in an unseemly manner, though it was the worst. We repeated several such scenes. To her, they were scenes; she was an actress. To me, they were ritual combat; I was a ritual studies scholar.

You are not supposed to write about such things, particularly if you are a man. And white. And a liberal academic. And a teacher in a religion department. The only reason I expose my sense of shame now is that I hope naming the beast may contribute to its taming. Men don't talk much about their own violence, but a taboo on talking only loads a spring in the psyche, where it awaits an occasion to uncoil. The cycles of violence that shatter so many male-female relationships are utterly ritualized, sufficient reason for trying to understand the connections between ritualization and love.

In a corner of the attic sits a wooden treasure box; it once transported soy sauce from China to Toronto. Inside the treasure box is a "poison box." Inside the poison box is a brass-trimmed glass box with a unicorn on top. Inside the glass box is half a wooden friendship ring, which I now regard as a mock wedding ring. It sits alongside the golden half-ring that was once my wedding band. The wooden one is a reminder of this second relationship, broken and then followed by another pain-driven rite aimed at ending a relationship. At the end of our two-year cyclone I performed a divorce rite even though we had not married. I was sure that the solitary performance would burn indelible images into my heart. I would remember. But it is vague, fuzzy, barely accessible, and it bleeds into the divorce rite that severed Mary Jane and me.

For the first and only time in my life, I felt I had experienced soul loss. Even though the term now sounds corny, I did—and do not—know what else to call it. For the rite I wrote one of my worst, but most necessary poems:

AN INVECTIVE
FOR EXORCISING THE MALE PSYCHE

i take you back give back my fucking soul you give it back to me where it sticks sweet psyche in the pitch of night dear psyche come home she is not your body i am or no one is i draw you wandering whore-soul i draw you out of her i suck you down to my innards into my loins through my mouth soul she wanted ownership but so do i we are not safe you fled me flee her soul of my soul i imagine you seed my seed for god woman or child i depos-

ited you to grow instead you hid i withdraw you goddamn you if you don't come out she hides with you where i cannot go soul you are no woman no man no son no daughter no god no self

soul come home:

> *soul invested in otherness*
> *is all there is to being a demon*

you do not need to have me; you are me.

The invective is swamped with a magical sensibility. Words are expected to compel some new, desired state of affairs. Did I believe in magic? No, but I acted as if I did. My bones believed whether my head did or not. In the poem I use symbols and language to coerce reality. On the one hand, I have projected my soul. It is out there, in her; not in here, inside me. On the other hand, the next to last couplet reclaims the projection by recognizing that whatever one demonizes is a fragment of the self treated as if it were other. Zen Woman, my dream figure whose hair is short and ordinary, not long and mystical, reminds me that I do not need to *have* a soul. I am soul. Were it not for Zen Woman, I would not have survived.

Near the time of the ceremony I was reading Erich Neumann's interpretation of the myth of Eros and Psyche. That soul loss was my problem, not Morag's, was obvious to me even then. From a Buddhist as well as a Jungian perspective (neither of which I hold with any consistency), I knew that no one takes my soul. Rather, I project it. In doing so, I become the demon that I imagine I am fighting.

In the process of ending a relationship (as when beginning one), everything threatens to become symbolic. The vortex generated by such activities sucks everything into itself and arranges the world into a set of symbols. And their relevance to this all-consuming relationship becomes unmistakable. Turbid lovers leap from world shrinkage to world inflation. Either everything else is locked out, or it is locked in. Either way, nothing is ordinary. Everything is loaded with meaning. This overload is the essence of ritualization. Rites are necessary to establish boundaries for ritualization. When the powerful undertow of symbols breaks the dike and spills over it, the results can be devastating.

I suspect that when a major relationship ends, ex-lovers are bound to ritualize the one that follows it. Though I make this sound like a law, maybe it is only a pattern—maybe only mine. Endings, like beginnings, drive me to poetry the way they drive some men to drink.

ROUND

Repeatedly.
We have come this way before.
See our footprints there.

We are returning.
I do the very thing
I do not want to do.

We hedged the possibility
with vows,
but here we go again.
It all comes round;
we can't kill it.
Again and again,
impulse and counterimpulse
arising from ashes
with new fire and wings.

Don't we wish
repetition were merely statistical,
the result of randomness
lodged in the heart of the universe?
But, no,
we press the drift of things
harder than percentages suggest.
The eternal return and original sin—
however tightly they are woven
into the fabric of the world—
are actively badgered by you,
coerced by me.
The viciousness of our circlings and cyclings
cannot be blamed on atoms and stars.

I am sick again; heal me.
I am angry again; calm me.
We are at it again.
It has all been said before.
It all.
It all revolves.
My poor back;
your poor head.
What a track we have beaten
into the pile
of this once-plush carpet.

Not everything we return to
at night or in the heat of day
is a pond for watering.

I return to sip poison.
You come to suck vomit.

This ritual of ours,
this wedding,
this funeral,
where will it take us?

The sages say,
"Trust your disease;
go where it goes.
Make love to it,
and it will heal you."

Mysterium tremendum et fascinans:
this circling, this disease.
Every vicious circle,
like every primordial deed,
is at a crossroads,
at a seam in time.
The primal crime,
the original sin,
did not begin at the beginning,
nor at some place else—
Eden or up in the sky.
Right here
is where
the fall,
it all,
began
and is still beginning.

This is the stuff of Freud's death instinct, Jesus' dog returning to its own vomit. How wonderful it would be if we only returned, ritually as it were, to repeat those things that nourish us. Unfortunately, we also return to whatever threatens to destroy us. Sages suspect there is wisdom in wounds. Perhaps there is, but recovering it is like mining uranium. Making its recovery our life's work is dangerous business, and we'd better take out soul insurance.

Poisons fascinate. Driven by curiosity, drawn by dread, we return, daring to face the threat of their hissing. Boxed, they appear to be under control. See them there? We are gawking tourists, peering at sidewinders in roadside serpent pits. We write about them, magically transposing complex relationships into objects safe for handling. Distanced, we can muse with irony about fate. We are free to wax wise about recovery and redemption. But boxed poisons do not lose their sting. Not for long are we able to convince ourselves that the alchemy of transmuting poison into medicine produces a safe and permanent chemical change.

Poisons leak. Each time I unload the contents of a treasure or poison box, I worry about contamination. Across the years I dispose of items. By doing so, am I rendering the remaining stuff supersaturated, hyperconcentrated? I return to the brown piece of meditation cushion fabric. I rethink the knife-blade rip. The more I ponder it, the less I am sure how it got there. Maybe it marked the ending of my affair with Morag rather than my marriage to Mary Jane. I should have left it intact. Cutting the cushion was a serious ritual error. The cushion had no substantive relation to either of the women I divorced. It was the cushion I sat on to court Zen Woman, the feminine I cannot have but am. For the life of me I cannot fathom why I destroyed it. From where I sit now the action appears self-destructive. Why I cut the wedding ring and the wooden friendship ring is obvious enough, but what deadly subterranean substance did I release in gutting the cushion? I do not know. I cannot remember. Ritual actions do not always work, and memorable gestures sometimes fade.

It is easy to exaggerate the degree of control we exercise in our lives. That we make moral choices or ritualize the inevitable makes it seem that we have power. Lovers imagine that they *decide* whom they will marry and how. On one level they do; on another they don't. Insofar as they do, lovers choose a marriage partner. Insofar as they don't, marrying just *happens*, which is why we say *falling* in love. Mating is enacted in the midst of an enormous undertow. Undertow can result in fusion, which is what happens when two become one without retaining the ability to remain two. Fusion is deadly. Sometimes we have sense enough to stop the process. Sometimes we lack the sense to recognize it.

If we have several weddings—a statistically probable event these days—they will likely bleed together despite our resolve to keep them separate. Most of us marry more than once—if not the mates of our dreams, then dreammates. These imagined mates, who dwell in the head, may or may not be tolerated by the mates we actually marry. Both partners can declare that she's not real, but surely she is. And certainly this polygamy will keep us busier than any Muslim, Mormon, or other man-with-many-wives that we can imagine.

7

A WEDDING
THAT WEDS

After thirteen years of marriage and a seven-year interlude marked by separation, divorce, and affair, I remarried. Friends and relatives wondered whether Susan and I would put into practice our high-flown, yet earthy notions about weddings. They, like us, were wary of do-it-yourself ceremonies. There were so many good-bad examples to choose from. But we had no use for standard denominational or merely civil weddings. Not only the ceremonies themselves but also the social processes they focused seemed pallid. So our only choice was to take the risk of constructing a wedding script, knowing that it might seem self-indulgent or imitative of California religion (which in southern Ontario is not an object of envy). We announced our coming marriage in a letter to which we attached a script and commentary.

July 1, 1984

Dear Friends & Relatives,

Although we have not folded your invitation to our wedding according to the dictates of the Vogue *wedding bible, here it is. Knowing us, you suspected we wouldn't do it by the book, right? This invitation is several things: an official summons, a broadsheet with cartoons, an order of celebration. In some respects our wedding is going to be more traditional than others; in some respects, less. So we thought we had better prepare you, since we want to be doing rather than explaining things on August 18th. We do not think of this wedding as a private affair but as a communal and familial one. We believe that not only does a minister marry us; you marry us. Since many of you cannot attend because of the distance, this little treatise will have to serve as a substitute—a wedding on paper. For you who can attend, consider these pages your cue cards.*

First and most importantly, we would like you to participate actively. Several clergy will be involved, but we are asking others to vest, sing, and pronounce us husband and wife. Also, we are inviting you able-bodied ones to join us in the preparations for the ceremony and the remainder of the all-day affair. The reception will be held in a circus tent in the back yard. We hope you will bring stories, anecdotes, songs, toasts, and lord-knows-what-else to help us celebrate. We do not want the usual, expensive, formal wedding gift; we want your presence, work, and participation. (Yes, we know this is asking for more, not less.)

If you can join us for the earlier phases of the day, wear work clothes. And bring your Sunday best for the ceremony at Wesley Chapel. Dress as formally or outrageously and celebratively as you wish.

Breakfast at Angie's Kitchen is on us. Munchies and cold drinks will be in abundance for helpers and devotees throughout the day. Supper is pot-luck in order to accommodate diverse palates and avoid caterers. Mexican food (prepared by us) will be available too. Susan is coordinating the flow of casseroles and caviar, so she will contact you to settle the epicurean logistics.

Accommodations are available for a limited number of weary travellers. (Please bring your own toothbrush.) When you reply, let us know if you're interested in staying overnight. Some friends have offered accommodations, or you may camp in the tent if you like birds and squirrels.

Unfortunately, neither the chapel nor our dwarf-sized house will accommodate more than forty people. So, in addition to not folding the invitations by the rules of etiquette manuals, we may not have addressed them properly either. There is simply no room to allow for the implied each-one-bring-one clause. We are inviting only relatives and close friends but cannot include spouses and dates. Please accept our apologies if this causes difficulties.

We are including a map, so you can show up when and where you choose. It will help if we have some idea how many are going to join us for the day's work. Send a note or call. We need to know: (1) whether and when you can come, (2) whether you want to stay overnight, and (3) if you can contribute to the potluck.

When you read the outline of the ceremony, you will see that you should bring: (1) a symbolic offering, (2) something to put on as a "vestment," and, if you are so inclined, something to say or do at the late night festivities. If you can't come, we would be delighted to receive letters or tapes filled with anecdotes, advice, and wedding memorabilia.

Finally, reading the description of the rite a couple of times will help eliminate paper-wrestling from the ceremony. And for you who cannot attend, imagine this epistle is a rip in the tent through which to view the circus.

Affectionately,

Ron Grimes & Susan Scott

Susan and I spent a year planning the wedding. Images and ideas were given the space and time to steep. We set aside Sunday breakfasts for working on dreams and noticing what they suggested about our fears and hopes. Both of us had made too many hasty mistakes to gloss them over. Disagreements were resolved slowly, often by incorporating them as tensed motifs into the wedding script itself.

The Order of Events

10:00 A.M.	*Breakfast at Angie's Kitchen, St. Agatha, Ontario*
12:00 P.M.	*Preparation of 13 Roslin Ave., North*
4:30 P.M.	*Preparation of St. Paul's Chapel. Rehearsal.*
5:30 P.M.	*Rest. Dress up.*
7:00 P.M.	*ceremony at wesley chapel, st. paul's college, university of waterloo*

Posting Angel & Ancestor

Our entrance into the chapel will not be a formal procession, nor will people sit and await the dramatic entry of the bride and groom. When the music calls, we will all enter together.

We will be led into the chapel by two totems called simply Angel and Ancestor. They will be tall enough to oversee the ceremony. In search of a luminous personality to preside, we decided an angel would be appropriate. As messengers and guardians, angels turn up in our dreams, courses, and postcards from afar.

The ancestors, whose presence we invoke along with that of the angels, include not only the dead but saints of both the early and latter-day variety. Not so many years ago weddings included a dance at the graveyard in recognition of the communion of the saints. Numbered among the angels and ancestors are the absent— friends and relatives who could not attend.

Vesting & Lighting

While candles and incense are being lit to banish demons from doorways, guests and clergy will vest. Clergy will not don their robes behind closed doors but in the middle of things. We invite you to bring something special to put on—a tie, a hat, a shawl. Flowers will be distributed.

Invocation

The opening prayer will be chanted rather than read or said. This may seem foreign to some, but we prefer this way because our experience of prayer is more akin to singing than to conversation (the usual Protestant way of thinking of prayer).

The Grimes and Scott Stories

Two friends (Moira reading for Susan, Hugo reading for Ron) will tell you a Reader's Digest version (rated GP) of our courtship. This is mostly for our own benefit. We keep asking ourselves, How was it we became a couple? How did we get through all that? We will not be responsible for any educational value the story may have.

The Stories

1943: *Wartime. Ronald L. is not born in New Mexico but in California—in exile. Son of Milton, a riveter, and Nadine, a dispatcher, at Consolidated Aircraft, he narrowly escapes being named Roxie (after the Roxy Theater). He is named after the co-star of* Bedtime for Bonzo *instead.*

Meanwhile, Susan's mom, Corporal Betty Johnson, alias Johnny, is packing parachutes at Sunnyside Air Base, Prince Edward Island. And Susan's dad, Gomer Scott, alias George, is trying to convince recruiters that it's possible to fly color blind.

1946: *Unsuccessfully, Ronnie tries to escape from nursery school. He tries again later on a tricycle and is rounded up by a San Diego policeman.*

Susan has not been heard from or thought of yet.

1950: *Ronnie is playing Tarzan in the desert, hankering after Jane (not "Doe"). Still no Susan.*

1951: *Ronnie, age eight, puts away childish things and takes up cowboy Christianity as a calling.*

Susan, where are you? It's getting late.

1955: *Susan Lorraine, as usual, lands in her own good time in Port Elgin, Ontario.*

Ronnie wants a Chevy but settles for a Cushman Eagle motorscooter. He wants to play football but gets a paper route. He wants to be an evangelist but becomes a Boy Scout instead. He wears a chip on the shoulder of his black motorcycle jacket.

1960: *Susan loses two front teeth and enters grade one. She thrives on reading, writing, and westerns. She is first in her class and Ben Cartwright at recess. Terrified of cows, Susan nevertheless loves cowboys.*

Ronald L. is elected Mr. Citizen of Clovis High School.

1961: *In search of greener grass (or any grass at all), Ronnie, having been fired from the church camp staff, packs his worldly belongings in a black '54 Mercury and follows the spirits to Kentucky Wesleyan College. He arrives three days later in a buckskin jacket and having changed his name to Ron.*

1962: *Susan leaves greener grass, packs up all her worldly belongings in a black '55 Chevy, and moves to Lunch Box City, Hamilton, Ontario. She enters grade three* *with limited urban social skills. She is the fat kid in class and The Rifleman at recess.*

1964: *Brother Grimes preaches his last sermon at Short Creek Methodist Church, ignores the heavenly voice, and gets married. He complains about the amount of new wife's worldly belongings and moves to Atlanta, home of civil rights, and the death of God controversy.*

Susan spends the spring of grade four in pyjamas, scratching rashes and bumps—the chicken pox, measles, and a tonsillectomy curtail her acting out. She daydreams about the Civil War and writes Southern stories in her scribbler. Barbie and Ken play Gone with the Wind.

1968: *Ron is reclassified by draft board and considers a quick trip to Canada. He survives teargas at Columbia only to flee to Paris, where police are parading with machine guns. Ron, who first tasted spirituous substances at age twenty-five, experiences drunkenness in rural France.*

Susan graduates with a perm from grade eight. She is awarded $15 for distinguished literary achievements and earns the citizenship crest but has no date for the dance. She cruises to the Dairy Queen with Mom and Grandma and stays up late to watch The Graduate.

1970: *Trevor Brant Grimes is born. Ron sends back his ordination orders when asked, "Are you going on to perfection?"*

The Scott family moves up in the world. Susan starts grade ten in suburbia and buys a buckskin coat in protest. Elected president of the youth group at church, she is confined to the basement at home. She is still waiting for her first kiss.

1973: *Susan gets kissed, ignores the heavenly voice, and elopes to North Carolina. Later, she huddles down for a long draughty winter in Niagara Falls, Canada, honeymoon capital of North America.*

1974: *Ron, his marriage flagging, moves to Canada, hoping a thaw will loosen up the family freeze.*

Rapunzel Scott goes to university and meets her first real live cowboy—in mysticism class. She dreams an A+ dream about cows and talks Dr. Grimes into buying homemade granola.

1976: *Scott burns the granola and goes to Grimes for marriage counseling.*

1977: *The Grimeses split the sheets (and everything else). Grimes goes to Scott for marriage counseling.*

1978: *Grimes and Scott seem to be passing like ships on a dark, foggy night.*

1980: *They reconnect in Religion and Therapy class, where they commiserate about dreams and archetypes. They try riding off into the sunset, but it's a mirage.*

1982: *Grimes spends a sabbatical chasing after Scott in Toronto. Annie Oakley gives Cowboy a run for his money.*

Ron lives out the title of a book he's unsuccessfully writing, Fiction and Ritual. *Things between the lovers seem made-up and repetitive.*

They consult the I-Ching. *The sagely Chinese book advises, "Gradual Progress: A tree on a mountain develops slowly according to the law of its being and consequently stands firmly rooted. The wild goose gradually draws near the tree. Perhaps it will find a flat branch. No blame."*

1983: *A Red-Letter Year: The Pilgrims Progress. Scott, Grimes, and Son make a pilgrimage to New Mexico. Three weeks later Son makes a pilgrimage to dwell among angels and ancestors. The father and grandfather make a cross for the mound.*

The Mistress of Arts merges households with the Doctor on Roslin. They set their house in order. They repair the leaky roof, refinish the ancestral table, and plant a Japanese maple tree.

1984: *Ten years after mysticism class the two contemplate divine union.*

The I-Ching *says, "Development. The maiden is given in marriage. Good fortune. Perseverance furthers."*

And, "The wild goose draws near the cloud heights. Its feathers can be used for the sacred dance. Good fortune."

Here ends the story.

Hymns

Hymn-singing is more important to us as a joyful noise unto the Lord than as a declaration of beliefs. If you can't sing wholeheartedly, use the occasion to stretch your legs.

Exhortation, or Musings on Married Life

We do not know what will be said here. We are asking someone venerable (that is, roadworthy) to address us with words of wisdom. We would have invited a saint, prophet, Zen master, Zadik (Jewish "righteous one") or martyr, but we could not afford the fee.

The Readings

I Corinthians 13

If I speak in the tongues of men and of angels, but have not love, I am a noisy gong or a clanging cymbal. And If I have prophetic powers, and understand all mysteries and all knowledge, and if I have all faith, so as to remove mountains, but have not love, I am nothing. If I give away all I have, and if I deliver my body to be burned, but have not love, I gain nothing.

Love is patient and kind; love is not jealous or boastful; it is not arrogant or rude. Love does not insist on its own way; it is not irritable or resentful; it does not rejoice at wrong, but rejoices in the right. Love bears all things, believes all things, hopes all things, endures all things.

Love never ends; as for prophecy, it will pass away; as for tongues, they will cease; as for knowledge, it will pass away. For our knowledge is imperfect and our prophecy is imperfect; but when the perfect comes, the imperfect will pass away. When I was a child, I spoke as a child, I thought like a child , I reasoned like a child; when I became a man, I gave up childish ways. For now we see through a glass darkly, but then face to face. Now I know in part; then I shall understand fully, even as I have been fully understood. So faith, hope, love abide, these three; but the greatest of these is love.

Wisdom Literature

SUSAN: *Three things are too wonderful for me;*
four I do not understand:
the way of an eagle in the sky,
the way of a serpent on a rock,
the way of a ship on the high seas,
and the way of man with a maiden. (Prov. 30:18–19)

RON: *A good wife who can find?*
She is far more precious than jewels.
The heart of her husband trusts in her. ...
She is not afraid of snow for her household,
for all her household are clothed in scarlet.
Strength and dignity are her clothing,
and she laughs at the time to come.
She opens her mouth with wisdom,
and the teaching of kindness is on her tongue. (Prov. 31:10–11, 21, 25–26)

SUSAN: *As an apple tree among the trees of the wood,*
so is my beloved among young men.
With great delight I sat in his shadow,
and his fruit was sweet to my taste.
He brought me to the banqueting house,
and his banner over me was love.
Sustain me with raisins, refresh me with apples,
for I am sick with love.

Lo, the winter is past,
the rain is over and gone.

The flowers appear on the earth,
the time of singing has come,
and the voice of the turtledove
is heard in our land.
The fig tree puts forth its figs,
and the vines are in blossom;
Arise, my love, my fair one,
and come away. (Song of Solomon 2:3–5, 11–12)

RON: *You have ravished my heart, my sister, my bride,*
you have ravished my heart with a glance of your eyes,
with one jewel of your necklace.
How sweet is your love, my sister, my bride!
How much better is your love than wine,
and the fragrance of your oils than any price?
Your lips distil nectar, my bride,
honey and milk are under your tongue;
the scent of your garments is like the scent of
Lebanon. A garden … is my sister, my bride,
a garden locked, a fountain sealed.
Your shoots are an orchard of pomegranates
with all the choicest fruits,
henna with nard, nard and saffron,
calamus and cinnamon,
with all trees of frankincense,
myrrh and aloes,
with all chief spices—
a garden fountain, a well of living water. (Song of Solomon 4:9–15)

SUSAN: *If two lie together, they are warm; but how can one be warm alone?*
And though a man might prevail against one who is alone, two will with-
stand him. A threefold cord is not quickly broken. (Eccl. 4:11–12)

A Zen Parable

A man traveling across a field encountered a tiger. He fled, the tiger after him.
Coming to a precipice, he caught hold of the root of a wild vine and swung him-
self down over the edge. The tiger sniffed at him from above. Trembling, the man
looked down to a place far below, where another tiger was waiting to eat him.
Only the vine sustained him.

Two mice, one white and one black, little by little started to gnaw away the
vine. The man saw a luscious strawberry near him. Grasping the vine with one
hand, he plucked the strawberry with the other.

How sweet it tasted.

The Way of Chuang Tzu: Keng's Disciple

If you persist in trying
To attain what is never attained,
If you persist in making effort
To obtain what effort cannot get;
If you persist in reasoning
About what cannot be understood,
You will be destroyed
By the very thing you seek.
To know when to stop
To know when you can get no further
By your own action,
This is the right beginning!

The Way of Chuang Tzu: Flight from the Shadow

There was a man who was so disturbed by the sight of his own shadow and so displeased with his own footsteps that he determined to get rid of both. The method he hit upon was to run away from them.

So he got up and ran. But every time he put his foot down there was another step, while his shadow kept up with him without the slightest difficulty.

He attributed his failure to the fact that he was not running fast enough. So he ran faster and faster, without stopping, until he finally dropped dead.

He failed to realize that if he merely stepped into the shade, his shadow would vanish, and if he sat down and stayed still, there would be no more footsteps.

The Way of Chuang Tzu: When the Shoe Fits

So, when the shoe fits
The foot is forgotten,
When the belt fits
The belly is forgotten,
When the heart is right
"For" and "against" are forgotten.

A Haiku Poem

Icicles and water—
old differences dissolved
drip down together.
—Teishitsu

Offerings

First we will make our offerings, then you may make yours. We will offer our wedding rings in a bowl of water. Water: washing, cleansing, the unformed and primordial. Rings: fidelity, eternity, simplicity.

Our second offering is symbolic of what we know to be necessary in any marriage: sacrifice. We will cut off locks of hair and offer them in a bowl of earth. Earth: the blanket that covers us all.

The bowls were a gift from Trevor. The idea of two small bowls for the sacrifice came from the I-Ching *when we consulted it about our marriage.*

Your offering, like ours, will be symbolic. The point is to give us something you suspect we will need along the way. We invite you to give it in a miniature, concrete form. We do not need blenders. How about balloons for days we're deflated? We already have plenty of matching towel sets, but we could stand a little more flexibility; a bunch of rubber bands would do. As a last resort, bring pennies. Penny weddings are an old English tradition, and a few more won't hurt—especially in these taxing times.

Ablution

Both of us have been married previously, so neither of us can ignore previous marital failures. In a bowl the color of the sky we will wash our hands, acknowledging our sins and expressing our hope for a clean start free of pollution.

Absolution

This is simply the pronouncement, in the name of what we consider holy, that our sins are forgiven.

Anointing

Anointing with oil is an ancient and widespread ritual act with two functions: healing and consecrating. Although neither of us attributes any magical powers to blessed oil, we are using it as a symbol of the grace that has brought us together despite ourselves. The anointing declares that we take marriage to be a religious, not merely a civil, state. Because it enacts what we sometimes refer to as the mystical connection, we find this part of the ceremony the most difficult to explain. To us this is not only chemistry but calling.

Silence

We considered naming this phase "just sitting," "prayer," "meditation," or "the solemn pause." What else can we say?

Robing

The preparatory actions completed, we will put on our marriage robes. Robes for bride and groom are common in the Middle East and Asia. Originally, this practice was a way of transforming a couple into royalty. For us a robe suggests the religious and celebrative nature of what is occurring. It also symbolizes our authority to solemnize the marriage.

Binding

"Tying the knot," or "getting hitched," is not just a synonym for "getting married." It is an actual practice still used in some churches. A pastor will bind our hands with a sash, an act later confirmed by the pronouncement.

Questioning

The law requires that bride and groom explicitly consent to marry. Bridal theft and shotgun weddings are illegal, so we must say what everyone already knows, namely, that we want to marry one another. We prefer the archaic wording to emphasize the gravity of the questioning.

You will not be asked whether anyone knows of any impediments or reasons we should not marry. If you do know of any, notify us now. By telegram. Or forever hold your peace.

Vows

By vowing, we will in effect be binding the future. We dare to say what we will and will not do, even though we know that we cannot predict the future or the conditions that may weigh upon our marriage. Despite what we know about human fallibility, we affirm these vows with hope and joy.

Exchange of Rings

The rings will be taken from the water of blessing and passed through a flame of purgation to enact the burning away of dross. In keeping with traditions more ancient than the modern penchant for matching sets, Ron's ring will be gold; Susan's white. Gold and silver are high on the alchemists' lists, the former symbolizing masculinity and the sun, and the latter, femininity and the moon. Wearing wedding rings on the third finger of the left hand originated with the Romans. They believed that an artery led directly from that finger to the heart. Whether it does or not, we will wear them on said finger because doing so most effectively deters comers-on.

Signing and Sealing of the Documents

Signing is the only ritual magic still recognized by the state. In many weddings this is done later, often after the service itself has ended. We've placed it here because we consider it a prerequisite for, not a consequence of, the pronouncement.

Bride, groom, clergy, and witnesses will sign various and sundry documents to assure our legitimacy so we can make insurance claims, sleep together at the Scotts', and live guilt-free. We will seal the documents in red with a Japanese-style stamping stone. The monogram consists of an interlocked "S" (for Scott) and "G" (for Grimes), indicating the spirit in which we retain our maiden names.

The Pronouncement

You who are assembled will declare us married. The philosophers call such a deed a performative utterance. Please join in reading the pronouncement: "We unite you and bind you to one another. We pronounce you husband and wife. Live in peace."

Having this declaration made by all, rather than by a single minister, reflects our belief that the power to effect a marriage resides with the whole community, not just the ordained. In early Christian practice priests did not perform marriages. The church merely blessed them after brides and grooms performed them.

The Kiss

Here we disrobe and kiss. Since the kiss of peace in some churches has disappeared altogether or degenerated into handshaking from its sensuous, early Christian style, we hope to set a new standard. You may kiss one another if you deem it appropriate or can get away with it.

Coronation and Investiture

The festivity begins. The bride is presented with a floral crown; the groom with a hardwood staff. The symbolism is too obvious to deserve comment. King and queen for a day, we get to parade around blatantly happy and only a little self-conscious. In this jubilant state we all sing a concluding hymn.

Benediction

Again, our final prayer will be chanted.

Recession and Bell Ringing

We will exit with some semblance of order: Angel, Ancestor, Queen, King, clergy, quasi-clergy, peasants.

Bells, missing from most churches these days, will be rung.

Then we will drive back to 13 Roslin.

Crossing the Threshold

A portal will already be erected in the back yard. The groom gets to carry the bride through it, and thereby, over the threshold. This is where you get to throw all manner of seeds, beans, corn, rice, and peas to insure our fertility.

Burial of the Locks, Release of the Doves

At a mound, over which a cross presides and upon which the Buddha sits doing nothing, we will bury the sacrificial locks of hair. This holy hill, like the one at Golgotha, is just a glorified dump. In it rest lots of things from times past; some of Trevor's toys are buried there. The two doves to be set free are from the market and soon would have ended their days in captivity. Like the one released from the ark, we hope these find the olive branch of peace.

Bread and Wine

We have put the love feast where we think it belongs—in the context of a real meal. We will honor our wedding guests by offering them bread (the homemade variety) and wine (vintage or Welch's). For some this may be communion; for others, the first course.

The Wedding Night: Feasting & Celebration

Food. Music. Song. Dance. Storytelling. Stargazing. We know what we're supposed to do on the wedding night. Improvisations of other sorts will be up to you.

The Morning After

Sleepers-over get to help wash dishes, clean up, fly the kite. Don't expect an early breakfast.

The Morning After the Morning After

Grimes and Scott hop the Great Bird to Mexico City. …

The most remarkable feature of the wedding was its collaborative ethos. Many who came spent an entire day working on the wedding. Several spent a day and a night, and a few spent two nights and a day. The result was a relaxed working atmosphere that stimulated imaginations and evoked creativity in ways we did not anticipate. Garlands and arbors appeared unplanned. A wedding certificate was crafted. Songs were sung, jokes told, naps taken, seductions attempted, and tempers tested.

As we approached the hour for the most formal portion of the rite, the group had surprising cohesion and trust. It was a jolly, tired, expectant bunch. Thunderclouds gathered suddenly, and it poured. We worried that Angel and Ancestor might drown, since their height required that we carry them to the chapel on tops of cars. We feared that the soil beneath our circus tent would wash out. Just as we arrived at the chapel, the massive, dark clouds parted, and a resplendent evening light broke through. We hedged our awe with joking about the heavenly scene; it would have pleased Cecil B. DeMille. We could hardly resist taking it as a good omen.

Our major difficulty was trying to write, direct, and star in the same production. Even Jack Nicholson, whom we both admire as an actor, becomes narcissistic when he directs himself. Susan and I had been so active in the construction of the scenario that we felt a strong desire to be carried along, to be wed rather than to wed. We were only partly successful. Such is the curse of mounting rites without benefit of long tradition or sustained community. We anticipated the problem and tried to circumvent it. Wanting someone else to direct traffic, we drafted two people to serve a function analogous to that of stage managers. But too much remained undone and uncertain. We found it hard to yield to the process of allowing others to marry us. Not only did we want to get everything right; we were also asked for directions and advice. We had to supervise the cooking and cleaning. We had to erect a gigantic circus tent. The errand list was endless.

"Did the wedding wed?" some inquired, knowing I had written an article on the question. We both assured them that it had—no doubt about it. The real litmus test, however, would take a couple of decades before we could read the results. A student in one of Susan's classes, himself in his forties and a divorcé, said the wedding script reminded him of a carpenter who, worried about breakage, uses several kinds of glue hoping to avoid splitting. "Overglued," he teased.

Upon seeing the script, an anthropologist friend chided us: We still lived in an enchanted world. His was disenchanted, he was sure. We still believed in too much. "Besides that," he observed wryly, "your script reeks of California, like it or not." After the actual wedding he changed his mind about the judgment. The difference between ritual described and ritual undergone is vast—a fact that makes me wary of putting ritual scenarios like this in print. Like the anthropologist, most published ritual scripts repel or embarrass me.

Two caveats remain regarding the belief that our wedding, in fact, wed. One is that weddings can generate a subtext or aftermath, sometimes both. A second is that the work of wedding is probably never instantaneous or complete. On April 24, 1985, I had this dream.

Mary Jane (notice, not Susan) and I are rehearsing for our wedding. It is dark. We are in the backyard. I am tying a fuzzy white cord around her knee; it is supposed to bind us together. As I look at her knee, it reminds me of Susan's, and I begin to cry. I run into the house, desperate to find Mom and tell her that I can't marry Mary Jane, that I love Susan instead.

Notes on dream of April 24, 1985: I find this dream immensely disturbing on two accounts—that Mary Jane appears in it at all and that Susan's identity overlaps with Mary Jane's. This fluidity between the two of them has appeared in several dreams over the past year or so. The repetition is driving me nuts. Awake, I am an-

gry about my stupidity in the dream, my willingness to marry Mary Jane again.
The dream reactivates bad memories of my first wedding. I am plagued by memo-
ries of the night before the wedding. The whole family came to Kentucky from New
Mexico. I slept in the motel bed with Mom and Dad, because there was room no-
where else to sleep; even the floor was full. I hadn't done so since I was a child. It
was a good way to spend a few hours with them before they had to turn around
and drive halfway across the country back to New Mexico. Desperately, I wished I
could tell them that I wanted out of the whole thing. Probably, they would have
understood, but I didn't have the courage. I thought I had to follow through on my
commitment. I had been taught that a man is true to his word.

I had no such fears or qualms in marrying Susan. The only emotional trauma
around the wedding with Susan was our conflict with her mother, who was of-
fended by our jesting comment that now we could sleep together at the Scott
household. She was also outraged about the absence of Christ from the ceremony.
And she was angered about having ritual at all. "Our church doesn't have ritual,"
she insisted. She threatened to boycott the wedding. Susan was devastated for a
couple of days and even considered not going through with the marriage. My feel-
ings about her vulnerability to her mother were confused. I admired her courage
in admitting how much power her mother had over her, yet I was disgusted at her
apparent crumbling in the face of her mother's opinions. I remember Mary Jane's
crying for her mother on our wedding night. What powers these mothers have!

I am unsure what this dream amounts to. Fear that Susan will become like her
mother? Fear that Susan will become like Mary Jane? Fear that I will uncon-
sciously drive Susan to become like either?

Having performed one wedding by the book, undergone one blood wedding,
and enacted one that weds, I have had occasion to reflect on the work of wedding. It begins earlier than we think and continues long beyond what we imagine. Probably, it begins in childhood fantasy and continues through childbearing
and divorce into dreams that persist after divorce. Likely, it has no clear beginning and no final end. The connections we make drop seeds, tiny and invisible,
and they are as persistent as the long-rooted ones that invade gardens. The big
seeds we call children, but there are small seeds, too; they are hardy, perennial,
and weather resistant. They hide in rocks, in boxes, in the dark corners of the
night. They spring up in the next relationship and the following marriage. In the
middle of this one, we are pulling weeds from the last one: weeding-wedding,
weeding-wedding. What a lot of work, especially if our politics don't allow us to
pollute the environment with chemical sprays.

As with all ritualizing, there are dangers in creating your own wedding. A
writer for *Time* magazine made this observation: "The vows that couples devise

are, with some exceptions, never as moving to the guests as they are to the couple. Too often the phrases, words overblown and intimate and yearning all at once, go floating plumply around the altar, pink dreams of the ineffable. Friends and family lean forward in their pews. The cleric beams inscrutably, abetting the thing, but keeping counsel. The guests are both fascinated and faintly appalled to be privy to such intense and theatrical whisperings."[12]

Nevertheless, some of us believe that designing rites is worth the risk. Whether or not couples construct their wedding ceremonies, they need domestic practices of a symbolic nature that lead up to and away from a wedding. Marriage requires continual ritual practice; a few showers and a honeymoon are not enough. And interpersonal growth is, by itself, insufficient.

The connection between a wedding and a marriage is often misunderstood. A wedding is a rite that effects a transition from the social state of being single to that of being coupled; much is packed into the term *effects*. Strictly speaking, people are never single—never simply unto themselves. We are always "the child of," "the brother of," "the aunt of," "the spouse of."

Consequently, a wedding rite is a ceremonial realignment, not just an invention, of ties that bind a couple. The ceremonial aspects of any rite are those that involve participants in negotiating power and constructing alignments. In a wedding two people ceremonially make relatives of each other. Relative-making, like lovemaking, is dangerous and difficult. Dangerous, because made-relatives (the in-law type) can be un-made by divorce. Difficult, because those things we make up, for example, fictions and weddings, also make us up. They may even outlive us. We cannot always unmake what we have made just by deciding to do so. When two people make love or make relatives, they generate or tap something (call it a force, thing, or institution—all are inadequate terms) outside themselves. It surrounds, or is between, them. And this "something" does not go away just because warm feelings wane and couples fight.

When two people divorce, observers are prone to attribute marital breakdown to social and moral factors. Seldom do they include ritual ones. They should. Wedding rites themselves can fail and not simply by the bride's tripping or the groom's forgetting his lines. There can be ritual failure as surely as there can be social or moral failure. Many denominational and civil weddings in North America are ritual failures. Marriages succeed despite them, not because of them.

This failure occurs for several reasons: lack of imagination, lack of living tradition, failure to think critically about rites, lack of community, too much or too little concern with personal expression. Any view of ritual that considers its primary task to be that of expressing participants' feelings or an institution's ideology is bound to flounder. Weddings fail as rites when they only *express* ideals and aspirations, when they *describe,* rather than actually *effect,* new states of being. Weddings must wed, not merely anticipate that a couple will later, somehow, make a marriage.

Certainly, weddings should express, but they should do more. They should transform. They should "do work" in addition to expressing. The goal is to wed, not just to ratify a legal transaction. Every couple approaching a wedding has a unique work, a magnum opus, to perform. The hardest part is divining what work needs doing.

Several years after my fieldwork in theater two former members of the company asked me to assist in designing their wedding, presided over legally and officially by an ordained colleague. The ceremony involved serious ritual work, and it incorporated motifs from the couple's habitual patterns. The groom insisted on being chased by the bride and the rest of the wedding party. The rehearsed chase was short, token. The enacted chase of the actual wedding was protracted: We spent the better part of an hour running and prowling through southern Ontario sugar bush. The scene predicted with uncanny accuracy how the marriage would end. Unfortunately, the bride and groom did not believe the chase divined their future. And even if they had, couples do not always call a halt to their wedding just because they discern the truth about their impending deed.

A wedding reaches forward and backward in time. It reaches forward, thereby ritualizing the future, by formal vows and promises, as well as by informal devices such as wedding pictures, gifts, legal obligations, and tacit understandings that outlast the ceremony itself. Ritualizing the future happens on those occasions after the wedding when the ceremony continues the work of wedding beyond the wedding ceremony itself.

How a wedding rite reaches backward into the past is less obvious. A priest, pastor, or rabbi may inquire about the couple's families and religious backgrounds. Something old may be worn and so on. But the most important, and most overlooked, heritage from the past is a couple's ritualization patterns, their routines of social interaction. Interaction ritual encodes unconscious elements such as family scenarios and personal habituations. It is crucial that the graft between interaction ritual and wedding ceremony be on good base stock. The ritual graft "takes" when the wedding rite itself permeates the marriage to the point where ritualization patterns are affected. What is usually missing in premarital preparation is any sense that ritual transactions between individuals have been transpiring long before a couple ever approaches an officiant.

Taken seriously, this idea implies far more than premarital counseling followed by an hour-long wedding and reception. It could imply, for instance, a week-long wedding with individual, couple, friend, and family phases preceded by certain ritual tasks (one might even say trials) during the preceding engagement period (for instance, periods of solitude and sexual abstinence). Such tasks would have to be designed to expose the dynamics of the couple's own ritualization and thus reveal both the strengths and weaknesses of their habitual patterns. Subsequently, a maker of ritual in consultation with a couple could design a ceremony to consolidate the strengths and compensate the weaknesses of the interaction rites.

Wedding-makers need to attend to the layers of a wedding: the couple's interaction ritual, a ritual maker's "divination" of that ritual, the ceremonial making of relatives, the ritualized aftermath. If these occur as they should, celebration is possible; otherwise, it is not. To enable a wedding to become a celebration of fidelity capable of permeating a marriage in these days of divorce, ritual-makers will have to learn to stitch together several pieces of ceremonial work into whole cloth. Such attention to ritual preparation is time consuming, and it demands work, both physical and spiritual.

Once in upstate New York I performed a wedding for two vaguely Unitarian artists from Greenwich Village. They approached the president of Union Theological Seminary, having heard the place was "with it." He sent them to me. They wanted it short. I had to plead and argue to stretch the ceremony to eight minutes. After it was over and the groom was slipping payment into my palm, he confessed, "You were right. I can't remember what just happened. The people had barely finished shuffling their feet when, suddenly, the service was over; I was shocked." Celebration in every culture is costly, and the effort to make it quick and merely expressive has led to its repeated failure.

" 'Til death do us part." What a ring this declaration has! At the very moment when a couple is becoming ceremonially glued, they contemplate becoming unglued: Old Death will part them. In this era of divorce and remarriage couples add an additional qualifier. We have become a society of serial monogamists, forced to drop a silent, bracketed interjection into the declaration: " 'Til death [or divorce] do us part."

My devoutly Baptist younger brother recently divorced and remarried with a rapidity that made our heads swim. The rest of his siblings had either contemplated the possibility or enacted the actuality of divorce, but Terry and his wife, along with Mom and Dad, were unimaginable as separate beings—in this life as well as the next. But the divorce happened nevertheless.

We were not invited to Terry's second wedding. The bride and groom wanted it small and private. But, as is the case in most weddings, there were social pressures that necessitated compromise. Sherry—among us siblings the fiercest advocate of family solidarity and the most persistent manager of attempts to assemble the whole family in one room—crashed the ceremony. Well, crashed is hyperbole. She "convinced" Terry to invite her. The ceremony was distinctly non-Baptist. In fact, it was a-religious, conducted by a justice of the peace. I wondered how could the bond possibly be eternal if eternity or its representative were not supervising the event. I had to work hard at swallowing the couple's desire to be married at a Putt-Putt golf course. "By the hole with the chapel over it," Terry said, hoping to stave off my criticism. How could my family be so oblivious to my ritual expertise? Here they were, sitting on a gold mine of good advice, and all they did was ignore it!

"Why?" I queried my brother.

"Because," he replied, "that was where some of our best conversations happened."

"Well," I laughed, "I guess Darrell and Cyndi [our brother and sister-in-law] have been together longer than the rest of us, and they were married at a wedding chapel in Las Vegas."

Terry's wedding set me to wondering what the genealogy of our family's weddings looks like. How did Mom and Dad marry? Grandma and Pappy? Grandpa Grimes and Nancy Ford? I became interested in what they actually did, even more interested in what they anticipated, dreaded, secretly imagined, and hoped for. Probably all of them paid lip service to the " 'til death do us part" clause, but I suspect they had a secret caveat quite different from the contemporary one. Neither Mom nor Dad, for instance, could make any emotional sense of the notion that death could part them. They agreed that it might, but only because Jesus had said that in death neither man nor woman is given in marriage. But did they always feel this way, even during the Depression? Was it years of marriage, four kids, and impending terminal disease that made them sure their marriage deserved to transcend death?

The act of wedding is still a mystery to me, even more so than death, about which I know nothing. Death, initiation, and birth themes are infrequent and thus special in my dreamlife, but marital ones have established squatter's rights. They recur with frightful frequency. My psyche works overtime at marrying. I have dreams in which I marry ceremonially, dreams dominated by an acute awareness of my current marital state, dreams in which I am married to the wrong person, dreams in which I completely forget that I am married. Night after I night I search for Susan, even though she is sleeping soundly beside me, even though I have no anxiety about being abandoned or any interest in abandoning. In dreams I lose track of her, search for her, feel heartsick that I have not seen her for years. Though we have a richly nourishing marriage that is immensely satisfying to both of us, the dreams persist and repeat themselves with the frequency and force of ritual. For years we have mythologized our relationship as a mystical marriage, flying in the face of conventional Jungian wisdom, which holds that such relationships do not occur within marriages. Although we are shy about such terminology and do not verbalize it publicly, we have no better words, and our view has persisted through arguments, diaper changing, and wrangling over budgets.

PART THREE

BURYING

Man is the only animal who stands abashed in front of death or sexual union. He may be more or less abashed, but in either case his reaction differs from that of other animals.

—Georges Bataille[13]

What should I send you [after you are dead]?
If I send an apple, it will rot.
If I send a quince, it will shrivel up.
If I send basil, without water it will wither.
I will send you a tear in a linen handkerchief.
But my tear was burning hot, and it dyed the handkerchief black.
I washed it in nine rivers, but I could not restore its color.
Then I washed it in a shallow stream, and I did restore its color.
But a partridge flew down to drink from the stream, and its wings were dyed black.

—Traditional Greek funeral lament[14]

8

BIRD DROPPINGS
ON THE BUDDHA

When the voice at the other end of the phone finished informing me that my son had "passed away" that morning, I created such a disturbance at the top of the stairs that the Zen master instructed a senior disciple to lead Susan and me to a storage room full of stacked, kapok-stuffed meditation cushions. Downstairs a celebration was just beginning. The garden and meditation room were packed with Buddhists and art aficionados who had come to see an exhibit of Korean calligraphy and ink paintings. The Zen center was raising money and throwing a coming-out party after several years of low-profile hibernation in Toronto.

Stunned by the news and wary of the exotic environment, Susan, then my fiancée, sat beside me, comforting me as best she could. Sitting there, I did not just sit, as one is supposed to do in Zen centers. Sitting, I raced. Down the road to Guelph my soul sprinted to be at my son's bedside. Then, scarcely having cradled him in my arms, I found myself doing more violence than I care to describe to his mother and her new husband. I punished them in a most unchristian, unbuddhist fashion for failing to keep their promise to call me whenever and as soon as Trevor was admitted to the hospital.

Sitting in the Zen center attic, my overheated brain raced to the Actor's Lab of several years ago. I began to dredge up meditation cushions from actor-training exercises that I had engaged in while doing fieldwork there. Following my own impulses in much the same way as I had been taught to follow my breathing in Zen practice, I had found myself kneeling and doing deep prostrations while lifting up a cushion as if it were some sort of offering. One afternoon, after numerous repetitions, I was struck with a clear image of Trevor; I was offering him up to ... to whomever. I was not sure whether to his mother, to God, or to something quite unknown. Those theater exercises had preceded by several years my knowledge that he had an incurable, terminal disease. When I originally performed the exercises, I suspected they anticipated loss by divorce, not by death.

Sitting in the Zen center overcome with grief and shock, I was flooded with an awful sense of appropriateness at facing a whole room full of meditation cushions. Later, I would haul twelve of them back to the Ritual Studies Lab, where I taught not only Rites of Passage but also a course called Zen Meditation, Zen Art. The irony was even deeper, since I had turned down the Zen master's invitation to become a Buddhist several months before, surprising myself by protesting, "I suppose I am inescapably Christian." At that time I had been practicing zazen for a dozen years but never thought of myself as a Buddhist. I had not worshiped as a Christian for a long time.

Sitting there, I continued to relieve and confuse my flagging soul with more memories and fantasies. I remembered having asked Trevor if he wanted to come to Toronto with us; after all, it was our weekend to be together. No, he had said emphatically, he was not interested in that old Buddha junk!

"Buddha junk?" I said, picturing him as an impertinent little sparrow pooping on Buddha's head. "I thought you liked Buddhas. You have a couple of your own, including the red one in the backyard. 'Buddha junk' sounds like a phrase your mom would use."

He had replied with a typical Buddhist answer: silence.

I went to wash my face, relieved that there was no mirror in the washroom. Susan and I sneaked down the stairs on tiptoe so as not to disrupt the celebration. We loaded the car with meditation cushions, each stuffed in a plastic sack—a dozen buddies being shipped home in bodybags after some godawful war in a foreign place.

During the drive to Guelph, I glimpsed myself in the mirror. I had broken a tiny blood vessel in my eyelid. I was not just crying; I was crying at—crying at Trevor, at the doctors, at the celebrating Buddhists, at the cushions, at the God who had refused to dole out proper bone marrow, at the stepfather who posed as father around nurses and doctors. Cowboys don't cry, but if they do—if they must—they cry mad.

Early in the summer Trevor had accompanied his mother and her fiancé to Europe. When he returned, having served as their twelve-year-old best man (so he announced), he referred to them as "my parents." I was still his dad, he admitted in the face of my queries, but they were his parents. They had bought him a new suit for the wedding, and his participation in the ceremony had magically transformed his act from one of complicity to that of family-making.

The only counter-ritual I had been able to muster was our annual pilgrimage to Clovis, a place where nothing ever happens. The presence of Trevor's grandparents, aunts, and uncles could at least dramatize the fact that he had two families, not one. Parents are always ogres in comparison to grandparents. I have a

half-baked theory: Religiosity has its real roots in grandparent-grandchild relationships, not parent-child ones, as Freudians imagine. In any case, Trevor had
felt sufficiently safe in New Mexico to confess, on the night before we were to return to Canada, that he had not wanted to come in the first place. He declared
that his mother and her husband (not his parents, I noted) loved him more than
Susan and I did.

"Oh, really? Why do you think that?" I asked, trying to appear neither hurt nor
angry.

"They give me money and buy me things. They're going to buy me a bicycle
when I get back."

"Good," I said. Then I informed him who sent the money. He was shocked to
hear that I sent a monthly check for his support. He was even more surprised by
the amount, though he had been reminded of it several times before. He said his
parents had told him that I sent only a little bit of money.

He paused, seemed to absorb for the first time the significance of what I had
said, and then changed the subject by asking if I had a will. I said I did. He answered yes when I offered to help him write one too, signed and sealed like mine.
I did not tell him that his mother and I had disagreed over informing him that he
had Fancones disease. I refrained from saying that it would likely take his life before he became an adolescent. Mary Jane had insisted on protecting him by hiding the fact. I thought he was being cheated by the deception. Although I was repeatedly tempted to trample her wishes underfoot, I accepted the doctor's
proposed compromise. The speed with which I would tell Trevor the truth about
his condition would be determined by the speed with which his symptoms became manifest.

We had left New Mexico for Canada certain that Trevor would be around for
several more years but suspecting that cancer would crowd the breath out of
Mom's lungs before we saw her again. Flying back, I was imagining her funeral,
not his.

But here I was, only two weeks later, barreling southwest down Highway 401 to
make his funeral arrangements in Guelph. He had said to me before we left New
Mexico, "Dad, I don't want to go to that new school in September. I don't want to
become a teenager."

He didn't.

When we arrived at the house where I had picked him up on alternate Fridays
and deposited him on Sundays, I shook a hand with a pastor at the other end of
it. His plastic-coated comfort had already been paid for, and I was told that the
funeral would be on Tuesday.

"It's already been set?" I queried, incredulous that I had not even been consulted, since Trevor had died only that morning. I knew that back in New Mexico
Mom was scheduled for radiation therapy on Tuesday, so she would be unable to
come with the rest of the family unless the funeral was postponed a couple of

days. On the way to the funeral home I did not bother trying to restrain my outrage, since it had become obvious in my conversation with the pastor that the funeral was going to proceed as if my family did not exist.

Mary Jane and her husband had left the funeral home just before Susan and I arrived.

"Where is Trevor?" I asked in a sickening voice that sounded too much like that of the funeral director.

"He's not ready yet."

"Not ready? Who is ever ready? I came to see him. I am his father. I want to see him now, ready or not. Where is he?"

"Down those stairs. Are you sure you'd rather not wait?"

I did not wait, and I was sure the funeral director considered me a boor for barging in on my son, who was not yet decorously dressed in his wedding suit but instead lay there in his birthday suit. He was barely covered by the white sheet. The overly protective director intruded, but I resisted by asking him to leave me alone with my son. I had more right to see Trevor naked and bruised by broken blood vessels from head to toe than he did. I wanted to wash him, sit with him, cry over him, but it was too late—not because he was dead, but because the funeral had already begun without me. Like a procession, it was already headed in one direction, while I was going in another. "This is it," I thought. "I have five minutes for a funeral." So I touched my son all over, as I had when he was born. I swore and I prayed without feeling any contradiction between the two kinds of utterance.

Upstairs again, I used the funeral home's phone to call Trevor's stepfather, the man who had said "passed away" instead of "died." I asked if we could hold off deciding the date of the funeral until I called my family in New Mexico. He said, "No, you are always doing things like this—disrupting other people's plans with your own ideas—and besides your mother, if she is ill, has no business coming anyway." I told him to go to hell and punctuated the invitation so loudly by slamming down the phone that the slick silence of the surroundings was thoroughly shattered. Later that evening I called back, and we agreed to bury the hatchet. As a token of his good faith, he agreed to put the funeral off by one day. I desperately wanted to believe in the integrity of our little gesture.

Two days later all the men and none of the women of my family flew into Toronto International. In view of Mom's condition, they decided it was best this way. A one-day delay in the funeral had not been enough. On the way home we stopped at the funeral home. After Dad and Terry stepped outside to blow their noses, Darrell joked and I complained about the soppy music floating above Trevor's casket. I became hysterical with laughter when Darrell said, "Oh, I don't know. Maybe it's appropriate. Trevor always liked K-Mart." Darrell didn't know that in my classes I described eastern New Mexico as K-Mart and Baptist country. On the way from Guelph to Waterloo Dad and Terry were solemn. Darrell and I were loony.

In southwestern, cowboy Christian families like mine the women do most of the emotional labor and the men, the physical work. Here we were, four men— their wives a thousand miles away and my fiancée at her apartment down the street.

Now what?

The day after they arrived I asked Dad to help me build a cross in the backyard. He said nothing as we stuck it into the mound where Trevor's red Buddha sat doing nothing. I knew Dad's Methodist sensibilities were probably being scraped by this pagan earthmound stuff, so I confessed, "I am not sure why I wanted to do this, but I don't expect much from the funeral tomorrow. I don't know who they design funerals for, but I am sure they are not designed for me."

"Me either," he replied, surprising me. "Must be for women. All those flowers."

I replied, "Probably not for women, but for some male funeral director's idea of women."

"Maybe so."

We dug in silence. Then Dad, obviously ruminating, said, "Making a cross is something I understand."

"Me too," I replied. "My religion is all in my hands."

The official funeral failed in ways too numerous to count. There was one limo, not two; those who pay are those who get served. The minister ministered to the mother and her family. Mary Jane, her decorum on full display, offered two front seats to us. We declined, choosing instead to sit together in the only place we could find five seats, the back row. Mary Jane's husband brought us a message: His wife would like us to step forward and view the body. Whatever affection my father and brothers had for their former in-law was squashed by this command performance.

We were excluded from the planning. In the funeral itself the only evidence that my family's wishes mattered was the presence of Hippie in Trevor's casket. Susan and I had bought the tiny stuffed hippo for Easter.

At the gravesite my family and I, along with the "others," were held back by a rope, while Trevor's mother and her family were admitted to the inner sanctum. Dad was so angered by this blatantly discriminatory act that he refused to go near the grave once the rope was dropped. Only one civil gesture transpired during the entire official funeral. After the graveside service my former father-in-law shook my father's hand as he confided, "Trevor sure loved you." It had been nineteen years since they last met and shook hands. The occasion was our wedding. The route from marrying to burying had been circuitous and devastating.

The minister's prejudices, along with the insensitivity of the funeral directors, so incensed me that grief had to vie with anger for breathing room. Noticing my dilemma, two former students, both already pastors, took me in hand. We kept our distance from the grave until the official ceremony was finished and the rest of the funeral party, gone. Then, to the horror of the gravediggers, we peeled back the astroturf from the dirt and began to lower the casket ourselves. We said some words and left a few things. When a busload of senior citizens stopped to view the grave, they stared at us as if we were grave robbers. Their eyes asked what sort of people would be so crude as to violate the decorum of a child's funeral.

Aunts and uncles had sent money for flowers, but the funeral became such a territorial battle between two divorced parents that we decided flowers would be taken later to the grave rather than to the funeral home. We waited until after the official funeral to deliver them. This ritual tactic seemed right to all of us men. Dad bought several buckets of gladiolus from the Waterloo Farmer's Market, having decided that the arrangements found in flower shops looked too much like those found in funeral homes. At sunrise on the way to the airport, we breached the gate of the cemetery and once again outraged the groundskeeper by violating the rules. We covered the fresh dirt with flowers not grown in hothouses.

After I put Dad and my two brothers on the plane, I stood wondering how they were going to tell this story to my mother, sister, and in-laws. How would Dad explain our putting a cross beside a Buddha, exposing graveside earth, depositing toys in the death hole, and raiding the cemetery to leave flowers not purchased at the florist's or sent to the funeral? Even though I suspected he had grown up seeing dirt at funerals and taking flowers from gardens rather than buying them in flower shops, I knew that under other circumstances he probably would not have condoned our behaving like the Dalton gang at a funeral. People are supposed to buy the whole package, even though in private they may complain about it. Would the women hear the story as just what they'd expect when males get together under duress? I wondered if anyone would report on the affection and solidarity we discovered among ourselves. They were not usually so overt.

The grief work was not done. In fact, it had not yet begun. Friends kept inquiring what they might do. I understood the need to do, so I began saying, "Come on the weekend; bring something to plant." Meanwhile, I was sorting Trevor's things. First, I would despair at having to see them at all. Then I would struggle to figure out who might be able to use what. And finally, I would become angry at how many things he had smuggled to Mary Jane's, since I was sure I would never see them again. I put up a tent in the backyard and laid some of his things in it: a white mask of his face, a stuffed dragon, a treasure box full of junk, Coyote (with a broken neck from being carried so much), Pink Panther (also with a broken neck), and a bolo tie from his grandfather. Trevor was afraid of the mask, even though he had wanted me to make it, because the students in my class were doing so. I doubt that he knew what a death mask was, but he seemed to sense death in the glossy, closed eyelids. For several days I cleaned the mound and sat in the tent with the mask, menagerie, and collected kid stuff.

When Saturday arrived, the tent was still up. I expected half a dozen people. Two dozen came. Some brought bulbs—tulip and crocus. Some carried small evergreens—a couple of cedars, a blue spruce. A kite arrived, slipped inside the back door. Food appeared as if conjured. The atmosphere in the backyard was gauzy. Things happened in a slow, hazy blur around me. I was permeable, a little elated, a lot sad. I lacked direction and did not mind that I did. I could hardly decide where to put the trees. People and food seemed to materialize and dematerialize. I was surprised that so-and-so showed up, just as surprised that so-and-so did not. A few friends sat on the air mattresses in the tent laughing, crying, playing with the toys. They milled around the lawn imagining what colors spring would bring. They nibbled, drank, and told stories about the horrible funerals they had been subjected to. They remembered their dead and tried to fly a kite, but the wind would have none of it. It was too early for kites; I wasn't finished with death, much less ready for resurrection. We buried some of Trevor's things near the mound. Only then did the obvious occur to me. By force of our ritualizing, the mound, not the cemetery where his body rested, had become his grave. In recognition of this fact we hung some deep-throated chimes in the tree above the mound.

Someone asked if I had seen the obituary in the paper. I said no. He remarked, "Good. Don't." Since he was the young Lutheran pastor who had observed, "At the funeral your family looked like the uninvited guests in the New Testament story," it was easy to guess why he was advising me against seeing the clipping. Usually parents keep such things as souvenirs. Who were in print as Trevor's parents? I wondered. Immediately, I began to imagine what was going to be on the tombstone. Whose son would the rock proclaim him to be? I sat in the tent smashing a tombstone thirty miles down the road, but the guilt of desecrating my son's already desecrated grave stopped me midway.

Funeral stories were told and retold in the tent. One mother was unabashedly continuing the funeral of her daughter. Her words and accounts were not reports but further enactment. Rites do not always finish when they seem to. They ride on the backs of other rites like trailer trucks mounted on flatcars.

Sometime after Trevor's two funerals Susan and I spotted a high hill with a large antenna guyed atop its crown. "Trevor liked TV," I said inanely as I pulled off the road. We flew the kite off to one side of the antenna. Finding a grassy spot free of cow pies, I lay on the ground watching the rainbow-colored, sperm-shaped kite flap its long tail and short arms as if swimming to heaven were a possibility. Trevor's left arm had been too short, one birth defect among others. I almost let go of the string, expecting to see the kite ascend into the beyond. Then I remembered that without a tether, kites come careening down to earth.

I tell university students that early Christians did not expect souls to ascend to heaven. They looked instead for the resurrection of the body, I say. Nevertheless, for the next month or so the kite convinced me that the ascension of the soul was a better idea. I was sure—no matter what I believed or didn't—that Trevor's soul was hanging around the wind chimes in the backyard.

I recalled having a similar sensation when Ken Feit died. One summer after Ken, Trevor, and I had spent much time together, Ken left to go on the road again with his suitcase of toys, his tales, and his Fool's Mass. A few nights later Trevor reported dreaming that Ken had come back. He was dead, in a car accident, and his hands looked funny. Trevor feared Ken's dream hands more than anything else in the dream. A few years later Ken died in an auto crash. Since I couldn't attend his funeral, I never got to see his hands. Even though I did not believe in heaven, I hoped Ken was up there in whiteface taking care of Trevor. The trouble with the fantasy was that I began to be afraid that Mom, in some unconscious way, might think it was her duty to go up after Trevor to look after him. Grandmothers do things like that.

I will not recount all the dreams I had about Trevor. My ritual life and dreamlife often consort, not because I consider it a principle to make them do so, but just because they do. Lured into theorizing, I would probably mumble something about the unconscious impact made by ritual symbols and actions, but I doubt that I would really be explaining anything.

In one dream Victor Turner, who died three months after Trevor, came in a dream. He wanted to go over the hill; the pun was obvious even in the dream. Others, including myself, did not want Vic to go. But in the end I assisted him. Something about the look on his face convinced me that I should.

When I awoke, I felt assured that Vic had been ready to go but, in addition, that he had come back to help me let go of Trevor. Turner is known all over the world as the scholar whose theory of ritual focused on liminality, the process of passing over a threshold, the state of being betwixt and between. He had taught me much about its processes and possibilities, and here he was tangled up in my ritual and dreamlife, a veritable ancestor.

If ritual has anything to do with repetition, then my dreams were a ritualizing activity of sorts. I cannot count the times I have dreamed that Trevor and I become separated—at train stations, on subways, in crowds. I look and weep and become enraged. Do not tell me about Demeter and Persephone; I know about that search already. Not believing in resurrection, I nevertheless dreamed him resurrected. I thought such a dream might be a turning point. I would not see him in my dreams again, I surmised. I was wrong. Of course, I have seen him since. Even resurrection, it seems, is not final. I wonder what it means to believe or not believe in anything. What I believe and what dawns on me are dissonant. I do not believe that Trevor literally fluttered about the wind chimes or that Vic literally came to advise me. I am not a medium. Yet my deeds, feelings, and imaginings suggest that I do not not-believe. I have no experience of ghosts or visions or gods except in the context of rites, dreams, and imaginings—all subjunctives, as Vic would have said, all as-if's. I have no interest in the occult. The nearest I get is liking ghost stories. But to me they are just that—stories, not reports.

Eleven months after Trevor's funeral Susan and I were married. We released doves and buried hair at the mound on top of which Buddha sat over the remains of Trevor's toys. I suspect Trevor did not want to weather another wedding. It is one thing to marry off a child, another to marry off a parent. Susan and I were left to plan our wedding without Trevor. No doubt it was easier that way. Second marriages have too much to prove as it is.

I forgot the first anniversary of Trevor's death; there was no ritual. But on the birthday following his death I constructed a scene in an indoor sandbox. I pulled out two of his birth pictures. In one he is stark naked. In the other the nurses have stuffed him in a Christmas stocking. December twenty-second, they had assured us, was close enough to make him a Christmas baby. I put the naked picture under the stocking-clad one. Around the picture I posted little guardians, mostly animals. Animals and children—a remnant of Victorian children's religion. To one side was a tiny purple coffin containing a skeleton with glass eyes. The skeleton had a key chain sprouting from its head, and the coffin, as I recall, once held bubble gum from the Short Stop on Erb Street. In a corner I stationed a black mountain. On the mountain was a tiny aromatic wreath made of cloves, and in the middle of it was a ceramic sleeping boy—a chopstick holder from my friend Koichi. At the foot of the mountain I put a small bowl containing an offering to Trevor, now my ancestor. It was a rubber Oreo cookie. Approaching the black mountain were three figures, two of them having been unpacked from one of those Russian dolls-within-dolls, the other, from Tetley or some other kind of tea. Half way through my sandbox ritualizing I recognized that by casting the three figures as wise men, I had made Trevor into the Christ child.

That evening *Three Godfathers* was shown on television. I do not like John Wayne because of his politics. Besides, he can't act. However, cowboy Christianity does not easily accept parenting, so I decided to watch, aiming to see if they got it right. The three crooks, who became in this allegory three wise men, carried a baby to—of all places—Jerusalem (not Bethlehem), Arizona. The Mary figure was dead and John Wayne was a poor substitute for the Virgin. Nevertheless, I believed when the wind whipped open the Bible and a voice told John Wayne that an ass and a colt were tied just over the rise. Humor helped me withstand the heavy draught of sentimentality that one had to swallow along with the "every child is Christ" message flogged by my sandbox ceremony and the John Wayne movie.

No one ever thought of Trevor as profound or precocious. His Grandma Nadine assured us he was smart as a whip, but she was his grandmother. Profound or not, he sometimes dropped lines—every kid does—that were worth scrapping together. I used to write them on the backs of used note cards and the edges of napkins. How strange they look, all titled and lined up neatly in a row like farm kids dressed up in their Sunday duds awaiting maternal inspection.

BIRD DROPPINGS ON THE BUDDHA

SAYINGS OF TREVOR
& CONVERSATIONS WITH HIM
BETWEEN 1975 & 1978

Yes, the sparrows,
if you treat them kindly,
will reward you with bird droppings.
(A traditional haiku)

Sayings

[While walking on frozen rain] Sounds crunchy. Sounds like cookies. My feet are eating cookies.

I've got this thought stuck in my mind. I can't get it out. I have a teddy bear stuck in my mouth. I am chewing on it.

I just love cartoons! I wish those guys, especially Pink Panther, were alive. I would buy a whole apartment building so we could live there, and I wouldn't play with my friends, just my cartoon friends.

Why do little people have to tell big people where they are going when big ones don't have to tell God where they're going?

I like God better than anything.

[The next day] I hate God. I hate myself.

Hey, God, I like rain. That's all. [uttered while walking in the mist]

I wish I had breasts so I could change my last name.

[Of a girl at school who sat in a puddle:] She's got things in her head. Dad, she's got animals in her head.

Are ants people to themselves? Do giants think people are ants?

I think I can. I think I can. I think I can. I can!

I wish I was dead. I don't want to be alive. I hate people.

[Later, lying in bed, chatting, chanting, singing:] You're IT! *Trevor, you're it! [Spelling out loud:]* T R E V O R ! !

God is not very nice. He won't even show his body—not even his head. Come on, God, show up! I want to see God. I want to see God. I can't see God.

I love Jesus and I really love God. And I love everybody. Also.

If God made Jesus come back from the dead, why can't he make my left hand strong?

God is stronger than the Incredible Hulk. He can kill anyone he wants.

Dad, what's infinity plus infinity plus infinity plus infinity plus infinity plus infinity? [Etc. for over a minute, until it sounds like a chant]

[After spilling chocolate ice cream on a clean tablecloth:] It's not my fault. Accidents happen, you know. Not my fault. Not God's fault. Nobody's fault.

Conversations

TREVOR: *What's that?*
RON: *Buddha.*
TREVOR: *Where is he?*
RON: *Right there.*
TREVOR: *No, I mean the real Buddha, not the statue.*
RON: *He died and was buried in India.*
TREVOR: *Aw, is that all?*
RON: *No. We say he is in us.*
TREVOR: *Where?*
RON: *Oh, the belly, I suppose. That's what Buddhists say.*

TREVOR: *Is that really Buddha?*
RON: *It is a statue.*
TREVOR: *Where is Buddha?*
RON: *In you. I told you the other day.*
TREVOR: *Is Buddha hungry?*
RON: *If you are.*
TREVOR: *Where is Buddha?*
RON: *I already said.*
TREVOR: *No, I mean, where does he eat and sleep?*

RON: *Still want to be a magician when you grow up?*
TREVOR: *[Angrily] No!*
RON: *What then?*
TREVOR: *God.*
RON: *God? You want to be God? Why?*
TREVOR: *So I can make you disappear for not giving me my dessert.*

TREVOR: *Hey, Dad, let's get bread and pray to God and Jesus and Buddha.*
RON: *Okay, there's some in the fridge.*
TREVOR: *[Checks] Nope, that's not good. We need—you know—the kind [he makes a breaking motion].*

RON: *A loaf?*
TREVOR: *Yep.*
RON: *We don't have one.*
TREVOR: *Then we can't pray. Maybe next time.*

TREVOR: *I have this feeling. When you light the incense and I go to sleep, I think those two guys [Buddha and Jesus] are up running around going to things. [Silence.] I have Buddha in my belly and Jesus in my heart, you know. I know a lot about God, you know.*
RON: *How do you know?*
TREVOR: *I've got him here inside my head. [A few days later Trevor's kindergarten teacher reported that he had announced he had Buddha in his belly—and Jesus, too. She wondered if Trevor got indigestion from the load.]*

TREVOR: *[After breaking his arm, sitting in the hospital] I wish I wasn't a person.*
RON: *Why?*
TREVOR: *[Thoughtfully, taking lots of time] I wish I was clay. ... No, I wish ... I guess everything gets crashed up. I wish I was God.*
RON: *Some people say God is everywhere.*
TREVOR: *Yeah? Well, he forgot one place.*
RON: *Where?*
TREVOR: *Here [long silence, crying]. No, no. ... Now I know. I wish I was wind. Wind never gets hurt.*

TREVOR: *What's that?*
RON: *A butterfly.*
TREVOR: *Why doesn't it fly?*
T'S MOTHER: *Looks like it's dying.*
TREVOR: *I don't want it to. Does everything die?*
RON: *Yes, everything.*
TREVOR: *Why?*
RON: *I don't know. Whatever lives dies.*
T'S MOTHER: *You guys stop the morbid philosophizing.*
RON: *You're the one who told him the butterfly was dying. Besides, I am only answering his question.*
TREVOR: *Dad, you're not going to die.*
RON: *Yes, I am.*
TREVOR: *I'm not.*
RON: *All living things die. Someday you will die.*
TREVOR: *Nope! If I see Death coming, I'll cut off his head with my yellow sword.*

[Several months later]
TREVOR: *Dad, will I die?*
RON: *Yes.*
TREVOR: *God won't.*
RON: *Perhaps not.*
TREVOR: *When I die, it will be okay.*
RON: *Dying is not bad, though we are sad when someone does it.*

TREVOR: *Don't you know I've had a hard day [tears welling up in his eyes]? Jen has been mean to me*
    all day,
    all day.
    I was going to marry her,
    but I'm not now.
    You're supposed to love each other,
    and all she does is make me mad
    and beg ice cream and money.
    And she's stubborn.
    I am not going to play with her until I am dead.
RON: *[Silence.]*

RON: *What are you doing?*
TREVOR: *Playing Muff.*
RON: *Muff died years ago. In the street. Remember?*
TREVOR: *[Silence.]*
RON: *Why are you playing Muff? Do you miss your dog?*
TREVOR: *No. When somebody dies, you have to play him. I just do it on rainy days [a long silence as he romps on the floor, chasing his tail]. When I die I want purple and yellow flowers, some rocks, and my animals and my birth certificate with me. Okay?*
RON: *Okay.*

Not long after Trevor's death, two friends long intent on having a child gave birth to a premature son. He was so early and tiny that he was expected to die. For his birth I gave him Trevor's autoharp; Brother Camillus, a kindhearted old Christian Brother who drank too much, had given it to Trevor during the Santa Fe Fiesta of 1973.

The imagination entertains all sorts of guests that the scholarly mind turns away at the front door. Late one evening I had let myself imagine that Trevor had come back as this new child. I said nothing about the fantasy. Later, I was glad I had not elaborated it.

After a few days Bob and Julie named the boy Daniel. He was still hanging on in the face of death, whose hungry maw was being held shut by some mysterious means. Within a few days Daniel's chances for survival jumped from 10 to 70 percent. With each new day there was increasing jubilation among hospital staff, friends, and the mother and father. We were beginning to think the couple would not lose this child.

But they did.

The tiny white casket sat atop a contraption, a maze of rollers, belts, and trapdoors. Staring at it, I was ten years old and sure that the trapdoors opened into the mouth of hell. What could be more like hell than the basement of a morgue? I had to correct myself: This is a chapel in a cemetery, not a morgue.

I hoped for silence and congregational singing, but neither transpired. This was going to be another prepackaged job. That I was working on unfinished pain and anger about Trevor's death became obvious as I discovered myself speculating that the funeral director worked for the Mafia.

Mourners and comforters were gathering. An aerosol spray hung in the air. No incense calculated to attract or repel the spirits, its fragrance was of Lysol spiced with Hai Karate shaving lotion, antiseptic and sickly sweet. Condolences were being extended, largely to Daniel's mother. Having had a belly full of "a child belongs to its mother," I could not help noticing. People appeared to assume that the father was in no particular need of comfort. Person after person shook Bob's hand and then lingered with Julie, talking with her, touching her. The emotional division of labor functioned to keep the mother's grief on display and to suppress that of the father.

During the funeral my only consolation was that the Anglican clergyman read scripture and refrained from preaching. But the comfort was short-lived. His homiletical silence was completely overshadowed by the fact that burial was not going to be part of the service. The funeral rite had a momentum and dynamic of its own that soared above the dead child, the grieving parents, and the rest of us, who were in a thick fog, not quite knowing what to do or how to feel. The traditions being evoked by the ceremony had no connection with the people gathered in that place.

Susan and I declined to attend the reception after the funeral and asked if we could come alone later in the week. Our friends agreed. Five days later we went with an apple tree. Initially, Susan would have been content with this expression of our sympathy, but I was not. I was restless and depressed about Daniel's funeral; what had needed doing had been left undone. I knew that in some vague sense I would be continuing Trevor's funeral, but I was likewise certain that Daniel's funeral was not finished for Bob and Julie.

I entertained the idea of building a casket but decided that such a thing would be too stark, too blunt. Daniel, I imagined, should be wrapped in a bundle, not put in a box. Not quite knowing why, Susan bought some tiny pots. We bought some nicely woven cloth, bells, and ribbon. I made a rag doll. At the last minute I fashioned a little Halloween ghost—the kind kids make by tying a string around a puff of handkerchief. Unsure what we were doing, and assuming that we might only plant the tree and leave, we arrived on our friends' front porch.

We were not sure how they would respond to this unplanned second funeral, and we were groping for a gestural vocabulary we did not have. Knowing we were treading on sacred ground, we hesitantly ventured to explain that we had brought some things. Our friends liked Susan's impromptu suggestion that we write messages and send gifts to Daniel on slivers of paper. Among other things he was given courage, warmth, and a pot to pee in (he'd had kidney problems).

Julie suddenly bolted from the room. Susan and I were afraid we had violated a taboo. But in a moment she returned with a piece she had been knitting for her child. She yanked the knitting needles out—a powerful, climactic act after which we were elevated (I almost wrote "reduced") to silence.

We stuffed messages in the tiny pots, which we then put in the rag doll. We tied the whole thing into a bundle and wrapped it tightly with yarn from the unfinished piece. Bob read something he had written. Then we planted the apple tree in the backyard (as for Trevor, so for Daniel) and buried the bundle at its base. Then we blew some bubbles.

When our friends applied for adoption, they were told that the waiting period would be three years. But one morning Bob saw Susan and me near the birth control counter in the pharmacy. He declared ecstatically, "We're getting 'one.' Soon!"

One summer shortly after Daniel's death the apple tree seemed to have died. Later it was thriving again.

When *Life* magazine decided to publish an issue in October 1991 containing some fifty photographs on rites of passage, I was interviewed by the author of the article. He wanted to know if I thought invented rites, self-consciously constructed rather than traditionally inherited, were ever effective. I was tempted to say no, because I knew of so many bad examples in which metaphysical pretensions had led to tortured self-deception. But I remembered the planting of trees for Trevor and Daniel, so I replied with a qualified yes. Most of the do-it-yourself rites published in manuals embarrass me. They lack awkwardness, tentativeness, ordinariness, and modesty. Even so, many people have no other alternative than to invent makeshift rites with which to patch the holes in the fabric of their ripped collective lives.

9

A FUNERAL
UNDONE

Grandma was president of the New Mexico Women's Christian Temperance Union. She bird-dogged her children and grandchildren until they signed pledges declaring that they would never let the diabolical stuff touch their lips. She was not tall. But she was big, an important woman. She was friends with the ex-governor. When he retired, he built her two lamps, one of which now lights the desk I write on. She wrote a book, paid a vanity publisher to print it, and gave copies to all her friends, children, and relatives. They are grateful for it; they feel guilty when they don't read it. Since her death, she has become wiser with each passing year.

Grandma ran the church. The pastors, whom Clovis Methodists would have called preachers, only thought they did. Grandma—not Mom, not Dad—was the dominant religious force in my life. She was the only patriarch I ever knew.

At Christmas Grandma sometimes played Santa Claus. In other southwestern families fat uncles or grandfathers played the role. Even though her verbal expressions of humility were profuse, Grandma was the only woman in the family whose sense of self-worth would enable her to play it. One Christmas, when I was about fourteen, she gave me a folding army shovel. I still carry it in the back of the car. I use it for digging up wild grasses to transplant into the backyard, where we hope to displace the domestic grass. We used it to plant two placentas beneath the smoke bush. It was an army surplus shovel, its purpose military. I use it like a ploughshare. Not that Grandma was a pacifist, mind you—she was a Sargent before she married to become a Williams. Sometimes you just had to fight, she would counsel, like the patriarchs in the Bible. Some of her sons had been in the war. In the Bible God sends people to war. That's how we know war is necessary. Yes, of course, we are supposed to turn the other cheek and be peacemakers, but sometimes you have to go to war. God blessed America. We have to defend her (though, Lord knows, she's not perfect), so she can spread the Gospel to the rest of the world.

Once, without knowing that I was implicated, Grandma called the police to break up a fight in the alley behind her house. I was a paperboy, and another news carrier had threatened to beat up Darrell, my brother. I had been taught to defend him, along with my mother's honor and my country, so I punched the guy. The other paperboys hurried the two of us across the street so the *News Journal* managers would not discover the brawl and call the police. The guy was bigger than me, but slower. I kept hitting him, knocking him over parked bicycles. He kept coming back, head ducked, missing me with the predictability and comedy of slapstick. I was winning when the police arrived. And I was threatening to hit the policeman when Grandma strode out to see what was going on. Caught in the act of violence, I publicly shamed her. Perhaps I now use her shovel in the garden to redeem myself.

I was to be her spiritual heir. I was chosen. She chose me; that made it a calling. She used to say "my child" to all of us, but I was special—so I thought and so she said—because the Lord had summoned me from among the sprawling family brood to spread his word. I was the first of her grandchildren whose ears were sufficiently tuned to hear the barely whispered call of the still, small voice. She and I were thick as thieves. She steeped me. I soaked up whatever she taught. I believed her; I was no fool. I knew where the power was—with God, of course, but God had his chosen vessels. She was such a vessel. Men did not cross her.

Grandma would have been proud. Going steady with a new girl, I had just returned from church camp. This one was not in faraway Texas but only a few blocks away, up Tenth Street. We were strolling arm in arm across the campus of Clovis High. A loud voice shattered our enamored gaze.

"Hey, asshole!"

The accusing voice belonged to Buddy Jacobson. He had beaten my nether regions to pulp when I entered high school last September. "Initiation," he had sneered, as he and half a dozen others lined up to see if they could break their oak paddles over Jimmy Stewart and me.

I ignored him.

"Hey, Greasy Grimes, motherfucker, I am talking to you."

I started to turn in his direction, but Marlene tugged at my elbow and we turned a corner.

The next day the scene was repeated. Buddy was surrounded by an audience of football players this time. His taunts were louder and more aggressive, but no more articulate. I had spent the night crying in shame, talking with Mom and Dad, praying, swearing. It was the morning after, and I had a strategy.

He reissued his unholy invitation: "Hey, you miserable son of a bitch, why don't you come over here and let me shove this fist up your ass? Motherfucker!"

I had prepared Marlene. She let go of my arm and slipped around the corner without me. I turned and walked toward Buddy, David approaching Goliath.

"What did you say?" I asked with uncharacteristic bravado. The group tightened around me. This was a huddle and I was a football.

"You heard me, shithead," he said.

"Yeah, I guess I did," I replied. He outweighed me by sixty pounds. I was five-eight. He was six-two. I was now a city kid. He was still a shitstomper, a country boy who gunned a pick-up with dual chrome stacks. I delivered papers on a Schwinn Phantom. He loaded hay. I tossed papers in people's yards.

I reached into the back pocket of my Levis and pulled out a Gideon New Testament.

"See this?" I challenged. Someone gasped. "This is a Bible. You ought to read it."

I shoved it toward the horns on his belt buckle. He leaped back as if the Good Book were radioactive.

"You goddamned son of a bitch," he screamed, his voice rising to girlish heights. "I ought to kill you!"

"Try it," I retorted, my confidence escalating rapidly. "Meanwhile, this will do you some good."

My talisman was working. I had his balls in a vice. Later, when I would tell the story, I would use St. Paul's imagery instead of truck-driver terminology: "I heaped coals of fire on his head."

Grandma was proud.

Just before I turned to walk away, I noticed Buddy's eyes. They were streaked red with fury, wide and white with hatred. Behind my back I could hear the astonished hubbub of the guys as Buddy's venomous stream of swearing pelted my back. I couldn't refrain from snickering at its adolescent inarticulateness. I whispered in a volume that he was sure to miss: "Learn Spanish, asshole; you could swear better if you knew some Spanish."

When Pappy became critically ill, I bused home from college, hoping to be with him in his dying and intending to participate in his funeral. When I arrived, relatives explained that the ceremony had to be moved from Trinity, which was small, to First Church, which was enormous and on Main Street. Trinity folks regarded First Church people as uppity, so I felt peculiar about our borrowing their sanctuary. But Pappy had lots of friends, the relatives assured themselves, and the crowd would be large. Recently, he had begun to drive an old Cadillac, so why not act like it?

He died of kidney failure a few hours after I arrived at Clovis Memorial. Upon his expiration, everyone but the orderly and I left his room. They congregated in the hall. Since I had barely arrived and had not seen him for more than a couple of hours, I wanted to be with him, to touch him. It seemed a desecration to let some stranger pull the catheter tube out of his white, fuzz-enshrouded, old man's penis, which I'd never laid eyes on before. So I pulled it out, shuddering at the pain the corpse must have felt. I pulled that plastic sidewinder out of him, by God (I could hear his voice in mine). The scene is etched in my memory. It, not the funeral, was the real gesture for me. I can remember almost nothing about the formal ceremony, although I helped conduct it—perhaps because I helped conduct it.

Meanwhile, a scene was transpiring in the hall. Grandma was uncharacteristically distraught, complaining to and about God in a way that shocked her grown-up children, who were huddled around her trying to contain her wail. Several years later she would confess that she had almost lost her faith. A daring few speculated that she had in fact lost it.

When Grandma died a few years later, I was home from graduate school for my annual summer pilgrimage. She had been in the rest home for months, gradually becoming incapacitated, knowing less and less, recognizing fewer and fewer of us. She, whose mother had been an esteemed member of the Ku Klux Klan, seemed to recognize only the black nurse who tended her with obvious solicitude and care.

Mom had long since intervened to prevent Grandma, now confined to her sickbed, from coercing the pastor into making a place for me in his pulpit. My statements about the Vietnam War had already made me an embarrassment to Grandma and numerous others of the Trinity faithful. To everyone's mutual relief I was no longer being asked to preach. Grandma was dying, disappointed in her grandson. I hadn't lost my faith momentarily under the stress of some crisis. Rather, I had deliberately rejected the sacred teachings lavished on me. Before she slid into senility and then into a permanent coma, she suspected, maybe even knew, that I no longer venerated a perfect Bible or put high stock in the virgin birth. She didn't dare ask what I thought about the resurrection, although she would occasionally torment herself by asking questions about my view of creation in six days. She had feared my spiritual corruption before I left to go back east, and soon her fears were confirmed. She was never good at concealing how she felt. She was never, as far as I know, accused of being diplomatic. Though no longer her spiritual heir, I am, unfortunately, her heir in both diplomacy and decorum.

When Grandma died, many assumed that I would preach her funeral. Probably, they thought that doing so would bring me back into the fold. I wasn't sure I even wanted to attend, much less officiate, at the funeral. Too much remained unfinished between her and me. I was still rebelling against her tutelage, and she was dead, disappointed with my liberal, communist, catholic ideas. I had never been able to tell her, as I had Dad, that I had learned everything they labeled communist at Sunday School, not at Columbia's graduate school.

Dad, seldom known to play mediator, averted the impending dilemma by having a violent muscle spasm in his back. He was walking across the living room when suddenly he fell, as if stomped from above. The scene was breathtaking. Lying flat on his back, he peered up at me in terror as if God had kicked him in the head from the sky. He lay there embarrassed and twisted with pain.

Dad and I missed Grandma's funeral. I drove him to a clinic in Oklahoma City and then one in Lubbock, Texas. We laid him out flat under a homemade, pink camper shell mounted on the bed of a pick-up. The shell leaned like the tower of Pisa. For the first time in his life he was dependent on me. I got to carry him on my back as he had once carried me on his when my leg was smashed in a tractor accident. He was ambivalent about missing Grandma's funeral, but I was happy to have a legitimate excuse. I was a man doing what was needed and necessary. I was saving my dad.

HEAVEN´S GATE

"Mercy!" crooned the granny,
saintly,
old, and
dying white.

Nigger Lady,
her servant friend
so-named for years,
had just pushed
with the gentleness of Jesus
a tube up her collapsing nostril.
She set it up high,
with altitude enough to make the wind blow.

The old woman raised a wail,
a low granny wail,
a howl coyotes wouldn't recognize.
Inside,
a trembling white girl
quaked at the sight of a hulking Negro
bearded,
holy,
male,
and tending the gate
of home,
waiting,

for whatever soul
by right was his.

She imagined she knew
who would greet her.

She kept it white
all her life.

Even her old man couldn't stain it
by dropping brothers and sisters
into its hollows and dens.
She was keeping it there,
safe and soft in a velvet vault,
waiting
for the Word
to deliver an invitation
engraved in gold
by the boss of golden streets.
He would call her
where no liquor
or color
could taint the taste of holy song.
She would fly away,
over there,
where He could pet her
poor old blue head
and touch her soul
in whatever part of her body it lay.

Six years after I missed Grandma's funeral, it happened of its own accord. The time was a lonely and painful one. I was entangled with Morag, stupidly and fiercely pursuing everything my marriage had not been. Trevor was with Mary Jane, and I was living alone in a cramped, nondescript apartment with grayish-green floors. It was sparsely furnished with cheap, creaking furniture picked up at garage sales and bought at the Goodwill Store. Christmas nostalgia suffused the winter air. Since the nostalgia reminded me of the family I no longer had, I both craved and hated it.

I am not a moody person, but an indescribable mood haunted me. I avoided mirrors, because a pall was draped visibly, like a veil, across my face—the wounded prince look, someone called it. My intuitions and paranoia were high. I felt sorry for myself. I was needy, hungry, and hurting. Blind as a sidewinder in spring, I would strike out at anyone who threatened to deepen or relieve my pain. I should have carried a bell or worn a sign: "Divorcing: Taboo."

December 22, 1978, was Trevor's eighth birthday and the first one following my final separation from Mary Jane. Intending to commemorate his birth—which is radically different from celebrating a birthday—I wrapped myself in my brown Zen meditation robe. I would meditate on his birth, following impulses as they welled up.

For no particular reason I put on burnt sienna facepaint. Looking in the mirror, I jumped back, startled. Some creature who had just escaped a fiery pit stared back at me with bloodshot eyes. Afraid of losing my trail in a dark wood, I pulled out a tape player and set it to record what was about to happen. Then I sat down on a black meditation cushion to wait.

I remember little of what transpired, but I still have the tape, which I avoided playing for almost fifteen years. In writing this chapter, I listened to it for the first time. I had to press my ear to the speaker as if overhearing a lunatic. Sometimes the sounds were inaudible, sometimes clear but deranged. Nevertheless, I could follow the emotional rhythm for its full, tortured forty-five minutes. I could feel my way through it, even though many of the sounds and words were too faint to make out. Even in private I suffered acute embarrassment listening to the tape. No one else has heard it, and I censor my account of it here.

I am making guttural sounds as if I have all the time in the world. They sound like vocal stalking; I am searching for something. I don't know what. Occasionally, the noises resemble sound stories that Ken Feit, Trevor, and I used to make up, but whatever narrative they seem to suggest soon breaks off for more animal-like growling and prowling. Words and sounds weave a braid through the tape. The sounds are probably the more significant, but I have no way of either describing them or saying what they mean.

Something like a word emerges: "Yitzaak." With variations it is repeated over and over. Eventually, it becomes, more or less, the Hebrew for Isaac. Recalling Trevor's birth, I am led to Isaac, whose father sacrificed him, at least in intention. I am swamped with guilt.

Suddenly, out of the verbal rambling comes, "It doesn't rain. Why doesn't it rain?" I am alluding to the drought that cost my family its farm in the 1950s. I had been about Trevor's age when I first realized that something was going wrong in the universe. I am also invoking T. S. Eliot's "The Wasteland," since I associate that poem with the Dust Bowl drought.

"I've got a knot in my belly," I say. "Are you going to kill him and eat him?" I ask. I suspect that I am amalgamating two stories here: Jonah and the whale, Abraham and Isaac. Abraham is not only going to sacrifice his son but cannibalize him as well. He will live off his son's flesh. I am playing with the story in ways that resemble Kierkegaard's retellings of it.

Eventually a long, rapid string of words leaps from the speaker. I no longer have to strain to hear them: "There is always sin and there is always dust and I want a mask on my face so my nose won't drip and my mother has got a bull ring in her nose and she is not a bull but a cow. I want to eat that cow. I don't want to eat that cow. Don't hit that cow between the two eyes. They're too brown to hit between her two eyes. When I am a hundred, I want to eat that cow. I am sick of pig and I am sick of beans and I don't like bacon."

This is an associative string intelligible to me, though probably not very meaningful to anyone else. (I wasn't engaging in this free-form, ritualized search for anyone else's benefit.) The string of words links sin with mortality, dust, and shame. In my alienated state I want to hide. I already have on facepaint, and now I wish for a mask too. The mask evokes the hay fever filter that Mom had to wear on the farm. All her male children had hay fever. Only Dad and Sherry escaped it. We used to kid Mom about her bull ring, the odd-looking hay fever filter she sometimes wore in her nose. The cow is the one Dad killed by laying a sledge-hammer between its eyes. We had no more steers, and we were too poor for bullets, the usual way of preparing cattle to become food. For some reason I was allowed to witness the killing and butchering of this one. As a child I grew tired of bacon and pork. I wanted to eat beef, but watching a cow's slaughter, especially with a sledgehammer, stunned me. On the tape I identify with the cow. As the words tumble out of the recorder, I remember thinking, What am I doing wrapped in a Buddhist robe with its nonviolent, vegetarian ethic when I am such a carnivore heated by such anger?

The words on the tape take a new turn: "You took my dog in a bag." I am complaining at Dad, since he hauled off more than one stray dog and cat in this manner. "You took my dog in a bag, in a toe sack, in toe sack" (which is what my family called a gunnysack). "And why do I have to wear a toe sack as a shirt? Shirts made out of sacks I don't want, not those flowered flour sacks. They are for girls, not boys." An acute source of embarrassment for me as a child was our poverty and the homemade, flour-bag shirts that advertised it.

I continue, the momentum building, "That bull is black but that bull is not a bull; it's a cow. It is black and it acts like a bull and it chases me." Blackie really was a cow, but since she chased people, we called her a bull—a primal source, I am sure, of some assumptions about gender and power.

Again to Dad, very rapidly: "I fell in the horse tank with my overshoes on, and my overshoes held water and I fell to the bottom and the ice was thick and you came and got me and I was hanging on by the side." If I had become the evangelist I aspired to be, I am sure this winter incident on the farm would have become fodder for an allegory about salvation.

"There I was on the tractor. ... You pulled me off and carried me. My leg was smashed. All I wanted to do was plant watermelons. You carried me on your back. You were my good horse." The reference is to a childhood incident. I was about ten and had convinced Dad to let me ride on the plow so I could scatter watermelon seeds in the rows of corn he was planting. At the end of a row, when the powerlift pulled the blades out of the ground, my leg got trapped between it and the tractor fender, smashing my leg near the ankle. As testimony to the accident, my right leg and foot are now shorter than the left. Sometimes I catch myself mythologizing Dad. Why does my memory try to ignore the fact that he, as driver of the tractor, was largely responsible for the accident? Instead of blaming him, I find myself praising him as savior and steed.

Given what eventuates from this stream of words, I suspect I was marshaling mythic male guardians to give me courage for taking on the Big Mama, Grandma. This childhood event, in which Dad carries me to the house and then the hospital, is reversed many years later when I carry him to Oklahoma and Texas, thus missing Grandma's funeral.

I continue spilling words and make the crucial turn in this verbose search: "She came down from the mountain, goddamnit. She was the man." When I uttered these words, I had no idea who "she" was. Eventually, it becomes clear that "she" is Grandma in her most mythologized form. Insofar as she comes down from the mountain, she is also Abraham. She is a patriarch.

As if frightened, I leap back into what I can only call grizzly speech. I growl and carry on like a bear.

"Grandma, God Almighty. God Almighty, Grandma." I acknowledge her functional divinity by using a version of profanity that I heard from Pappy. She would have denied the status (I deny it too) and been less than happy with his using God's name in vain. Nevertheless, the child who grew up under her tutelage experienced her power as divine in its exercise.

"That's what Pappy said to you. He would say, 'God A'mighty, woman, get off it. Shit!'"

I sometimes wished he would say this to her. I doubt that he ever did.

"What were you doing out in the hall, Grandma, losing your faith? You don't have a right to lose faith." We in her church and family trapped Grandma as surely as she trapped us. We couldn't bear for her to have the same doubts that plagued us.

"I didn't go to your funeral, because my dad hurt his back. Dad carried me on his back, so I carried him on my back. I was a turtle. I didn't go to your funeral. I didn't go to your funeral. You were always on my back. Get off my back, Grandma. You were heavy, a real heavy."

In the Babylonian creation epic the god Marduk has to get drunk to bolster his courage before he lops off the head of his mother, Tiamat. Here I strut and accuse as if I weren't afraid of Grandma's power.

"Gray-headed old lady Abraham. Grandma Abraham. Grandma Abraham." The chant continues for some time.

Then I begin to wail. At first it is forced, pushed, pretended. "I am not afraid of you. I don't have to be your chosen one, your performing seal, your preacher boy."

Grandma, the only patriarch I ever knew

I begin whining. But there is a very sudden, startling tonal shift as I declare, "I don't want your shawl." By now it is obvious to me that I am, in fact, conducting a funeral. I tell Grandma calmly, decisively, that I refuse to assume her spiritual mantle.

"I don't want to be a woman in the house. I want to be a house."

Now a threshold is crossed, and I am faced with a basic conundrum. Declaring that I don't want to be a woman in the house means that I don't want to be domesticated. But I want to be a house, that is, domestic. I want to be or to have a home. I begin to weep in earnest, repeating the petition, "I want to be a house. I just want to be a house."

Then the theme shifts, "I want to be a watermelon." Watermelon: sweet water in a dry land. Watermelon: seeds, thus progeny. Watermelon: the desire for which precipitated the tractor accident.

After a flood of tears, sounds emerge that eventually become recognizable as "Aidio, adios, a-dios, ah-dios." A second round of crying sets in. Here the real grief of missing Grandma breaks forth. For the first time since her death I let myself miss her. Now I am crying for her rather than at her or for myself. "Adiós, mamasita. Good-bye, Grandma." Overwhelmed by grief, I begin choking and coughing. Eventually, the crying becomes almost musical. No longer self-conscious, the crying follows its own course for several minutes.

I conclude with what sounds like a new, surprisingly affectionate farewell: "Big Grandma Book. Good-bye, Big Grandma Book. Goodbye, Grandma."

What I intended to be a birthday commemoration for a lost son quickly turned into an exploration of my relationship with Dad. It, in turn, evolved into an active, even aggressive meditation on my grandmother as first spiritual master. Finally, it became a funeral. Funeralizing sometimes happens despite our intentions.

Missing the funerals of those who shape our lives either for better or worse is a decidedly bad practice. Since stumbling into enacting Grandma's funeral, I have become shy about advising people to skip what are predictably awful rites of passage. Defective or not, they sometimes enable transitions that nothing else can facilitate.

A funeral avoided leaves business unfinished, and there are few things worse than some ceremony's trying to work itself out through us when we are either resistant to it or unaware of its covert manipulation. A missed rite enacts and reenacts itself in surreal ways. If we flee a major transition, it will pursue us. If we don't do the work of passage, it will bird-dog us until we pay it proper attention.

LAST FRONTIER

The gnarl of this grizzly's human hand
pounded the limits
of earth's slim possibility.
Bent on peace and good order,
a bowed spirit-broom,
servant of the mothers-in-waiting,
turned the bear's blow
and banished his bluster
across the prairie,
beyond the ditches of heaven.

He was no match
for one whose roots
tied her more to mother
than a man can swat
or love.

Grandma:
Would you dismember
*   by caring and carving?*
Would you mash a mere hammer
*   with pillows?*

His thin questions
were little enough with words,
hardly protection
for a hairy male.

The years have instructed him.
The fears and grandmas are his,
so he'd best unplug the projector
and call the old woman home.

All a foreshortened bear's arm can do
is kiss the hands
that are his own
and hope the old lady
will grow gentle
with age and fat.
Surely this is more delight
than rage or smothering.

For man the animal
the last frontier is a household,
and the kitchen
is the heart of darkness.

10

WORDS FOR
A BUNDLING RITE

Varch 4, 1985. The roaring winds of a snowstorm awaken me from a dream about Jean Genet, who is wielding a knife in a roller-skating rink. Somehow I know the dream means that Mom is dead or dying. *Why* the dream means this or *how* I know this is its meaning escapes me. Perhaps the connection is that death comes as a thief in the night and that Genet is the epitome of night thieves.

Susan and I go for breakfast at Angie's Kitchen. We are forced to walk, trudging through a whiteout, wondering if our favorite local restaurant will be open on such a morning. Over blueberry pancakes and scrambled eggs I tell her the dream and confess that I am not sure how I have arrived at its significance. Then I walk to work at the university. When I enter the door, the phone is ringing. It is Sherry, my sister, saying that Mom is dying. Mom dies an hour later, while I am trying to shovel the car out of the driveway.

Trevor died early in the fall just as school was starting. Mom died in the dead of winter. She was buried on her wedding anniversary, a synchronous twist at once diabolical and perfectly appropriate. The coincidence squeezed many a tear from her friends, kids, and mate.

I had to pay a neighbor to blow my driveway free of snow. Since traffic could not move in the direction of the airport until the next day, I arrived too late. When would "on time" have been? Mom had been ready to die.

The previous summer she had been morbid, self-indulgent, manipulative. Without success we had tried to love her out of her all-consuming self-pity. The next summer she was assured, calm, even radiant. I found her puzzling, tantalizing.

I almost did not hear the story. I was packing my bags to return to Canada when Sherry came into the bedroom.

"Has Mom told you anything yet?"

"Anything? What do you mean?"

"I can't say. But you'd know if she had. I'm not supposed to tell."

"I see. I take it there is something to tell."

Sherry grinned in her toothy way and muttered as she walked out of the room, "Remember, I haven't told you anything."

An hour or so later Mom ambled into the room where I was reading. "Hate to see you leave," she said.

"Yeah. I hate to go, but it's time for Trevor and I to start school."

Silence.

"You and I have not had our talk yet," I urged.

"What talk?"

"You know. We always have a talk."

"Sometimes we do. Sometimes we don't." Silence. "Sherry told you. I'll kick her butt!"

"Sherry didn't tell me anything except that there was something to tell."

"It's nothing."

"You're lying."

"I'm just not telling everything." She grinned sheepishly.

"Well, then, let me ask you a question. What has happened that you're so different this summer? Last summer you were unbearable. Remember when you asked us what we would say about you when you were dead? Then we got into that tortured discussion about what Grandma had really been like. You of all people—you, the realist in the family—were giving us that romanticized crap about her and trying to elicit similar stuff about yourself from us. You know very well how much you are loved. And it was you who taught us that we could love people and still face the *whole* truth about them. 'Warts and all,' you used to say. Anyway, it's obvious that you're at peace with yourself, and I want to know why."

"You have to promise not to make fun of me."

"I won't. Why should I?"

"You're pretty flat-spoken, sometimes harsh, about these things."

"What things?"

"Spiritual things."

"I want to know what happened."

"You have to stop being a professor."

"You sound like my Zen master."

"What?"

"Never mind. Forget it. Just tell me. No laughing, no judgments. I promise."

She turned beet red with shyness. For a moment I was gazing on a young girl who had just been asked out on her first date, a wife about to be seduced by her new husband. Her voice began to tremble as she talked. She would not look me in the face. Her eyes searched out the corners of the ceiling and scanned the floor.

"One night I was reading the Bible. All my life I have heard about assurance, but I have never been sure. Oh, I always went to church and prayed and all that, but I never quite felt what they say you're supposed to. Anyway, I was reading the Bible. Your dad and I have been reading it a lot lately, every night since we found out ... you know. We read and I pray for just one thing: to know the presence of ... of, well, I guess you'd say the Holy Spirit. I wanted to know for sure. The presence, I mean."

She looked at me squarely in the face, searching to see if I was going to laugh or raise a skeptical eyebrow.

Then she continued, "I fell asleep. Later I woke up feeling strange. I thought I was going to choke to death; something stopped up my throat. I was afraid, really scared. Then suddenly I could feel something—like a cool breeze coming over me. It blew on me. I could feel it. It was real. And the windows were closed. When it blew across me, I could feel the choking in my throat being lifted away."

A long silence followed. Finally, she broke it. "That's all. I told you it wasn't much."

"Not much, my ass," I said, trying to deal with the problems in my own throat.

"Well, it was important to me. But I didn't hear voices or see visions or anything like that."

"But look at you."

"What about me?" she retorted.

"You're beaming," I said.

The description made her shy and self-conscious again.

She asked, "Then you believe me?"

"Of course, I believe you." Besides feeling hurt at having been excluded from her confidence, I was so taken by what she said that I began nervously to fill up the silence. "What made you think I wouldn't believe you? Look, I hate the phony versions of religion so much because I am awestruck by the real ones. I know my way of being religious is a puzzle, maybe even an embarrassment, to you and Dad, but it's still a way of being religious. I am not a dirty old atheist, you know, even though I'm not quite what people around Clovis like to call a believer either. What you're like now—I mean your attitude and your face—convince me. Words by themselves don't, but you're obviously a changed person."

"The way I feel now, I'm ready to die and I'm ready to live, I guess you could say."

At the funeral home I went in alone. Everyone else had already visited Mom. I cried, but not a lot, which surprised me. I remembered the summer talk. I was not as upset as it is proper to be. I put my Eagle Scout medal under her pillow. Now that I was over forty, it was time to give up being a good boy. I was returning my good-boy heritage to its source. I knew from dreams that the eagle in me was a mother, good at hatching eggs, fierce at defending the nest. I didn't need the medal to remind me anymore. Mama Eagle was now an ancestor, resident of soul space.

"Who's doing the funeral?" I asked my sister.

"The preacher at Trinity. Stanley is going to assist."

"Stanley? Our cousin Stanley? You mean our Baptist preacher missionary cousin?"

"That's the very one."

I said nothing. But I spent the next few hours angry, confused, jealous.

The phone rang. It was the minister asking me if I felt I could do something at the funeral. "Yes, of course," I said without hesitation. We were to meet in the morning to go over the details. I could hardly believe what my mouth had just said. I would be dishonest if I claimed that my yes was motivated solely by love for Mom. Damn the competitive spirit that fights for what it no longer even wants!

The knot about Stanley was untied more easily than I would have guessed. Death softened me up. My Baptist cousin, whom I had not seen since he was a kid, was gentle and unpretentious. More pious than me, to be sure, he was no less observant, no less thoughtful, no less human. I could not continue to dislike this person whom I had dismissed on the basis of his good Christian reputation in west Texas. I gave up my jealousy. I was relieved that someone had picked up the flag that Grandma was sure I had dropped when I failed to become a preacher. Stanley probably didn't even know there was a flag.

Minister, cousin, sister, and brother—we planned the service. I suggested what I thought were minor changes, all in the direction of being more, not less, traditional: congregational hymns instead of solos, scriptures that expressed pain and suffering as well as assurance and hope, and time to linger and speak parting words at the grave. The minister raised his eyebrows about allowing time for last words but did not object very strongly.

The service was simple. It felt good. I was not busy shredding the funeral ceremony for its ineptitude. It did what it was supposed to do in the traditional, Methodist way. And the tradition, for a change, was good enough for me. People, even old people, commented how much they liked the new way of doing things. When I asked what they meant, they said, "The hymns." Few of these Methodists had ever sung congregational hymns at funerals. Always, it had been solos—tear-jerking songs whose effect was to pierce the heart and isolate mourners instead of welding them into a congregation and community.

The dirt at the grave was covered with astroturf. I did not rip it up (K-Mart was only a few blocks away). The minister tried three times to stem the tide of testimonials about the impact of Mom's life. Farmers and ranchers, known never to utter words in public, said surprising things. On the basis of old westerns I had surmised that talking to the dead at the gravesite was a solid part of cowboy Christianity among the elderly. I had seen it done scores of times on the screen, usually on a hill overlooking Tombstone, Arizona. But these people confessed that they had never been invited to do this before. They, too, knew the tradition only by way of movies.

A day or so after the funeral I dreamed Mom was sitting on the countertop in her kitchen, swinging her leg as she might have done at twenty. She was laughing at the fuss we were making over her. Had she been alive, she would have been embarrassed at it. Not only Dad but other men wept openly and freely, without embarrassment—an action totally foreign to the "stand up and act like a man" training I had suffered as a child. Clearly, cowboy Christianity was changing in ways I did not understand from the distance I had put between it and me.

The day after the funeral Dad asked us "kids" to go through Mom's drawers and closets, taking what we wanted and giving away the rest. He said he couldn't stand to do it. In addition to all the supposedly important things, we found some unfinished letters and scraps of paper containing handwritten dream fragments that Mom had scribbled. The letters were false starts. One of them was a more or less cheery letter meant to preface the dream accounts: "Dear Ron and Susan, Today I feel almost good." Obviously, she had entertained the notion of sending me the dreams, because she knew of my interest in them. She had changed her mind.

The other letter, also never mailed, began, "Dear Ron and Susan, Well, here we are ready for another important event in our lives," with "Wedding Letter" scratched in the margin.

The seven dream fragments stopped me in my tracks. They starkly revealed the doubt, fear, and isolation that she had suffered near the end:

- Trying to find my way out of a very big, complicated railroad work yard. Can't—no one to help.

- Out on lonely road in country. Come out of rink. All cars & people & (husband) leave while I stand there. I am left alone. No way home. Long, lonely dark roads.

- On Boston-like streets. We pull car into opening in store. Milton talks to man. I leave by doorway. Then can't find car or door we came through. Very dark, lonely, no way to find my way home.

- In school building everyone disappears except myself and one little one. Building becomes dark. I don't know how to get out!!

- By the time I go in (to the circus) all my family gone. I sit on bleachers and try to find family but no one is there!

- Many cars pass but no one will stop and give me a lift. [Things] become dark and deserted. I am left alone and my [probably she meant to write "no"] way to get back to my family.

- [The only dream with a date on it:] 1-1-85 Butchered beef—everyone curing the meat. One lady puts full quarter beef down in creamy looking mud, says it flavored it well. I reach down and lift it high enough out of mud so I could cut a large chunk off. It cut easily but other large pieces fall off. All this time people are leaving. All that is left is me and one large chunk of mud-cured beef.

Mom was not a keeper of dream journals. Her New Mexico Christianity had not been, as they say there, Californicated by ideologies that construe dreams as primary spiritual data. Her dream notes are a bleak, concluding self-portrait that stands in tension with her experience of assurance by the Holy Spirit. As I write this, I feel her spirit brooding and stewing over what I am saying.

"Now, son" (a form of address she never used except when very serious), "you said you weren't going to play professor with me. It would have been bad enough while I was alive, but you don't wash dirty laundry in public. So what do you think you're doing, telling everybody my dreams after I am dead?"

"I am not playing professor, Mom. I am moved by both experiences—the one of your encounter with the Holy Spirit and the bleak dreams. I suspect you wanted to be remembered both ways—as one who had a brush with the Spirit and as one who, even in the midst of an affectionate family, felt lost and alone. You wrote the last dream, even dated it. How can I pretend I do not know that the dream came after, not before, the breeze in the bedroom? You are the one who taught me such dogged truth-hunting. I am neither laughing nor poking holes in your experiences. I am honoring them. I believe both stories—the one that transforms you into a beaming, shy child of the Spirit and the other that makes you next of kin to one large chunk of mud-cured beef."

"I must be a contradiction. How does anybody hold together such drastically different views of life?" she asks from the other side of the grave.

I give her back one of her own phrases: "With spit and bailing wire."

WORDS FOR A BUNDLING RITE[15]

(what happened)	*(what she said happened)*
When they call her,	
she slips away.	
She is slipping.	
Her limbs	
are naked of leaves.	
She is in a blind	
remembering,	
stargazing.	
She packs herself away,	
rolls up	
in tissue.	

She ravages her books.
She glues herself together
cover to cover.
Her tent is a tatter of messages.
They hatch her
in a hut.

> *I built it.*
> *myself.*
> *It's all of a piece.*

Her notes float
in streams;
serpents guide them
until they are music.
She's old in cycles,
sometimes twenty-eight moons,
sometimes forty-four days.

> *I just have spells*
> *when I like stars*
> *and autumn nights,*
> *that's all.*

She fishes the heavens,
flags the spirits
with the odor of prayer.
They come to bind her wounds.
Their song is gauze.

> *I scavenged*
> *some rags*
> *and pads*
> *and batting*
> *and stuffing*

Where there are periods,
they powder her with commas.
She is put away.
They bind her
with latex and lace
and hang her damp bones
crack-open
to dry.

She can but assent.
She is in her time.
She is sitting
well padded with age.
They strap her together;
with leather
she is well preserved.

                                                and tied them up
                                                with string
                                                and glue.

She has done this before;
she will come once again.
She is not yet too old;
she is barely young.
Living still,
she sits in state.
She waits on wheels
to see
what is flowing by to see.

                                                Happens all the time—
                                                cut myself
                                                with the scissors.

That's where
the splotches came from. Really.

Nightly she is feverish;
she unzips the bag
and de-feathers it.
Though stripped,
she is well cottoned.
Her coffins are sentences.
Her books are batting.
She is dying
to spirit away
their lines.

                                                I said to your aunt,
                                                "I should build a fence
                                                around those things
                                                or hide them in the woods."

                                                Then I laughed,

The heavens spread:
she reads
what is written
on leaves to read.
Her limbs are bound
and hard
but panting still to grow.
She is bent.

They straighten her with sticks
and string.

        and then I got
        the boards cut
        and the screws put in.

They dismember her rotting
cords
and lace her back
into gifts and bundles.
Monthly they open her
and enclose
a scroll
a man can hardly read.
They teach her knots
to tie;
they suture
the door of her tent.
They send her screws and wire
by canoe,
nets and secrets by sail.

        One day
        I'll give back the tubing,
        and my kids
        want the wheels.

She is a branch afloat
on a pond of spirits.
They say she is
brooding with cures.
She crosses the threshold
and carries on

        with spit and bailing wire.

11

OH, GIVE ME
A HOME

When Mom died, Dad held the fort, but he began to plant tulips around it—tulips on the high plains, where cactus used to grow. "Yes," we assured each other, "he has the will to live." We ignored his inability to stay at home. When I was a kid, Dad taught me to sing, "Oh, give me a home where the buffalo roam." Though we never said so, we all knew there was no such place anymore. For me, Mom's absence was there among the tulips. For Dad, it was everywhere. He felt sorry for himself and confessed to frequent depression. Gray and rainy days got him down. Before her death, he had hardly noticed the weather even though he had been a farmer. His loneliness was palpable, but we marveled at his new burst of willpower. He gave up smoking. On innumerable previous occasions he had insisted that he was unable to stop. He never said so, but I think he wondered whether his smoking had been the cause of Mom's lung cancer.

After Mom's death Dad began to mirror her in surprising ways, as if the division of labor between them had not been final or absolute. He refused to let her ways of expressing affection go to the grave. He wept without shame. He hugged us. He said, "I love you" at the end of long-distance phone calls. The change was so pronounced that my image of him was transformed. Three years after her death, his eyes would still flood. I had grown up thinking he was an unemotional man.

Anger was an exception. It was a permissible part of the southwestern male repertoire. Dad had once attacked an abusive drunk in the skating rink. He exercised such vehemence that the air was shattered with the drunk's piercing scream. I wheeled up close to see the fight. I stood gawking, awed at Dad's swollen knuckles, which were bulging high on his gnarled hands. The guy's eye was so distended and blue that he had to be taken to the hospital. Anger comes naturally to cowboys. What comes hard is the soft stuff. But after Mom's death, the soft stuff sprouted like wheat from an irrigated field.

After Mom's death Dad traded cars and began to drive inordinately, coming home to water the flowers. We considered the cars and flowers an expression of his will to live, but we couldn't convince him that walking would be better for his health than driving. He bought a new Olds, as if aspiring to a higher social class. Then he bought a boat and put a pink TV in the motor home that he and Mom had bought. He had always been against buying one's way out of depression, since he had grown up in the Great Depression. "She would have wanted me to enjoy the money we saved," he argued, obviously feeling sheepish at his rash of purchases. He still had plenty from his pension if he got sick, he assured us. And he had insurance. Besides, the motor home and boat were for the kids. We, the kids, humored him by using them a couple of times, but for the most part they sat unused. We were not a boat or motor home kind of family. We found such suburban toys embarrassing, a betrayal of our upbringing as modestly poor people. The motor home was more conspicuous consumption than I could take. When Dad got low, he would say that he was going to sell all his newly bought junk. He never got around to doing so.

There was a spot on his lungs. The doctors assured him it wasn't cancer— probably just something left over from pneumonia the year before. Dad was afraid of cancer. He had watched Mom die of it. Slowly. He confessed that he did not have her tolerance for pain. We knew him as the master of pain. It never occurred to us to believe him.

Susan, Caleigh, and I were on sabbatical in Santa Fe for the year. Driving from the heart of New Mexico to its windy Texas edge, we saw herds of antelope playing. "Oh, give me a home," we sang. I had assumed that all the antelope had been shot or were penned up for breeding purposes. Clouds hung darkly and dramatically on the horizon. It rained gloriously, and baskets of bright sun spilled through tunnels in the clouds as if divinity itself were poking through a mineshaft with a flashlight. The antelope and light seemed a good omen.

When we arrived in Clovis, we drove to the milk plant to get Terry's key to Dad's house. Dad had already gone to Lubbock for tests. My youngest brother quickly exchanged his good-to-see-you look for furrowed-brow seriousness. He started out as if he were going to make a long story of it. Then he seemed to change his mind. He blurted out in plain speech, "Dad's got cancer."

Silently, we let ourselves into the house for a quick pee before scurrying across the railroad tracks that mark the Texas–New Mexico border. As we paused in the motherless kitchen of home, we noticed an open box of doughnuts on the counter. They were hard. Not much was in the fridge. Mom's old medicine bottles were still in the cupboards where hungry visitors once were assured of finding food. Caleigh began howling and wouldn't stop. We could not determine the reason. I took her to the backyard, where we found a tiny ear of dry, purple-grained corn. I reminded her that her full name, Cailleah, meant "cornsilk." "This is from your granddad," I said. She gurgled and wanted to jam it into her mouth. I ambled to the front yard and stooped under the birch tree, where I had convinced Dad that we should bury Mom's hair. He had topped it with tulip bulbs. The bulbs never came up; the spot was too shady.

Back on the road again, we commented on the eerie sensation; the house seemed truly empty. The texture of the stale doughnuts kept haunting Susan, a portent of something forever changed. The doughnuts' abandonment seemed to suggest how life would be someday when Dad, too, would be gone and there would be no one left to go home to. How strange for me, a grown man, to feel that my parents' place was still a refuge that I might call home. Feeling this way was even more peculiar, since the house on Vivian Street had never really been home for me. The folks had moved into it after I left for college. And Clovis had not been home for over twenty years. Where is home? I knew the Christian answer. I knew the Buddhist answer. But I did not know my answer.

When we arrived at the hospital, Dad was still under the anesthetic. The report came that he was doing well and that they thought they had gotten it all—"doing well" and "gotten it all," a chant intoned in oncology wards across the country. We seldom think of these as ritual utterances, preferring instead to hear them as reports, as diagnoses. We fail to recognize how stylized, repetitive, and symbolic they are. We fail to notice the performative nature of doctors' dress, decorum, and pronouncements: doing well, gotten it all, doing well, gotten it all. These words are just as magical as any Navajo singer's chant over his ailing patient. Look at the dances we do when we hear them.

Though Dad had been born in Texas, it seemed a crime that he had to die there. Texas: Bigger is better. New Mexicans always feel like poor cousins in comparison to Texans. But I had to remind myself that it was his death to choose, not mine, and he died in Texas—an act I would resist as stoutly as he resisted cancer.

In the video of Dad playing with his new granddaughter a few weeks before his death, he already has his death mask on. He is opaque. When we talked to him, we seemed to be interrupting something. Why is he wearing those awful see-yourself-in-my-sunglasses in the shade? He is tired. But everyone knows he's strong. And his father lived to be almost ninety. Dad still fished, hunted, worked in the yard, traveled, fiddled around, sat at Sam's Truck Stop sipping coffee with the other widowers—retired schoolteachers and the cowboy truck drivers who were always exclaiming, "Bet that really torqued your jaws!"

We had tried to talk Dad out of his irrational fear. He didn't want to die of cancer. "I saw what that was like for Nadine, and I don't have her courage," he would repeat. He was afraid cancer might be catching even though he admitted that his conviction was "against science." We gently ridiculed him, knowing that he had no reason to suspect he would die of cancer. "Hey, Old Man, you ain't gonna die of cancer. The sit-on-your-butt disease is gonna get you though," we taunted. Or, "You may run into the ditch showing off your Olds. But cancer? No way."

To this day Sherry and I debate what he died of. She was adamant that he died of negligence. She wanted to sue the doctors. The persistent cough was supposed to have been the result of too much smoking or of the only real disease of his life, a brief bout with pneumonia the year before. There was a little spot on his lung, they said. Was it cancer? Was it cancer? he wanted to know. No, they kept telling him, just a bit of scar tissue or something.

Then they sent him across the border to Texas. We didn't reflect on the fact that he had been born in that overblown, overdrawn state. There they have money, big hospitals, equipment, and specialist doctors. Whenever you crossed the tracks into Texas to see a doctor or visit a clinic, you knew you were in serious trouble.

"Let's operate and see," they had said. They always say that. They open you up, and what is supposed to be a little spot becomes a whole lung. "Cancer," they say. "Cut it out," they say. And cut it out they do. Meanwhile, we wait in the intensive care lounge. An old cowboy with considerable overhang at the beltline has made himself into a page. He answers the phone every time it rings. The whole lounge holds its breath, each family hoping and not hoping it's for them. The man is supportive as he calls first one, then another to the phone. He steps discreetly around the corner. He's mushy in the way cowboy Christians are when pain is stalking the halls. There is an odd mix of community and distance in the room. Some have been camping out here for weeks. Their stories make ours seem minor.

Dad wakes up from the operation, having given the nurses a hard time, thrashing and fighting even under sedation. He looks at us through glazed eyes and a snake's nest of tubes. He grunts, then motions. His fury takes us aback. The veins in his neck stand out. They are the same shade of blue as the tattoo of the Lady Liberty on his forearm. Sampson will break his chains. We untie his hands. He touches the tubes but does not pull them out.

"It was cancer, wasn't it?" he manages to whisper hoarsely.

"Yes. You were right."

"Do they think they got it all?"

"Yes, they think so."

"They always think that."

"How did you know it was cancer?" we ask.

"I always knew," he said, as if we should have known better than to doubt him. "Besides, I heard the orderlies," he added.

He rolls over and the conversation is thereby declared at an end.

Later, he declares to his bedside onlookers, "I love you all." Tears are in his eyes. We imagine he's imagining Mom. He never seemed to have stopped doing so.

That night after a belly full of second-rate, Texas-style Chinese food, Sherry acts out. She cries and carries on. The three of us brothers and the three sisters-in-law try to comfort her, telling her that he will be okay, that he's survived surgery well.

"No," she objects. "I am afraid I won't see him tomorrow."

She was right. We were wrong.

That night, not knowing what was coming, we sat around watching some old eight-millimeter films that Sherry had got put onto video. The local photo lab had superimposed random, sentimental music over the old silent films, some of them dating from the 1940s. The way the music bounced off the images was often unintentionally hilarious, but much of it was painfully tragic. There were Mom and Dad in their newly married youth showing off their firstborn; they are younger then than we who are watching the film. We had no idea how we were setting ourselves up for what was about to transpire.

Harley announced to no one in particular that he was going to skate on the horse tank. The family called it that even though they owned no horses. Being too poor to afford them was a source of acute embarrassment to Harley. The tank froze only once or twice a year, and the cows lacked the god-given good sense to use their damp noses for breaking the ice while it was still thin. He walloped the cows on their rumps to make way for his grand entry. Then he crawled over the edge of the tank, which was almost as tall as he was. For an hour he stomped across the ice in his overshoes. The roundness of their toes never quite matched the points of his boots. With the help of a rusty sucker rod from the windmill, he chipped a watering hole for all the stallions thirsting in his head.

Pretending he was a little Dutch boy on a canal, he began to slide around. Ice water trickled through the cracks in his boots as he sang "Little Dutch Mina" and yodeled like Eddy Arnold. Mr. Arnold was the Tennessee Plowboy, but he probably spoke Swiss since he yodeled. The cattle twitched their ears at the strange music.

Harley skated and fell, skated and fell. He poked the sucker rod through the drinking hole again, this time pulling out a salmon for Sergeant Preston's breakfast. "Mush!" he ordered the cows. They blinked and blew more white smoke.

Someone had said that the snow, so rare here, was God's winter blanket. Harley didn't believe it, because it wasn't warm enough and there was no pillow. But he was sure frosty breath was the Holy Spirit visible and invisible. He played Holy Spirit for a while. He was a ghostly, black, wild stallion blowing the whitest of cotton out his flared, steaming nostrils. Each time he bucked or kicked, the whole universe thundered and lightninged. Harley mumbled something that eventually became, "I listeth where I will, I list, I list, where I will, will, will." Skidding, then sauntering across the ice, he imagined listing as a lazy lope, and he was listing across the border into the Texas panhandle, where his nostrils, now those of a coyote, twitched at the aroma of camp bacon.

Without warning the ice gave way. A crack skittered across the tank from the water hole Harley had chiseled. The boy sank to his armpits before he managed to grab the side of the tank. He gasped. A shiver cut a trail down his back as he shouted, "Dad! Dad!" He hollered toward the barn, as he tried to lift a leg over the

edge of the tank: "Dad!" His boots were filling with water from the Yukon River.
The water's weight plastered them deep into the squishy green moss on the bottom
of the tank. "Dad!" he screamed again, beginning to panic.

Dad came flailing through the snow, ripping the crotch out of his pants as he
climbed over a barbed wire fence. When his father's arms tightened around
Harley's chest, the boy echoed his grandma in a whisper: "Cradled like a child in
the arms of God."

Laboriously, the boy was hauled out, a load of dripping laundry. His chin was
quivering and his arms, quaking. Icicles were forming in his hair.

"Dad," he said later when his belly was full of hot chocolate, "are there really
ghost riders in the sky?"

Dad was silent, a captive of the horizon that could barely be seen through the
steamy kitchen window. Harley, as was his habit when an adult ignored his first
question, posed a new, harder one: "Dad, hey Dad, when I'm an adult, will I be big
enough to save you?"

On the way to the hospital the horizon was infinite in the premorning light.
My gaze was fixed on the Texas license plate of Darrell's car as it raced silently, far
above the speed limit. Emergency flashers were blinking two or three miles
ahead of me on the flat highway running from Levelland to Lubbock. Gradually,
the car grew small. It became the heavenly chariot bearing Elijah to heaven. Elijah, the man who was "translated" without the usual detour through death.
Darrell's car penetrated the horizon that I could never hike to when I was a kid.

At first I too drove with my flashers on, trying to keep up with Darrell and
Cyndi, driving as far above the speed limit as they were. There was nothing in the
world but those red flashing lights and the sound of breathing emanating from
Susan and Caleigh. We were engulfed by an endless early morning, straining toward a big-sky dawn.

Then it all turned on its axis. Someone, somewhere in the universe, flipped a
switch. To be in synchrony, I switched off my emergency flashers and slowed
down, letting Darrell and Cyndi go on ahead. Suddenly, clearly, I knew there was
no point. I could feel a great sigh of relief in the universe. I was sure Dad's travail
was over. With the flashers off I drove the speed limit into the hospital parking
lot.

The family gathered in a private waiting room—only there was nothing to wait
for. Caleigh was seven months old. She watched with wide eyes as her family
cried. We tried to imagine what she was thinking. We wondered if she would remember her grandfather. We wished she had known her grandmother. We were
glad to be carrying this blond bundle of life. In the next few months this death
would lead us to decide that she should have a sibling.

There lies Milton. How wrinkled Grimes faces become when they cry or age or die. I replay a scene from Steed Memorial Funeral Home: Dad is crying for the first time in my life. His dad has died. I can't understand why Dad is crying, because Mom had said that Dad's dad used to beat him with a chain.

Dad's arms were bare, exposing Lady Liberty on his forearm. Before I was born, he had had clothes tattooed over her. Not long after he started going to church, he began to wear long sleeves, not just in church but everywhere. Occasionally, we could harass him into letting us see her; we tried to imagine her naked. Now here she was for the world to see. We put our hands on him, talked to him, cried over him.

"Cardiac arrest," they reported, "his heart gave out." We were numb. He was supposed to be recovering from lung disease, not dying of heart failure. It would be a few hours before we would entertain the notion that he had in some decisive, unconscious way willed to go. With Mom "over there" and with the prospect of a year or two of suffering, he had packed his shorts and socks and left— just like that—leaving us kids to dispose of that big pig of a motor home, which always looked like it belonged to some other family.

The funeral was a minor note in the events of the next two weeks. It was conventional. None of us helped lead it; we just went to it, letting the current pull us along.

The real event was disposing of all the stuff: the house, the car, the tools, the dishes, the clothes, the lawn tools, the knickknacks. Living in the heart of K-Mart culture, the folks had horded stashes of bargain paper towels, canned fruits and vegetables, and notebook paper. The closets were full of old clothes, stacks of shoes, and scores of ties. The memory of the Depression had remained real to them long after they had made it squarely into the middle class. Dad found it excruciating to throw away anything—old hats, old ties, pieces of metal, sunbleached pieces of wood. I have his genes.

We thought we could make our decisions and plot our course of action within two or three days. It took ten and required the labor of all four siblings and their mates. We stayed up late, slept in, laughed like hyenas, and cried in closets or in the middle of the living room floor. We felt claustrophobic. We overate and underate. People streamed in and out; the sympathy-card pile grew. We stacked underwear, guns, knives, fishing tackle, dishes, and shoes on the floor. We plowed through mounds of papers and photographs.

Mom and Dad had two kinds of offspring: the travel-lighters and the carry-alls. The first kind wanted little or nothing of parental worldly goods. The second wanted everything. Darrell and Terry avoided the growing piles, as if they risked carting death home in taking anything at all. Sherry and I amassed boxes of stuff, as if we might overcome death by keeping tabs on the family baggage. She had the watch and wallet that Dad had carried to the hospital. She wanted some of his old clothes; their smell reminded her of him. She called Dale, her husband, to come with a horse trailer to haul the memorabilia back to Lubbock. Watching her, I began to feel burdened and so gave away some loot to her. We had a small car and I had to choose: baby stuff or dad stuff.

In some ways Sherry had grown up the most independent among the four of us. She had competed in collegiate rodeo when ladies didn't do such things, and she had driven all over the state, pistol in the glove compartment, doing court reporting. Even though she was once chosen Curry County Fair Queen, she defied many of the conventions of southwestern womanhood. Yet she remained the most directly dependent on Mom and Dad. Now she was orphaned. So she held the center of the family's grief. The brothers, if we wept much at all, did it privately. Sherry cried copiously and publicly. She moaned that she would no longer have Dad for advice or for emergency cash. He wouldn't be there for Mary, her youngest daughter, to visit. Mary seemed to have no reaction to the absence of her grandfather, even though she had spent extended periods with him and they had become buddies. We surmised that she was in shock. The silence of a child in the face of death is awesome, puzzling, and probably more attuned to what's actually going on than adult wailing or avoidance of wailing.

The nearest we came to a family fight was over the pictures on the walls. When should they come down? For Sherry, once they came down, it was all finished. The house was no longer Dad's, Mom's, or ours. The family abode would soon be on the real estate market. The pictures probably symbolized the same thing to us brothers, but we wanted them down and out. Sherry wanted to sustain the pain; we wanted to end it. She feared the family would never convene as a family again.

At first we wanted to have a monstrous garage sale to get rid of what remained. But appalled at how much rubble the family had collected, we decided to announce to friends and relatives that there would be a giveaway. As they trucked in pecan pies and bean casseroles, we invited them to truck away worldly accumulation.

One of Dad's buddies rifled through a garbage bag full of baseball-style hats, the kind cowboys and truckers and Boy Scouts and urban policemen wear now, the kind that every tractor or seed company in New Mexico and Texas gives away as advertising. "I feel terrible," said Dad's friend, "like a vulture, going through all this stuff and taking what I want. You should be selling it." Most of Dad's friends and relatives had his tendency to pinch pennies until Abe Lincoln yelled for mercy. So this family potlatch caught them coming and going. On the one hand, they were happy to capitalize on the situation. On the other, they were suspicious about the cosmic results of getting something free. "Well," someone muttered, "I guess it's a good idea—having something that will remind me of Milton." But people hesitated. Did they really want to be reminded of Dad every time they picked up a hammer or donned a hat?

As far as I know, the occasion was the first one in which the Grimes clan mingled with the Williams clan. Dad's family was reclusive and irreligious; Mom's, gregarious, competitive, and fiercely Christian. We had grown up closer to Mom's family. They were close-knit, wealthier—land owners and cattlemen, not dirt farmers like Dad and his dad. We had sometimes been a little embarrassed or puzzled about the Grimes side of the family. But this time I was proud to be one of them. They were without pretension, and their consolations did not have to be disentangled from pious formulas easily mouthed in times of trouble.

We ordered pizza and smuggled in beer. We had to smuggle, because our teetotaling Methodist parents were still hanging around the eaves, spirits not quite departed. "Well," we rationalized, as we popped caps and corks, "they probably did things their parents didn't approve of. We're in our thirties and forties, after all." Oversleeping, undersleeping, pizza, rich country-style food, beer, grief, relief, and a desperate feeling that the center had been blown out put us in a time warp. The emptying, sorting, and deciding knocked us into an altered state of consciousness, much as chanting or whirling or intense meditation does.

As the beds were stripped and the pictures on the walls lifted from their pinheaded nails, there was howling. The house moaned. We could feel the umbilical cords being cut. Cutting seemed to be a neverending process. Several years after Dad's dying the last legal knot was untangled: The final check for $1,600, money I'd not earned, finally arrived.

I inherited the Chili Wagon, a lumbering '76 Dodge van, faded red as a ristra of chilies exposed to too much southwestern sun. I tended it for the next six years as one would tend a grave. With the folks buried in Clovis and me living in Santa Fe, it became a coffin on wheels. I drove it back and forth loaded with my inheritance: the pink TV, an old microwave, some tools with M.L.G. scratched on them, cheap sleeping bags, three lamps, and several pieces of art that I had sent the folks as Christmas presents. I waxed the van's dead paint, re-covered the seats, put in new carpet, and made the engine rebuilders install a new motor in honor of the warranty they had written for Dad. They resisted, but the Grimes brothers threatened to go to Cook's Truck Stop telling the story of their attempts to screw a dead man out of a few bucks. We milked the system out of another engine, a new mechanical heart for dad-become-van. The Chili Wagon was a casket or a fish, depending on the angle of one's vision. A chili made of red felt hung from the mirror. I would have put up a pair of them, but Susan wouldn't abide the obviously phallic symbolism. Every time I fixed one thing on the Chili Wagon, something else would go. If it wasn't the motor, it was the brakes or the right door or the exhaust pipe. Once the entire passenger seat collapsed with Susan in it. When vehicles get old, Grimeses keep replacing the parts, but some day they won't stock parts for those old guys anymore. Then what would I do? Maybe Bryn or Caleigh would like to play with the wheels.

Mom used to complain that the Grimes driveway looked like a used car lot. It normally sported several vehicles: an old Packard undergoing restoration, a '55

Chevy (the Bit O' Honey) that the boys drag raced, an old fishing and hunting contraption—all in addition to the socially respectable vehicles.

We wanted to sell Dad's Olds but got snared into a go-round with an uncle who treated us like tourists in a cow trader's den. Not only did he haggle over the price (we expected that); he also accused the three of us brothers of ganging up on him and trying to cheat him. We were so insulted by his accusation that only Dad's Depression-minded ghost prevented us from giving the damn car away.

Dad surprised us with his decisiveness. Just like that, he crossed over. In good Grimes style most of his children made major purchases shortly after his death. Fearing I would lose my roots, I bought forty acres of New Mexico. The land has nothing on it. With my inheritance I bridged an arroyo, paved a long driveway with fool's gold, and put up a gate—a kind of idiot gesture declaring my roots in this quarter of universe and trying to protect them from the ultimate break-and-enter we all know is coming. I know that in the final analysis there is nothing to protect, because nothing is truly owned. But meanwhile, the K-Mart corner of a panhandle soul drives me to accumulate the most for the least so at the end there will be a pile big enough to make the kids and relatives pause for more than a minute or two.

With the center gone, we have to work at cohesion. Bryn and Caleigh now look at albums and videos. One says, "There is Grandma Milton."

"No," we reply patiently. "It's Grandma Nadine and Grandpa Milton."

"Yeah, and they live in the cemetery," asserts the grandchild, "in Clovis." The kids are still too young to know why I threaten to wring their necks when they ask whether that is in Texas or New Mexico.

In most North American towns Jessica Mitford's scathing attack of 1963, *The American Way of Death*,[16] made no permanent impression, even though her book was widely read and discussed. The ecclesiastical and mortuary establishments closed ranks. Little changed between her exposé and Philip Ariès's declaration in *Western Attitudes Towards Death*[17] that our society has tamed death. The major difference is that we now know—because Elisabeth Kübler-Ross taught us—that we go through stages in the taming process. There has been a great deal of psychological reflection on death and the grieving process but very little on the funeral rite itself beyond the fact of its unnecessary expense. Ritually, we are about as ignorant as we were when Mitford launched her attack or even when nineteenth-century Bostonians moved Mt. Auburn Cemetery out to the edge of town, removing the dead from the churchyard, center of town, and thus the center of American awareness. Despite the proliferation of death and dying courses in universities across the country, death is still largely pornographic. We whisper about it, fantasize about it, and pay other people to dress it up on our behalf. We consider funerals best left to experts. We know they are necessary—everything must be recycled after all—but we don't want corpses in our backyards where squirrels dig and robins twist and tug for worms. Composting garbage is difficult enough without adding further organic matter to the soil.

Compared with the other rites of passage, funerals find us at our most conservative. We're wary of innovating during them. If we innovate, we do so cautiously at weddings or perhaps births and initiations, but certainly not when people are racked with loss and grief. Once a death has occurred, it is usually too late to begin inquiring how to make funeral rites more meaningful. And before a death occurs, people want to avoid contemplating funerals for fear of being considered morbid or for fear of precipitating a death: Imagining something makes it so. So there is no good time to plan the final passage. Before death we are too busy. During it, too stricken. After it, still recovering.

So we remain confused about what funerals are supposed to do. Weddings should wed. Initiations should initiate. But what should funerals do? Funerals ought to fune, I adjure my students. "What we need are funerals that fune," I repeat, trying to get them to laugh in the face of anxiety about death. I do my best to avoid the psychological jargon to which North American culture is addicted. I do not say, for instance, "Funerals should enable us to work through grief," even though it is true they should.

Perhaps we need two funerals, the unreal public one at the funeral home and the real—but surrogate—one at home. Maybe we should give over dead bodies to funeral directors and just work with effigies instead. We could hold big stuffed dolls, fondling them, spilling tears on them, filling them with beans and seeds, and then burying them in soil so they can sprout in the spring. We could work through our grief by shouting at these manikins. We could cuddle them without having to worry about the stench of decaying flesh or the disconcerting presence of teeth, hair, and bone particles that might work their way to the surface from six feet under.

We Norte Americanos should learn from Mexicans, our more creative, less squeamish neighbors to the south. We should take lessons in making sugar skulls and death toys, the sort that kids use to crank souls up out of hell and into the mouth of the church (unless they are left-handed and crank the toy counterclockwise). Mexicans visit their dead with picnics and tease Old Death with dolls and puppets of himself (or herself)—Mexicans are not misogynist about Death. My favorite is a bride and groom in tux and gown—both skeletons. At the reception, which can be bought for a few pesos more, there is a skeleton band playing for skeleton relatives. Our society produces and sells death toys but only the sort for delivering death to someone else, not the sort that remind us of our own mortality. If we want to have funerals that fune (surely we need such a word), we have to learn to dance our own deaths.

PART FOUR

BIRTHING

There seems some reason to believe that the male imagination, undisciplined and uninformed by immediate bodily clues or immediate bodily experience, may have contributed disproportionately to the cultural superstructure of belief and practice regarding child-bearing.

—Margaret Mead[18]

By making the naturally transformative process of birth into a cultural rite of passage, a society can ensure that its basic values will be transmitted to the three new members born out of the birth process: the new baby, the woman reborn into the new social role of mother, and the man reborn as father.

—Robbie E. Davis-Floyd[19]

He feared his son might meditate on his abnormal privilege and discover in some way that his condition was that of a mere image. Not to be a man, to be the projection of another man's dream, what a feeling of humiliation, of vertigo! All fathers are interested in the children they have procreated (they have permitted to exist) in mere confusion or pleasure; it was natural that the magician should fear for the future of that son, created in thought, limb by limb and feature by feature, in a thousand and one secret nights.

With relief, with humiliation, with terror, he understood that he too was a mere appearance, dreamt by another.

—Jorgé Borges[20]

12

FIRSTBORN

Sometimes Harley got really angry, supermad he called it. He would say words he did not dare write, because if someone big or supernatural saw them, they might think he was breaking the commandment tablets of stone, which were heavier to carry than his Big Chief tablet. The side of the garage, which was leaning precariously, was so dented from cuss-rocks that it looked like two million helmeted bees had flown a suicide mission into it. "Damn it," Harley would exclaim each time he hurled another stone.

When Harley got sad, he usually got mad. More than one person had pointed out this peculiarity. He learned, in turn, to point out the idiosyncracy to others. He hoped they would take warning and avoid his tender spots. They didn't always, and today the din of stones banging on the weathered west side of the garage echoed like machine-gun fire. He augmented the warlike sounds with a rat-tat-tat or two, but his rocks were loaded, mostly with furrowed brow and secret invective.

"Shit!" he whispered fiercely as he hurled a smooth flat rock. "Damn!" and off sailed another. He avoided taking God's name in vain, and he circumambulated the f-word, though it would later enter his adolescent vocabulary with a peculiar vengeance.

Stokey Horner, the kid who could stick out his belly so far that a Campbell's soup can could sit on it, had told Harley that men and women made babies by doing something Harley would not say, because it was a bad word and a sin. Stokey Horner was from town, and people said he was poor white trash. Harley usually countered this accusation by arguing that Stokey was a poor white child of God. All children were children of God. This was what Uma had told him to say; it was no crime to be poor or white or a child.

Harley and Stokey were friends. Sort of. They were rivals too. Maybe the friendship was at an end. Stokey had said Harley's mom and dad did it, and he illustrated the procedure graphically with the extended middle finger of his right hand and a circle made from his left forefinger and thumb. Harley had shrieked that his parents were not cows or sheep and that his father's you-know-what had

155

one purpose and one only. Stokey had insisted that he could demonstrate to Harley another purpose, but Harley stormed away to play Tarzan and Jane with Kittysue, who was hanging upside down on the monkey bars.

When Harley got off the bus from school that afternoon, he would not look at Mom when she addressed him. His eyes searched the corners of the kitchen. Later, he sneaked behind the granary, where he peed down the hole of a red ant bed. Afterward, he fetched the milk bucket of rocks that he had gleaned a week or two earlier for just such an occasion. He lugged the bucket to the garage and did not notice who was watching through the front screen door.

Pelting the sun-faded, splintery side of the garage, he could not imagine being made in God's image in the way Stokey Horner had described. Once Harley had kissed Kittysue while standing in line at the water fountain, but Stokey's description of what was in Kittysue's panties had deeply offended Harley. Stokey had compared it to a wet, slobbery cow's mouth. Now he was stoning to death images of all the naked girls and women and men and boys who crowded his head all day while making lewd gestures. Mom heard the hail of cuss-rocks but did nothing. Usually, Harley would explain things in a day or two.

Late that night, around nine-thirty, Harley, who was supposed to be asleep, wandered out, rubbing his eyes with the backs of his fists. Mom, reading an article in the Illustrated Home Medical Encyclopedia, *recognized the regressive gesture: Harley was feeling like a three-year-old.*

When something was on her son's mind, he usually talked around it for a while. This time he blurted out with surprising directness, "Did you and Dad make me by fucking?" He spat the last word out with forceful disgust.

Mom blushed but didn't bat an eye. She was a farm wife. Harley and his mother conversed for two hours that night, almost until midnight. This was the first time in his life that he had been up so late. What Mom said about love and children and Adam's and Eve's nakedness he only vaguely understood. What he remembered most was Mom's undressing two dolls so he could ask about the details that were burning his brain. Gently, Mom put the dolls face to face. Harley still did not quite understand. He complained that he did not see how it was any different from pissing in a red ant den. Mom laughed, hugged him, and sent him back to bed with a remark about the birds and the bees that left him puzzled but content.

The next day Harley and his mom were uncommonly shy around each other.

Rites of passage are rooted in the facts of life, but the facts of life are not merely factual. Even when we can explain them, they remain mysteries. They are mysteries because they are bigger than we are. Faced with a fact of life, adults are rendered children. Theologians may pad birth and death with rumination, and preachers may hedge it with storytelling. Doctors may make the inexplicable seem matter-of-fact, but only temporarily. Scientists may explain the chemistry of life's facts, but birth and death still stop us in our tracks. Frozen, we cower; then we pelt them with philosopher's stones. They remain intractable. In the face of their intractability we make do; we ritualize.

Trevor's birth was not a ritual, but I make it one now by telling and retelling the story. With each repetition the narrative exercises power like one of those primal myths that says how it was in the beginning and thus how it should or should not be today.

Caleigh once inquired, "Did I see Trevor before he died?"

"No, you weren't born then."

"But I saw Grandpa Milton, didn't I?"

"Sure. And you've also seen him on the video, wearing those ridiculous dark sunglasses and with a big cigar peering over the top of his shirt pocket. He's nuzzling around on your cheeks and neck."

"Why didn't I see Trevor?"

She knows that he's dead and that his mother was not her mother. Never mind, one of her teddy bears is Trevor today. That way she's in control. She has drafted him into her pantheon of dolls and stuffed animals. She and Trevor have a connection. People say they look alike.

One sunny afternoon in Pittsburgh, before Susan and I had considered pregnancy, a self-designated prophetess came to my office high on the twenty-sixth floor of the Cathedral of Learning and said, "Oh, don't feel bad, your wife will soon be pregnant, and I've been led to see that your new child will be Trevor-come-back." I seethed. Tight-lipped, I said I appreciated her attempt to comfort me, but that I considered the whole notion an insult to both the dead child and the unborn one.

If Caleigh is Trevor-come-back, then who was Trevor?

The differences between Trevor's birth and the births of Bryn and Caleigh could not have been more stark. There is a photograph of Mary Jane looking pained, hand on belly, eyes trained on a watch. She is timing contractions. There is another picture of me. I am in the labor room, and for some supposedly medical reason, I am draped in a white smock and raising the victory sign. If you didn't know the story, you would think the photo was taken after, rather than before, Trevor's birth.

Not allowed in delivery, I hung out in the waiting room, trying to weather the smoke and other people's anxieties. I had few of my own, at least for the first couple of hours. Delivery was supposed to take thirty to forty-five minutes. I heard calls for pediatricians but had no inkling that they had anything to do with me.

When the pediatrician, whom I did not know (instead of the obstetrician, whom I did know), emerged from the obstetric sanctum talking about artificial limbs and surgery, I listened as if to a radio broadcast. This was a melodrama about somebody else's life. It would be years before there would be a definitive diagnosis. By then Trevor would be dying of Fancones disease.

When the doctor left, I was fine, just a little dazed. Since I was not yet allowed to see either wife or child, I called the folks. When Mom's voice cracked and Dad had to take over but couldn't think of anything to say, I fell apart. After I got off the phone, I went to the public restroom and did what I always do when hurt: I became angry. I raised my fist and gave God holy hell. Anger vented, I was free to cry.

Trevor's thumbs were missing. His left hand jutted out; it was perpendicular to his ulna. His radius was missing. Why? What now? What else?

Trevor's birth provoked a major religious crisis. There were, and are, no adequate ritual forms for such events. I was teaching philosophy of religion at the time and knew that the conventional way of framing my dilemma was in theological terms. I was experiencing the existential dimensions of the so-called theodicy problem: How can we explain the presence of evil in a world created by a reputedly loving and just God? The event taught me how useless it is to approach such occurrences on a philosophical or theological level. My problem was not what to think but how to feel and what to do. I needed a sanctuary, a nest, a place responsive to wailing and hollering. Surround me. Touch me. Loan me a boat that will carry me when I am too tired to row.

The nurses stuffed Trevor into a red and white stocking cap. He was a package under the cosmic tree in this seasonal celebration. It was December 22; therefore he was defined as a Christmas baby by the canons of nursing ritual. Sure, we wanted a Christmas baby—doesn't everyone? Only if one doesn't think about it. The original Christmas baby was a man marked for death the moment he was born. Medieval artists used to put a cross in the Christ child's hand, even though crucifixion was thirty-odd years in the future. They knew all too well how soon Jesus would be departing from his mother because of the demands of his father.

What worried me most were not Trevor's obvious birth defects, because we were still unsure how to name them and thus to know what they predicted about the future. More disturbing to me were Mary Jane's feelings of failure and then her protracted depression and guilt. She had "just known" that giving birth was what she was made for and that having a baby would bring happiness.

It didn't.

Her years of depression deepened, and I felt I had no room to bemoan Trevor's birth defects. A good guy, my job was to be supportive. She consumed all the emotional space in the house, and I let her. In retrospect I imagine that my wailing might have been a relief to her, might have released a healing balm between us, but that possibility did not occur to me then.

Eventually, Mary Jane took Trevor and left for home. Home was where her mother, not her husband, was. Alone, I sowed seeds elsewhere, hoping and praying they would not take root and sprout. When Trevor's mother returned, I confessed my sin, but soon I began to barter for an open marriage. It was the early 1970s so why not? The nuclear family was in decay. New models were needed.

The pressures and complications of the arrangement were too much for both of us. Within a year we were in marriage counseling.

I dreamed a dream that we both considered apt. The therapist, doing the work of a surgeon, is about to amputate my leg. It has gangrene. As he begins to saw away, I scream. He is cutting off the wrong one. The scream wakes me up.

Weekly, the counselor would greet us with a new therapeutic strategy. Last week it was Jungian; this week it is Gestalt; next week it will be transactional analysis.

One week it was Zen. "Grimes," he said in his testy, winsome way, "I'll bet that when you walk you don't walk, when you eat you don't eat, and when you shit you don't shit."

"What's that supposed to mean?"

"It's Zen."

He had been reading Alan Watts's *Psychotherapy East and West*. I'd read it already.

"Since when is Watts Zen?" I queried.

"Hey, you're the scholar, not me. I don't care whether he meets your academic criteria or not. It's you that's in therapy, not me. Watts is right, whether or not his book passes professorial muster."

Despite the therapist's bulldozer tactics toward me, Mary Jane was sure that he was blaming her for our troubles. I had received too much clinical training to take any of his judgments seriously, which made me a terrible client. Mary Jane's view was confirmed one afternoon after a week punctuated by two suicide threats. He blamed her. She ran out of his office and across the middle of a busy intersection. We ran after her. The therapist caught her arm, saying that he would commit her if she didn't commit herself. She spent a couple of weeks resting in the psychiatric ward. Even though she felt that it did her good, she was glad to get out. Then we joined forces in turning against the butcher.

Beware: What you set yourself against will pursue you. It wasn't long before I was reading everything Watts, Suzuki, Kapleau, and others had written about Zen. One of the therapist's darts had landed in a tender spot. I had put his bet to the test and he had won. I did not walk when I walked; I daydreamed. I did not shit; I planned. I did not eat; I talked, fantasized—everything but taste the food I was eating.

When I call all this to mind, I become mindful. But then I lose concentration as soon as I realize I am mindful. I am plagued by the Saint Peter principle. I can walk on water, but as soon as I recognize what I am doing, I sink. (After I wrote this section, my computer asked me if I wanted to save the document before I exited. Mindlessly, I said no. Exiting, I did not exit.)

In the short run Mary Jane went to the psych ward. In the long run I went to a Zen monastery. She got out in a few days. I've been in and out ever since.

In retrospect Trevor's birth seems like the beginning of his death. It also marked recognition of a deep crack in the foundation of our marriage. Every birth is an initiation into death, but the telescoping of our son's short life had the effect of stabbing his funeral back into the heart of his birth. Birth lives on death; death lives on birth. Children live off their parents; parents live off their children.

Commemorating Trevor's birthday two years after he died, I wrote a poem shorter than a haiku: "The kite flies, the seeds drop." A few years later for another commemoration of his birthday, I painted a rice-paper poster that read:

TREVOR BRANT GRIMES

b. Dec. 22, 1970
between Buddha's enlightenment
and Christ's birthday:

No east
No west
No birth
No death
No mother
No father
No son
No teacher
No student

The most puzzling part of what I wrote is not the Buddhist no-saying but the last couplet, "No teacher, no student." I suspect I meant—I have to guess at it now—that between father and son, the father is the conventional teacher. He's older and wiser. But sometimes the boundaries dissolve, the roles reverse, and the child becomes the father of the man.

Standing between Trevor and me at his birth was the medical priesthood with its "procedures," many of which were, and are, ceremonial. They are ritualistic insofar as they have little or no medical justification. They are performed instead for symbolic reasons: They inscribe messages about authority, control, and ultimate values, especially those rooted in technocracy and the cult of expertise.

In many hospitals it is now possible for fathers to be present in delivery rooms. It was possible in 1970, but only in larger cities in more liberal parts of the country. Hospitals now have birthing rooms furnished to resemble domestic bedrooms or living rooms. In some states and provinces midwives have medical and legal sanction to participate in hospital births. If I believed these and other changes had dealt with the infelicitous ritualization of hospital birth, I would not bother to write on the topic at all. But the changes are largely cosmetic, mostly a matter of packaging, so I remain skeptical. I know of felicitous hospital births, but most of them transpire despite, not because of, the medicalization of birth.

In many cases the birthing room is window dressing, and midwives are co-opted into a medical model to operate on the basis of a ritual script that demeans fathers almost as much as it does mothers. Robbie Davis-Floyd,[21] who characterizes the scenario well, shows that obstetrical procedures meet all the criteria for ritual. They are patterned, ordered, formal, repetitive, and symbolic enactments of ultimate cultural values. These values are primarily technological. The female body is treated metaphorically as a machine, and the doctor is a technician operating that machine. The initial wheelchair ride, pubic-hair shave, backless gown, and enema are purgative ceremonies. They are forms of ritual purification, tacitly implying that there is something unclean about women or female genitals.

The importance of these and many other procedures is ritualistic and symbolic. They dramatize power relations and values held sacred. Their medical utility is typically minor, sometimes demonstrably harmful. Scientific jargon too often is the rationalization that justifies the ritualization. Entering in a wheelchair, lying in bed, being hooked to a fetal heart monitor, and undergoing a host of other procedures symbolically identify birth with illness. The very fact of birthing in a hospital establishes the metaphoric equation of birth with illness. Birth is not normal; it is a species of sickness.

Episiotomies and the use of forceps, many instances of which are unnecessary, are a kind of initiatory hazing. Washing babies before giving them to parents, putting silver nitrate in their eyes, and giving them vitamin K injections function as an unwitting baptism.

I do not claim that medical personnel in hospitals *intend* to be ritualizing but that their procedures, consciously or unconsciously, function this way. They restructure and transform female physiology and psychology to conform with sacred values. They communicate to the psyche and body messages that become deeply embodied. Obstetrical interventions encode a largely unquestioned set of values and inscribe them in ways that have the same long-term effect as initiations that depend on physical exhaustion, bodily scarification, and genital mutilation.

Even though women work on hospital staffs, the upper echelons of power are still occupied by men. Most of the nurses who assist in hospital births are women following the orders of doctors, most of whom are males. So the hazing of women at birth is something men do, wittingly or unwittingly, to women. Even so, males—babies and fathers—are no better served by the system. They are made ancillary to the process, either objects or spectators but not real participants. Fatherly alienation from birth only weakens the foundations of marriage and enhances the likelihood of violence against children. The ambivalence, and sometimes even indifference, that many men feel about birth masks alienation and rage at being excluded from one of the most profoundly creative human acts.

The male-dominated medical establishment is not even remotely patriarchal, at least not in the etymological sense: "rule by fathers." It has no more respect for fathers and fathering than for mothers and mothering. I reject the feminist label "patriarchal" as a way of naming male domination. Hospital birth is misogynist. It is andro- and technocentric, but it is not father centered. Doctors are not symbolic fathers. They are metaphoric priests of technocratic ritual. Men as wielders of tools, not as fathers, are the masters of hospital birth. Fathers' roles in hospital births are less dramatic but no less ritualized than those of birthing mothers. The scenario is prescribed. Excluded, papa frets, stews, watches TV, and smokes. Fathers in such positions get spiritual whiplash. They are at the edge of a hurricane. Off center, they experience neither the fullness of a pain received dead center nor the swell of jubilation that arises from the bottom of the feet and courses through to the crown of the head. They are emotionally and physically removed from one of the two most fundamental events in human life. There are few truly universal human events. Birth is one of them, and to miss it—never to witness it, much less participate in it—is to be made less than truly human. This may seem a harsh statement to people who have not been part of birth, but I believe it to be true.

Fathers no longer have to be excluded. Now included but marginalized, they are made to feel that they are an encumbrance. They are witnesses who make doctors uncomfortable, get in the way of nurses, and threaten the civility of the performance by indulging in uncontained emotions: fear, joy, anxiety, or revulsion. Or worse, they go into emotional overload and shut down. The new routines still make fathers into appendages, props for a show of technological prowess. At best they become breathing coaches positioned safely by their mates' sides or heads, while others do the real work down below. Fathers' participation is not like that of Lakota mothers who prepare to watch their sons do the Sun Dance by cutting off bits of their own flesh as a way of joining them in the dance. Rather, fathers are more like an audience at a Broadway play: they emote decorously in the middle and clap at the end. They may be deeply moved, but they contribute little to the performance.

I sometimes ask myself, "Is a father made or born?" My answer: "Made. But by being born." But how? What would make birth an event capable of birthing a father? I doubt that I know the whole answer to the question. A tentative beginning would be full inclusion and deliberate ritualizing. Full inclusion of fathers in the pregnancy process and birth will not guarantee full participation in childrearing, but without this initiation at birth, subsequent involvement is unlikely. Deliberate ritualizing is necessary to inscribe the event in the personal psyche and in family history as well as to counteract the unwitting ritualization enacted by the medical profession. Birth is a social and spiritual event, not just a biological one. For this reason it requires ritual work. Upon birth into a nuclear family, not only must a fetus be made a child, but also a man must become a father and a woman, a mother. Done right, birthing does not just produce children. It produces parents, sometimes two, sometimes one, sometimes more.

Embraced fully, perhaps the birth process might not need to have ritual added to it. Birth itself would be a spiritually transforming enactment of values held sacred by those most centrally concerned. In my experience fathers are not born unless there is blood on their hands. Such involvement alone does not make a father. If this initial baptism in birth blood is not followed by regular baptism in vomit and shit—that is, in the repetitive routines of childrearing—it probably will not take.

Few of us are capable of fully attentive participation, so most of us require explicit ceremony, a more focused way of attending to the world and our place in it. Such ritualizing should coincide closely with the actual birth. Critics might say that I confuse the event with the ritual of the event. They could argue that the two should be separate, that a birth rite is important precisely insofar as it is *not* the event of birth itself. In this view the event of birth is a biological phase best followed by a social and ceremonial one. My objection to this sort of sequencing is that it rarefies birth. Rarefication is the process whereby the fundamentally incarnational nature, the primal bodiliness, of an action is forsaken for the sake of some merely spiritual or social meaning.

I suppose it is possible for fathers to be born without having actively participated in the births of their children, but I am suspicious of the claim that direct physiological involvement is not necessary. The labor of giving birth to a father is probably more protracted than that required to give birth to either a baby or a mother, which is to say, the work of becoming a father continues well beyond the limits of any one rite. Becoming a father takes longer, because birth, even for the most actively participating father, is experienced in a manner necessarily more diffuse than that of a mother. Becoming a father, I suspect, is the work of a lifetime.

13

BIRTH BY BELLY

When Caleigh was conceived, I was determined to share in the birth in whatever ways a determined man might. I had no desire to be lead actor, but I did want to play attentive servant and trustworthy messenger. One way of participating was to write the birth announcement. I composed, and Susan edited, a broadsheet to tell the story:

Sometime in 1987

The usual birth announcement doesn't tell anybody much of anything. Why not chronicle actual thoughts and events so we don't forget them, and so our friends and families can know what really went into producing whoever it is that's on the way? As parents-to-be we'd like to have a record in case No-Name Scott-Grimes asks.

If calculations based on the size of the bulge and the phases of the moon are correct, this baby (and thus, this newsletter) should be ready for delivery on or around March 17, 1988.

June 25, 1987: Living Flame of Love

Susan's birthday. We've just barely arrived at the University of Notre Dame for a summer teaching session. Susan discovers a seminar on Carmelite spirituality and finds herself in the midst of two hundred nuns and monks. She spends her thirty-second birthday absorbed in John of the Cross's erotic-mystical Living Flame of Love.

Birthday dinner is at a swanky fish joint overlooking the river in illustrious downtown South Bend. "What will the coming year be like?" is the prevailing topic of the evening. In his usual elliptical fashion, Ron utters: "This will be a very significant year for you—more significant than you know." Susan doesn't let him get away with that; she insists that he explain. Ron mumbles something about her turning thirty-two.

Later, to add the finishing touches to a romantic evening we retire. Why? Well, to work off the double chocolate cheesecake, what else? We indulge in what you could call bodily poetry.

July 10, 1987: Great Expectations, or, A Dread Come True

"Guess what?" she asks.
"No," he says. "Really?"
"Really," she says.
"How do you know?" he asks.
"I just know. I've double-checked my date book. I'm never late."
"This means you'll be a pregnant pilgrim traipsing after mystics' relics in Spain," he muses.
"This means I'll become a mother around the Ides of March," she frets.
"This means the great lumbering house we bought inadvertently will come in handy," they sigh.
"This baby is well organized," she laughs.

August, 1987: Does It Rain on the Plain in Spain?

Hauling our little unknown commodity overseas, we spend five wretched weeks in Spain. Apart from a little Berlitz Spanish and a lot of heartburn, we manage to secure the blessings of the great Castilian mystics, Saints Teresa of Ávila and John of the Cross.

In Salamanca we share quarters with thirteen others in the blistering summer heat. The Spanish food is grease-laden and the air, smoke-laden. Between bouts of morning- (and home-) sickness, she searches endlessly for whole wheat bread, fresh produce, peace, and solitude. The last of the great contemplatives, we decide, are the storks that nest atop the spires of Salamanca's cathedrals.

Eventually, the weary pilgrims are refreshed by a short trip to Lourdes. Ah, the curative properties of holy water. And a little French cuisine.

September 10, 1987: The Doctor

On Susan's first visit to the doctor what we've known all along is officially confirmed. The due date is March 17—a good saint's day.

October 16, 1987

Ron meets the doctor:
"We'd like to use the birthing room in the hospital," he declares.
"Yes, that's fine, provided there are no complications," she replies.
"We'd like to have a midwife with us as well."
"Well, if you like, so long as she doesn't get in the way of the nurses."

November 26, 1987: The Midwife

What does a woman with tendencies toward the nonstandard route in life and who has no experience whatsoever with babies do when she discovers she's pregnant? She looks for a midwife—a substitute aunt, someone to talk to about everything from dreams to diapers to the politics of medicine.

Francesca turns out to be the right person. She spends hours in our living room drinking tea, telling birth stories, pulling books, slides, and mysterious objects in and out of her great Guatemalan midwifery bag. Gradually, as she educates us about childbirth options, we become converts to home birth.

December 18, 1987

The doctor begins to squirm when we inquire about circumventing some of the routine birth procedures at the hospital. We'd like a natural (that is, noninterventionist) birth. Surely that's not asking too much, is it?

"Hmmmm. Let's not be heroic," the doctor cautions. She gets visibly upset (lots of hand-wringing) when asked what she thinks about home birth. She is worried about being sued. We offer to sign a waiver. We tell her home births are routine in Holland, which has the lowest infant mortality rate in the world. Waterloo, however, is not the Netherlands.

The physician indicates that she will withdraw even prenatal care should we decide on a home birth. We get lectured about cooperation and trusting our doctor. We leave the clinic depressed and stranded. Now what?

January 8, 1988

We find another doctor, one who is supportive of home birth—the only one in this area who will risk involvement in such unorthodox procedures. Like us, he doesn't believe that birthing is an illness automatically requiring hospitalization. He believes in allowing people who make informed choices to take responsibility for their own decisions. As a consequence of this position, he's admired by his patients and ostracized by the obstetrical profession.

Dr. Geppeto is a gentle soul who's traded in his lab coat for crystals and incense and who does guided imagery with his pregnant mothers. We come away feeling heard and respected, not to mention relieved. We are edgy about the incense and crystals. Is he reading Shaman's Drum *when he should be reading medical journals?*

January, 1987: Young Driver of Canada Driven Crazy

The New Year brings a big surprise. Susan, a confirmed nondriver, begins driver training. In a race to get her license before the baby arrives (the road test is scheduled for March 16th), she skids and stalls up and down slick wintry side streets.

Her instructor is satisfied with her progress; her spouse is less than thrilled with her technique. The big question is whether driving is preparation for birthing or birthing, for driving.

January 12, 1988: Prenatal Class

Prenatal classes are initiations into parenthood. Every Tuesday night for seven weeks, a dozen pregnant couples converge on St. Jacob's Birthing Centre for classes. These are led by Ankara, a childbirth educator whose gentleness and toughness delight all except the medical profession; her clients ask too many questions. She instructs us in the mysteries of reproduction and the perils of birthing in the standard Canadian way.

Ron is one of those sensitive-male types, an involved father, so says Susan. He asks hard questions and (also according to Susan) acts out in class. The standard role for fathers-to-be these days is that of labor coach. A coach is a kind of educated bystander who coaxes and soothes the birthing woman—as if birth were an athletic event. How do the men in the birth class practice their coaching? By pinching their spouse's Achilles tendons (to simulate the pain of contractions!) and by monitoring her breathing. This exercise helps women learn to enter into the center of pain and to deal with it by breathing their way into it rather than running away from it. What it does for the men is still undetermined.

February 23, 1988: The Hospital

Last prenatal class. Prospective moms and dads visit the hospital. We're happy we're going to use the living room instead. We notice the claw marks on the handgrips in the delivery room. We examine the forceps and wince at the stirrups.

And what about the hospital's "natural" alternative—the birthing room? Not impressive. Not even very homey. It has all the atmosphere of a Waterloo County middle-class restaurant. Between the bed and the coffee table sits the fetal heart monitor, which looks like a roving air conditioner—not the thing you want plugged into your anatomy as a matter of routine. Then there's the perineal lamp, for all intents and purposes a miniature microwave dish for a TV. The nursery is full of newborns stashed under bright fluorescent lighting.

We come away with our decision confirmed.

February 27, 1988: Belly Enshrined

One sunny Saturday Susan sits in the living room. Connie, a friend who is a mask-making artist, has arrived. She and Ron cover Susan's body, neck to navel, with vaseline and plaster-impregnated gauze. Susan's beautifully ballooning self is now enshrined in plaster. Later comes the clay. Later still, perhaps the child will point at the strangely dark art-object-become-fruit-bowl and ask, "Mom, was I really in there?"

February 29, 1988: Home Birth Prep Party

Typically, the Scott-Grimes strategy regarding ritual events is to involve their friends as much as possible. And what better way to have one's community participate vicariously in this momentous occasion than to beg and borrow the items needed for a home birth?

Susan drafts her cronies into volunteering everything from ice packs to pillows to Pampers. They lounge around these strange objects assembled on the living room floor (the intended birth site) telling birth stories, while a great vat of medicinal herbs brews on the stove.

Women come with domestic offerings, memories, and advice. They tend the acrid brew, preparing a postpartum bath to heal mother and child. They are amused, amazed, and curious about one another's experience with the great mystery of birth.

Now everything is in place. All the necessary items are ready. Susan is prepared, content. Her nesting instinct is satisfied.

Dreams

The Scott-Grimes family develops a nighttime routine. In her dreams Susan changes diapers, sews, checks the crib, and labors in a row boat, while Ron dreams it's a girl, then a boy, then a girl, and so on. Awake, both are sure it's a girl.

Susan dreams of birth helpers. One night it's a British midwife doll called Sylvia Breachbottom Bathwater. Another night it's a great white bear that gnaws on her collarbone.

Ron dreams of birthing babies. One night it's girl with a shock of blond hair sticking straight out of the top of her head like Woody Woodpecker or a corn tassel. He dreamed her name was Peaches. But the poor girl couldn't say her own name. Instead, she said, "Cheeches."

Another dream leaves Ron with a Sphinxlike question, "You, young man with your birthright and your death rite, how will you spend your last hour?"

In another he is dressed as a woman hiding in a pile of living female bodies. Then a hand snakes through the heap and takes hold of his important parts. A voice says, "It's a man. There's a man in here." He wakes up knowing that, however much he wants to participate in birth, he will participate as a man, not a woman.

March 10, 1988: The Rehearsal

A pleasant day. Francesca arrives for her usual Thursday visit. She examines Susan, who mentions she's having mild cramps. Francesca says that's a good sign; it means the body is preparing, rehearsing.

The foremost matter at hand now is, Who should attend the birth? We have no interest in a communal birth with family, friends, and video camera. But what about Romana, Susan's friend of some twenty-odd years?

Dream in hand, Ron at first wants to add no more women to the list of birth at-tendants. Already, there's a midwife, a backup, Susan, and, no doubt, a girl on the way. (Ma & Pa agree all along that's what "it" is.) Eventually, a compromise is worked out. Romana, friend and intensive care nurse, will also serve as backup midwife. Who cares if she's seen more deaths than births? So Ro meets Francesca for the first time. The four of us discuss everyone's respective role during labor. The only problem remaining is one of logistics: how to choreograph the birth so every-one arrives on time.

Late that afternoon, Susan walks Ro downtown to catch the 3:00 bus back to Toronto. They hope to see each other one week from today—on the due date, of course.

That night, Susan tells Ron she'd felt a bit of cramping on and off during the day. He playfully predicts labor. She accuses him of trying to condition her.

March 11, 1988: The Big Event

12:00 A.M.: *Susan makes several trips to the bathroom. What else is new? Ron saws logs; he's heard these sleepy footsteps before.*

2:30 A.M.: *She says, "Knock, knock." He is instantly awake. "I think I've begun," she suggests tentatively. She's shivering. It's the cold. No, maybe it's nerves.*

"Let's time a couple," he suggests. Five minutes apart, forty-five seconds dura-tion.

"Do you think I'm really in labor? It's not time." She is shaking.

"You should see your face. You're in labor. And besides, the contractions are five minutes apart."

2:43 A.M.: *Ron calls Francesca (Susan is preoccupied). Francesca drives from Guelph—no hesitation.*

3:00 A.M.: *Ron calls Romana. The first bus from Toronto is not until 7:30 A.M. Two phone calls later she's in a cab underwritten by her fiancé, who knows what she'll be like to live with if she misses her friend's labor and delivery.*

3:53 A.M.: *Francesca arrives, checks Susan, is astonished. Eight centimeters di-lated (ten is normal for birth)! This baby is wasting no time.*

5:00 A.M.: *Romana arrives, showers off the cabbie's smoke, visits Susan, who's on the toilet, her preferred site for riding the waves of contraction. "She looks like an angel," Ro exclaims in a whisper.*

Susan sits, open, hands lying loosely in her lap. Her hands are in the form of a Hindu mudra (a meditation posture), although she doesn't know it. The Benedic-tines say, "Laborare est orare"—to labor is to pray. This is true. No tension, just rid-ing the crest of the waves of energy coursing through the body. Between contrac-tions, which have escalated rapidly, Susan is so relaxed she almost falls asleep.

The lights are low. Classical guitar music is playing on the stereo. Everyone is quiet, attentive, waiting. The birth attendants prepare the living room for the next phase—pushing the baby out. Susan is too absorbed to be able to tell anyone where the home birth prep items are. The perfectly organized home birth becomes makeshift.

Between contractions, Ron reads a few of the "labor relations" messages that were elicited from friends and relatives for use during the event. Only a handful of notes have arrived. We thought we had another week before the messages would be needed. First babies are usually late. Good thing the notes that did come are short. One contraction is barely finished when another surges.

6:00 A.M.: Susan emerges from the bathroom. Francesca sets aside the book she's reading (an autobiography of a cellist) and picks up the fetal scope. It's time to push. Francesca checks the baby's heart; she can already feel the head.

Ever since she learned about the ease and efficiency of birth in the squatting position, Susan was determined to squat. With Ron and Ro to support her, she bears down and finds herself slowly cracking open. Like a great tuber, like a begonia bulb that splits apart for the sprout to emerge, she births the baby. Ron exclaims that the sounds she makes are primal.

"Each one will receive her own reward according to her own labor" (I Corinthians 3:8).

7:00 A.M.: There is a wonderful, earth-shuddering groan—terrifying, erotic, and utterly convincing. The head clears the pubic bone, and the rest of No-Name Scott-Grimes is lying belly down, face to the side, in what Christians call "this" world. Ro insists she saw the spirit enter the body. (Thomas Aquinas, move over.) We allow the child to lie there for a moment without our knowing whether it's a girl or boy. She whimpers a bit, but no scream. Then she opens her eyes wide and looks at Ron, who has caught her and is wiping her off. Francesca places her on Susan's belly and then prepares the cord for Ron to cut.

Whom does the baby look like? Not me. Not you. She just looks like herself. Red hair. The child of two brown-haired parents.

A lucky series of sevens: 7 hours of labor, 7 pounds (well, 6 lbs, 14 ozs.), 7 in the morning.

Why March 11? A day on which virtually no famous person has deigned to enter the planet. (Yeah, we checked everything from Butler's Lives of the Saints *to* Who's Who*). No doubt, she decided to avoid the solar eclipse, new moon, and St. Patrick's Day—all of which would have fallen on March 17, her due date. She wanted to avoid the heavy cosmic agenda.*

The placenta comes quickly. Placentas come in all shapes and sizes. This one is heart-shaped. Ron washes it, freezes it, and saves it for planting under flowers in the spring. The umbilical cord is first offered to Jesus and Buddha in the attic (no telling what they thought); then it's tied around Ron's chili-bedecked walking stick—the one used at the wedding.

Susan takes her herbal bath. It looks and smells like swamp water, but it soothes stretched and bleeding flesh. Ron absconds with the baby, hating to see the tiny body put in garlic-flavored water. Ro finds him in the attic, chanting to the newborn a Buddhist hymn about compassion. The child has fallen asleep in his lap. Reluctantly, he gives her up to the women and the water. Fortunately, the kid who just came from water is happy to return to it, at least for a couple of minutes. Then she screams for dry land and Dad.

Ron makes crepes for breakfast. All of us exchange stories, check the uterus, watch the baby sleeping contentedly. We recall the babies crowded under neon lights in the hospital nursery.

The afternoon is filled with ecstatic phone calls and rapid-fire computer messages. Suddenly, Susan remembers her driving appointment. When her instructor arrives shortly thereafter, she greets him at the door and announces that, having given birth this morning, she guesses she'll not be going driving today, thank you very much.

After dinner by candlelight, we discover a scene that students have built on the lawn. There are diapered pink flamingos, a crowing cock, a box of Huggies, lots of chocolate eggs. The scene is hedged with a white fence and guarded by two daunting cardboard nuns labeled Medieval Mystic #1 and #2, respectively. The former and larger of the two (Saint Teresa, no doubt) brandishes a cross with the greeting, "Welcome to the planet." Nearby is a pole strung with balloons and small toys and a sign shouting, "Happy Birthday." A kite is hanging from the porch light, and a basket of chapati (Indian bread) is nestled in a corner of the front porch. We retrieve the bread and chocolate and tiptoe up to bed. Just the three of us.

March 12, 1988: The Boys' Night Out

The Saturday before the birth was supposed to be the boys' night out. The point was to drum up appropriate masculine energies for the birth.

But La Petite disrupted—or rather, redefined—these plans. Instead of being preparation, the get-together is redefined as celebration. The boys, all sufficiently endowed and well enough aged to be worthy of manhood, meet at the Laurier Athletic Complex sauna—dressed in their birthday suits (like newborn babies). These guys do not know one another, but casual attire makes a good impression when you shake hands for the first time. Ron's hare-brained scheme is met with some skepticism but is tolerated; these are his friends, after all.

One thing leads to another, and the first thing you know they're at the Old English Parlour telling birth (human and bovine) stories and eating chocolate cheesecake.

Can you imagine what happens when you convene a poet-farmer, a philosopher-gardener, a nurse-father, a child educator–postman, and a ritual-making academic father? Conversation ranges from how cows eat the afterbirth but goats don't, to still being enraged at how one was born, to why obstetricians are embarrassed by perineal massage, to how one can be so full of joy at holding his newborn that he is, as they say, ready to die.

Afterward, they stop at the Scott-Grimes household to see the baby and get photographed passing her down the line like a seven-pound football. They sit around contemplating this tiny creature and her mom, who has so recently dismounted the Great Mare of Birth.

March 14, 1988: The Name

Usually, this part comes first, but in fact it actually came last. On a little blank, white doll we had penned several names, each the result of hours of research, day-dreaming, and twirling words around in the mouth like pebbles or jelly beans. We had decided not to choose a name before we had a chance to see, handle, and listen to the baby. We hoped she would help inspire the right choice. In fact, maybe she'd even tell us who she was. Some of the names were made up. We got out the old Scrabble game one night and started playing with sounds and letters. Friends cringed at the possibilities: Brook, Bevin, Sage, Willow, Felicia, Terra, Calla, Wyndra. But in the end none of these was chosen, so, dear friends with babies on the way, please feel free to use any of them.

After a few days the name presents itself:

CAILLEAH WYN SCOTT-GRIMES

Pronounced phonetically: kyleeah win skot-gryms. Acceptable nickname, Caleigh (phonetically: kaylee). In the first version of her first name the accent is on the second syllable; in the second version it is on the first.

Where did we get the name? We made it up, because we liked the sound of it. We are indebted to Stephanie's diligence with her Gaelic dictionary, which says that the word cailleach *means "the curled wisp at the top of a cornstalk" or "veiled, like a nun." The former meaning picks up on Ron's dream; the latter takes care of her mother's mystical yearnings.*

Wyn is old Welch for "fair." Fair was the springlike day on which she was born. Fair also is her disposition (except between suppertime and midnight). To us it also suggests the wind, which is holy, the spirit of the wind chimes, and the shudder of a breeze stirring autumn cornsilk.

Don't forget the hyphen in the baby's last name, Scott-Grimes. If you total us up, there are a Scott, a Grimes, and a Scott-Grimes. What happens when this hyphenated little girl meets a hyphenated little boy is anybody's guess.

March 18, 1988: Why This Newsletter Ends So Abruptly

Diapers, feedings, laundry, greetings, squawking, cooing, gazing ...
Need we say more?

———

For many, a prebirth shower and a postbirth announcement are the sole ritual gestures marking birth. Other rites such as church blessings are both rare and cursory, and they almost never celebrate birth as such. They sometimes give thanks for the life of a child, but not for a couple's sexuality, a mother's labor, or a father's care. The notion of a life is implicitly disembodied and despiritualized. Even birthday parties are segregated from the original acts of conceiving and giving birth. Instead, they are typically forward-looking, concentrating on the advance of age. Child-centered cults that tend to decline in ceremonial elaboration as the celebrant grows in age, North American birthdays ignore both maternity and paternity. They overlook the very event they are supposed to celebrate. Of all the rites of passage, birth is the most undercelebrated.

Though our announcement tells more than most announcements, much is missing. In retrospect it is obvious. We are jubilant and decorous at the birth, but we omit most of the painful ambiguities. Four years after the newsletter a birth performance made me acutely aware of what had been left out of the announcement. Carol Weaver and Judith Miller, a composer and a poet, were joined by several others in a performance called *Birthstory*. It was composed of several layers: instrumental music, poetry, and a tape of excerpts from women's birth stories. Portions of Susan's birth story were included in the performance. By coincidence it fell on Caleigh's fourth birthday, so we took her. The chapel was full, mostly of women.

Partway into the performance Caleigh whispered, "When will it be finished so we can go home?" She put her head in my lap and drowsily contemplated the fiery reds in the chapel's stained-glass windows. I thought she was going to sleep. Instead, she looked up and whispered, this time loud enough for the woman behind us to hear, "Was there a hole?"

"A what?"

"Hole! You know, for the baby to come out of?"

"Yes."

Silence.

Then, "How big?"

Embarrassed because I knew we were being watched and overheard, I tried to avoid showing her. "Big enough," I whispered, "for your doll-sized head to come out."

"Oh."

More silence.

Then, "Is there blood?"

"Yes," I said, "a little, not too much. And some water."

Five minutes passed.

I was beginning to think that she had let go of the conversation topic when she broke into the music again, this time insistently, "How big!"

When I showed her, she was content and did not speak again until the crescendo near the climax of the performance, at which point she interrupted, "That's loud!"

The intentions of performers only partly determine how a performance is received. My sense of *Birthstory* was strongly influenced by Caleigh's counterperformance. For me, the "hole and blood" conversation has come to suggest what was absent from our birth story as we performed it in the broadsheet. It depicts us as undaunted by the skepticism of acquaintances and the resistance of the medical establishment. It assumes an air of superiority over other styles of giving birth and implies, at least in its tone, that there were no ambiguities—no holes, no blood—in our pursuit of home birth.

For example, it says nothing about my fear of becoming a father again. My night out with the boys was a low-key attempt to deal with a lack of male support in the process of becoming a father. The night was enjoyable. We did, in fact, tell a few birth stories and share some hysterical moments about childrearing. We mustered a buoyant but temporary sense of togetherness. However, after that one night it was impossible to strike up more than a thirty-second conversation about birth with male friends. No one really wanted to hear the story. Men friends indulged me for an evening (I bought the beer and chocolate cheesecake), but they showed no sustained interest in the topic, even though most of them were good fathers who genuinely loved their kids.

I cannot say what birth is for a newborn or for a woman. Newborns cannot talk about their births. Women, even women who never give birth, ponder it more than most men, but their experiences can never be mine, even though the reflections of women have been instrumental in evoking mine. A man is left very much alone with his experience of birth. Men's birth experiences are sometimes admittedly paltry. The poverty of their stories is not entirely their fault. Much of the time it is. We must admit our failings before we have the possibility of making it otherwise.

The newsletter does not say how terrified I was that I might have another child with birth defects. Nor does it chronicle differences between Susan and me. Except for a line or two, we are the exemplary couple, one in mind and heart. But marital unity is always momentary, partial, and fragile. Left to my own desires and plans, I probably would not have had another child. On my own I might have been unable to resist hospital birth, despite my deep alienation from such institutions. I agreed to have children because I trusted our marriage. A child in the abstract meant little to me. I agreed to home birth because I trusted Susan's intuitions more than I did my own fears. In making the decisions to birth at home, she took the initiative. I trailed along, at first reluctantly, then enthusiastically. Now I am an advocate.

Since I had had a child, I was able to imagine the hole a child would knock in the fabric of our life together. I knew the cost in available energy, time, and space. I actively and openly mourned this loss before Caleigh's birth. I knew it would be impossible to do so once she was a real person cradled in my arms. Sometimes my foreknowledge (which was really history projected into the future) was an asset; often, a liability.

The physiological blood and hole that concerned Caleigh during *Birthstory* were small when compared with the psychological blood and hole that a birth necessarily entails in the life of a couple. Sure, the birth was a joy, and, of course, this specific child was truly amazing, and, naturally, the birth was natural, bordering on supernatural. But no one ought to imagine that the joy makes the pain any less painful.

The birth announcement does not say how much Caleigh looked like Trevor. Other people who had known him remarked on the resemblance. Even Susan, who for obvious reasons would have preferred not to see it, saw it. Had Caleigh been a boy, the resemblance to Trevor would have precipitated considerable ambivalence. For those of us who imagine that identity hinges on difference—on being a distinctly different person from every other person—such continuities present a problem, especially when the resemblance is to a child of another marriage. Sometimes I say that Caleigh has her mother's smile, her Grandma Nadine's hair color, and so on, but we carefully control and contain discussions of such continuities. They are not the stuff of birth announcements—ours or anyone else's. Rather, they are the substance of family folklore. They are ways of accounting for what would otherwise seem anomalous. We sometimes mythologize Caleigh's behavior by referring it to one of us or to a relative but never to Trevor. That would violate a family taboo. Now she asserts herself as her own person. "She doesn't look like either of us," we say. "She just looks like herself."

We knew that naming was a powerful act, so we chose the name Cailleah and nickname Caleigh wittingly. What we could not have reported in the newsletter—because we did not know it—was the taste of the name Cailleah in our mouths. It felt elevated, large, beyond the child. It sounded like something she had to grow into or achieve. It was too much to lay on a mere baby. I noticed that both Susan and I hesitated slightly each time one of us uttered it aloud. Eventually, we both began to call her Caleigh except around people who knew her by her more formal first name. The name Cailleah had an air of mystery about it that deepened two years later when we learned of its association with displaced Irish goddesses. We watch to see what she will do with her name or it, with her.

14

BIRTH BY HAND

If Dad had not died, leaving me a fatherless child, I probably would not have agreed to becoming double-dad, the father of two. If Susan had not witnessed the Grimes siblings working in concert after Dad's death, she might never have suggested that we have a second. These "if … then" sequences are always psychological, never logical. They are not conclusions to be argued or proven but trajectories to be followed or refused.

One would have thought we would be better prepared for Bryn's birth than for Caleigh's. We had birthed once; we had performed well. Nevertheless, we were less well prepared. The world that would greet Bryn would not be the world that greeted Caleigh.

Susan was distraught with my lack of readiness. She complained that I was less involved in Bryn's pregnancy. She was right. I was lagging behind its development, anticipating further losses of freedom and an increased energy drain. There was no birth class to choreograph our rhythms. It did not occur to me to take one and to frame it as a ritual preparation rather than the transfer of information, which I obviously did not need.

Some days I felt I should write a second newsletter, but I flagged. The medium belonged to another era and another child. I aspired to design a formal birth rite, but I couldn't. I was stuck, unable to imagine it, unaware of a source from which to borrow it. There were no cultural or religious communities with rites capable of buoying up our sagging energies.

I was concerned with Susan's fear of having a boy. My preoccupation kept me from doing my own preparatory work. When Bryn was in utero, I was certain he was boy. Susan was afraid he was. She has no brothers and comes from several generations of dominant women and absentee men. So she had little experience with rearing males and admitted that she didn't know what to do with little ones.

Susan and I had known that Caleigh would be a girl. Once the first pregnancy was known, the sex was obvious. We were delighted. So were our friends. Like us, many of them intuited her sex. Some even said she *ought* to be female. Feminists, they were busy undermining the widespread, prejudicial preference for boys. Since such comments were offered in jest, I let them pass, because I knew serious issues lay behind the bad humor.

Neither of us was happy with the roles carved out for boys. One day Susan, pregnant with Bryn, went to buy some boy's clothes. She came back upset. The shopping trip occurred not long after the murder of fourteen women in Montreal by an antifeminist male toting a rifle. All the boys clothes she could find looked like programming devices, ideological statements in cartoon form: BOYS PLAY BASEBALL, BOYS DRIVE TRUCKS, BOYS CAN FLY, BOYS SHOOT GUNS. It is one thing for boys to learn to shoot their guns, another thing to have to sleep with them emblazoned across their backs and chests. Neither of us has much use for the package that awaits boys. There are alternatives, but one has to work hard to find them. This society may have no focused initiation to make boys into men, but it has a diffuse one that begins at birth with color-coded cribs.

When Bryn's pregnancy was announced, no one suggested that he *ought* to be a boy or that having a boy was a better option than having a girl. Fair enough. Historic justice was busy righting an imbalance. The only person who might have expressed a preference for a boy was Susan's dad. But he wasn't around to utter his farmer's preference for a dandy boy. The world was not tipped forward in anticipation of Bryn's birth.

Susan labors in the bathroom where no one can reach her. I hear the music of her breathing—deep, aspirated. Sitting on the toilet, where she finds the most comfort, her chin rises, her eyes close, her thumb and forefinger curl into an oval. I sit meditating, ready to do whatever needs doing. I am relaxed, alert. I enjoy playing servant, second fiddle, handmaid ("handman" is a word that should exist). I guard the door. Who knows from what?

Eventually, Susan comes out of her bathroom-become-cell and goes down on all fours in the middle of a flowered sheet spread out on the living room floor. The midwives help but keep their distance. Our friend Grace keeps vigil. The midwives know—and say—that Susan knows what she's doing. "She does it the way it's supposed to be done," they observe. I am awed by this panting animal with a head of hair that would provoke envy from a Clydesdale horse. She does not birth the way women do in movies and birthing films. They grunt and howl, driving the painful thing out with all the force that attendant nurses and doctors can muster.

Susan waits, follows, rides the waves. My love and admiration are boundless. I ride behind, clinging to the saddle. She births the way she does every other important thing. She appears to be doing very little or nothing, and then everything changes. The transformation is deep and complete; its sources are invisible and its means, incomprehensible. When Susan works, everything shifts on its axis, but from underneath. Then something entirely new, utterly old enters the world.

The labor began at almost the same time of night as Caleigh's, and Bryn's birth, like hers, happened shortly after daylight. Both babies were born in the same spot, the middle of the living room floor, where we wrestle and tumble nightly before their story, snack, and tooth-brushing. The floor has never been the same since the two births. When we sit on it, I remember. When we move from our house on Dunbar, I will probably turn toward it as to some Mecca in prayer. From afar I will utter petitions and praise to the constitutive forces of the universe that gathered at that spot. Birth, like burial, anchors one to the place of its occurrence.

For me, the births were strikingly similar until the moment of crowning, at which time Bryn's dark hair suddenly made him not-Caleigh. She had been born almost bald and faintly blond. For Susan, the differences between the births were pronounced. She described Bryn's birth in transcendent tones and unabashedly religious language.

Larger than Caleigh, Bryn squirmed into my hands with less grace but more directness. He pushed his way into the world. Born in May, he and I are both Taureans. My skepticism of astrology notwithstanding, he and I are bullish. We paw the ground and a primal scene emerges. Two bucks in the forest, we butt heads, reveling. Two bulls, we chase each other. I chase him, and instead of running away, he charges me.

As soon as Bryn cleared Susan's body and the midwife and I rolled him over, I noticed his toes. I was afraid, certain that he had birth defects. Both Susan and the midwife laughed off my perceptions. In the end they were right and I, wrong. His toes were fine. But for several days I was afraid and depressed.

It is not true that new parents always feel their own kids are beautiful or that they instantly and automatically love them. Bryn looked like Bunyip, a homely creature from one of our favorite children's books. The creature is always asking other animals who he is and whether he is handsome. When he encounters a human being, the man asserts with pomposity, "Bunyips do not exist."

Bryn emerged with a face that reminded me too much of Dad. I should have expected it, since Dad's death had precipitated the decision to have a second child. Bryn did not have wide-open eyes like his sister and mother, but turtle eyes and blackish, oily hair. His eyes avoided contact as if he did not want to be looked at. He had Dad's way of avoiding too direct or too long a gaze. And like his grandad, whom he would never know, he seemed to retreat so deeply into himself that I suspected he was not there even though he was right in front of me. The world was too bright and noisy for him, and he wanted to confront very little of it directly.

When he wiggled his way into the world, he was already old, well baked. His placenta had begun to calcify, a sign that it was overripe. It was sturdy, not shaped like Caleigh's bleeding heart bag. We buried Bryn's placenta beneath a new smoke bush a year after his birth. Now the tree is fanning its glorious peacock tail in the backyard.

Soon after Bryn was born, Susan and I began to regard to him as an old soul. Even if he had been born in some other month, I probably would have felt that he was in some peculiar way older than me. For a while he was father and I, child. We both arrived in May—he, on the twelfth and I, on the nineteenth. Anticipating his second birthday, I said to Caleigh, "Well, Bryn will be born next month, and I will be born the week after." She looked puzzled, knowing that fathers are supposed to be born before their sons.

The friend who had made a casting of Susan's belly when she was pregnant with Caleigh offered to make a second one. I rejected the proposal but for a time was unsure why. Eventually, I had a dream that jolted me into knowing what I needed instead: a cast of my hands. Instead of two belly casts, a redundant set in my view, we would have a complementary pair—Susan's belly, my hands—one from each birth, her kind of labor coupled with my kind.

As with Caleigh, my hands were there to guide Bryn into the world. Both children issued from their mother, but they slid into these hands and gazed at this face. That made me father as certainly as paternity did. I was there to imprint on; I was not absent. This initial contact was a mythological moment; it continues to form me. It declares that I was not marginal to my children's births and reinforces my desire not to be absent from their ongoing lives.

The hands made, I then knew what I must do for Bryn's birth. I would write no newsletter or invent no new ceremony but build a wagon instead, a classic oak one. The wagon, I announced, would outlast my books. Probably, the kids would never read them anyway. Like Mom, they might display books I had authored, but they would not likely read them. I had to secure my immortality in whatever way I could, so Bryn got the Mercedes-Benz of wagons—late, but of fine workmanship. I had no idea that he would treasure tools by the time he was two.

In some traditional societies men with children on the way take to their beds in dramatically ceremonialized pregnancy. This pattern is called couvade. Wagon-building was my couvade. The wagon sported a curved tongue, removable-slat sides, and magnificent red wheels. When we strolled to Waterloo Square—the two of us, draft horses pulling our precious cargo and the two of them plutocrats for all the world to see—heads turned and the orders rolled in. But I turned them down. "One of a kind," I boasted. Susan would smile. We looked great, the four of us, cruising down the sidewalk in our oaken prairie schooner. We made a quaternity, a perfectly balanced picture: two males, two females. No gender imbalance here.

Two months after Bryn's birth he was hospitalized. Screaming, he resisted two nurses and a doctor, all of whom made a pincushion of his plump body as they tried unsuccessfully to find a vein. The night after this ordeal the wagon showed up in a dream. Dad is in it, and he is an ancestor. Now one of the old men, one of the grandfathers, he appears with great numinosity. As in many other dreams about old men, I can see only the back of his head. Dad is riding in a cart with wooden sides, reminding me of medieval pageants, Penitente death carts, and

Bryn's birth wagon. Because Dad is in the wagon, he seems in some sense to be Bryn.

The dream scene shifts. I detonate some powerful device, creating a blinding flash in downtown Clovis. The explosion transforms the skating rink we used to own into a men's hairstyling place and boutique. It is a successful business, but not a very manly place. Dad then tells me—or somehow I know—that such things (saving a business, accomplishing, achieving) are not really important.

I woke up knowing exactly what was important: Bryn. The dream forced me to notice an irony. My son, given birth to at home and thus out of the hospital's reach, was not fully born to me until he was in the hospital. Bryn, who evoked such ambivalence by reminding me of Dad, could become Bryn only when I let him merge with Dad in a dream. For several weeks following birth, that is, until Bryn's hospitalization, I had been affectionate but ambivalent. This child looked too much like my father. But for some reason I do not understand, the hospitalization and dream allowed both the identification of Bryn with Dad and the worry that he would have birth defects like Trevor to dissolve. For the first time since his birth, Bryn seemed to be truly alive, fully himself, and very important. Finally I was able to embrace my delight at his emergence.

Fathering is labor. Lack of sleep drugs the spirit. Changing diapers is penance. Leaving for work is purgatory. Making a great picture isn't all there is to it. Spiritual travail and bodily exertion continue. After Bryn's birth we lapsed into a sleepless stupor. Susan suffered chronic boundary loss and lack of a spatial refuge, and she had no time to shower, walk, or pee in private. No one told us that the leap from one to two could be greater than the leap from zero to one. With two children there was no rest. We entered a twilight zone, a fundamentally altered state of consciousness that appears nowhere on the lists of transcendent states. I complained, "I wasn't cut out for this; I'm too old. All my friends' kids are off to university or taking their first jobs. My colleagues' nests are empty, and they are free to roam the streets of Europe after twenty-five years of hard labor. I'll never have such a time. Bryn will still be in high school when I retire."

Fathering is sometimes hell. Often purgatory. Occasionally heaven. So I return to the births, replaying them like old records. They give me courage. When life is less than transcendent, which is most of the time, I recollect the children's births.

Bryn was born at a time when gender relations were fraught with public drama and compulsive ritualization. In the preceding year men had loomed particularly large in the public eye as rapists, murderers, and abusers of both women and children. The day of his birth no students showed up on the lawn with flamingos. Few gifts arrived. Friends who had fussed and cooed over Caleigh just looked at Bryn. Those who had held Caleigh and cuddled her stood back from him. Later, when he opened outward, becoming obviously good-looking, lavishly affectionate, and outgoing rather than homely and introverted, they still held back. And now that he forthrightly declares to everyone, while hugging their knees, that he loves them, they marvel, but most women continue to keep their distance.

Part, but not much, of what I am describing can be attributed to Bryn's being secondborn. "Pure yang," Susan says of Bryn, but she now revels in it. Female friends did, and do, not. They remain wary, though they'd probably never admit it or even recognize it. In the social circles I inhabit these are hard times to be born male. Men make wars and oppress others. Bryn looks too much like a truck driver or hockey player, even though he smiles like an acre of sunflowers and is as mushy as a bog swamp. The sexism that would entrap a boy in masculine stereotypes is there from the beginning and is not perpetrated only by men. So who's to wonder if a son resorts to Ninja Turtles or turns every stick into a gun?

Susan marked Bryn's birth with a postpartum ceremony among women. When she showed me the script for it, I strenuously objected to a line that became symbolic of deeper issues. Her words suggested that the rhythms and demands of the three of us (Bryn, Caleigh, and I) dominated her own needs. If the statement had been a private one, I would have been sympathetic. But it was to be public and ensconced in ceremony. I asked her to delete or rewrite it. She refused on the grounds that the line expressed how she felt. Did we in fact dominate her? I asked. No, she replied, but the line stayed; she was expressing feelings, not describing facts.

Eventually, we understood each other's point, but mutual understanding does not always solve problems. She performed the rite. I resented it. The issue remains unresolved. For her, the action was a rite of passage that accomplished two goals. It began, she said, the work of negotiating the terrible slide from ecstasy to servitude, and it marked her full entry into womanhood.

For me, it was a major marker as well, though I could not articulate the meaning of her rite for almost two years. The event drew a line that reminded me that I was a male and therefore on one side, not the other. No matter how much I empathized with Susan, participated in birth, worked for the hiring of women, or introduced students to feminist thought, I was still a man.

Two years later we reargued the postpartum rite. Neither of us had changed our minds, but I recognized that my sense of what it meant to be a feminist male (though I had never used the term) had made a significant shift as a result of that rite. I was used to being excluded from women's caucuses and women's groups. The reasons for them were valid and obvious, so they did not bother me. I remained angry, because I had participated in birth and childrearing to a degree atypical of most men, and yet my only appearance in the rite was as an oppressor. I argued that the slide into servitude, as we called it, was shared. It was not something men did to women. It had little to do with being female or male and everything to do with being a parent. Suffering postbirth burnout was not an experience that divided us on the basis of gender, although it was obvious that parenting implicates women differently from men. In my view women who had not experienced birth and parenting knew less about birth than I as a father did. In

Susan's view editing the one line in her rite would have been catering to a neurosis: I was being merely egocentric, controlling, and territorial. In my view editing the line would have constituted recognition that a man and a woman, not a group of women, gave birth to our children. She argued that the rite was an initiation into womanhood. I argued that it did so by invoking a caricature of fatherhood.

Not many fathers are territorial about birth. I am. That I am unwilling to turn birth over to the medical profession is evident. I am also unwilling to treat it as the sole preserve of women, feminist or otherwise, since feminist writing (as well as my experience with hospital birth) led me to become seriously involved in birth in the first place. It is easy for men and women alike to get territorial about birth, just as it is about other rites of passage. In the past it was assumed that weddings and births were the domain of women, even though women were treated as the property of men and male births were preferred. In such a milieu women supposedly entered their own enchanted arena when marrying or giving birth. For many, it is still the sacred preserve of women. This is true even of women who encourage male involvement in birth.

Womanhood has been defined by some women—in some cultures, in certain eras—as the act of, or even the potentiality for, giving birth. One can mythologize this ceremonial territoriality in several ways. One way would be to imagine that birth has always belonged to women, who have successfully resisted the incursions of men into their domain. Another way would be to assume that in some distant mythological past things were different. Once upon a time men and women shared equally in birth and then, and then … there was a fall. Fearing the death of offspring, men abandoned their posts to specialists, the medical profession. Alternatively, the story would maintain that women kicked men out of the delivery room or that men, driven by squeamishness in the face of blood and pain, headed for the hills and waiting rooms, where they chewed nervously on cigars as they awaited the outcome, at which time they reasserted their control. Another version would tell how men gave away their share of control over birth as a consolation prize to women in exchange for the right to remain lords of the political turf.

Who knows how it really was? I don't. And I don't like any of the myths.

There is no denying the physiological primacy of mothers at birth. A father's role is necessarily that of supporting cast. However, the notion that birth somehow naturally belongs only to women is like the notion that the professions and other expressions of public power naturally belong only to men. There is nothing natural about such arrangements. They are cultural. The sort of male participation in birth that we now see emerging in Europe and North America is almost unique in world history. It is no accident that this participation accompanies the rise of feminism.

My way of mythologizing the quandary of birth is clearest in the following dream, which happened long before the birth of Bryn.

November 12, 1978. I am walking with a woman and her husband. She is preg-
nant, near term. We go toward a large, urban building, though we are in the
midst of a flat, New Mexico–like pasture. At first I think it is a hospital. But it turns
out to be a bank that is also a kind of manger.

The woman says we must hurry as she hands me a large, ripe watermelon.

We arrive at the bank-manger and open a garage door leading to a small room
the size of a large closet. The woman and her husband enter.

I am holding the melon. The end grows soft and mushy. I realize that I have a
womb in my hands and that the baby is coming out of it.

I look through an opening at the side of the partly closed door. The husband is
bending over the wife, who is lying down. There are cloths and hot water.

The baby drops its head and shoulders out of the watermelon I am holding. I
am afraid. What if the child is dead or defective? I am scared to look down at it.

I think, "The woman will feel left out if this child is born in my hands. She will
be angry at me if it is defective."

I finally work up the courage to reach down into the watermelon. I lift up the
baby's head. It is smiling, healthy, and happy. With great joy I slip the melon con-
taining the baby to the husband so he can give it to the woman. She will finish
giving birth.

One can read this dream in several ways. In one reading I am a usurper, a male
who obstructs the birth process or, worse, presumes to give birth. Even when I
hand over the baby, I do not hand it directly to the woman but to her husband.
The watermelon birth suggests womb envy, a man's jealous appropriation of an
action unique to women. I've never been troubled by the notion of womb envy. I
make no bones about it: I've wished I could give birth. I also am glad I cannot. I
am happy to be a father. I would make a poor mother, even though Susan says I
have a fierce nurturing instinct.

In a second reading I know my place. Although slow to do so, I recognize the
way things are: Ultimately, I cannot give birth. So I remain on the outside of this
urban manger, and the real birthing, in which I merely assist, goes on inside,
properly the domain of the woman accompanied by her husband.

A third reading is also possible. In it the dream is not about literal birth at all
but about creativity, for which birth is a symbol. In this interpretation I hand
over to the couple what is properly my gift, my responsibility. I disown my own
capacity for giving metaphoric birth, that is, for creating.

And yet one more reading: The three of us share the birth of the baby, each of
us doing our part. The birth is a communal action, all phases of it and all roles in
it equally necessary. The woman both begins the process by giving me the watermelon and ends it by giving birth. In the middle we two men assist with our
hands.

The last interpretation is the one most consonant with how I felt when I woke
up from the dream. I was jubilant. The other interpretations have occurred to

me since. They reflect feminist critiques as well as studies of birth and child-rearing practices in other cultures. Even though the dream precedes the births of our children by many years, it anticipates a thorny issue: the gender politics of birth.

Men badly need vocabulary and images for what fathers can do at birth. God the father is a bad example. Jesus had no children. Buddha abandoned his. And Abraham would have sacrificed Isaac. We need human examples. The mythic ones offer little that I care to emulate.

My way of giving birth will inevitably be that of a man. In literal births I am of necessity a facilitator, one who has hands to assist. My self-image as father comes from this basic fact. The two plaster casts in the attic commemorate two different kinds of birthing experience. The cast of Susan's belly and breasts suggests that she "gives" birth. It depicts her as container (monastic cells are recurrent images in her own religious vocabulary), laborer, and feeder. The other casting depicts me as catching birth. I give a hand, lend support, fetch what needs fetching.

Once I began to imagine myself as birth catcher, I spun out an analogy rooted in adolescence. I was a baseball catcher for the Clovis Pioneers. My best friend was the pitcher. Although I was the captain of the team, he was the star. Newspaper reporters interview hitters and pitchers, not catchers. On a baseball diamond pitchers are central, and in the eyes of high school students and the public, pitchers and heavy hitters are stars. Catchers, well, they are necessary but boring. The stereotype is that catchers ground teams. They are levelheaded and earthy; they can see every other player. They are solid, stable characters. They guard home plate like mama eagles. Pitchers, in contrast, are glamorous, moody, temperamental, and high-strung. Catchers get awards not for catching but for hitting; pitchers get awards for pitching. They don't need to hit well.

The analogy is not perfect. Susan is not moody or temperamental, and she avoids starring roles. But during birth there is no question about it. She pitches; I catch. Catching is hard on the hands. A good pitcher bruises a catcher's hands badly.

I have a hand mystique. When I remember Dad and his dad, I recall their hands. I see their hands in mine. I imagine my kids as remembering my hands. I revel in the fact that I helped guide our two children out of the cave with my own two hands. I remind myself and others of this fact. Forgetting is the stuff child abuse and wars are made of.

The experience of birth has imprinted on my psyche in ways that surprise me. I replay my two kids' births once or twice a week, especially when I am relaxed. But even when I am mad at them, I sometimes say silently to the miniature Bryn or the Caleigh of my imagination, "I caught you, kid. When you opened your eyes, it was my grubby face you were looking at. So cool it." This is my crude way of reexperiencing the moment of first sight and of reminding myself that my children are now as indispensable to me as I am to them.

Male or female, whoever engineered the gender arrangement whereby men hunted or smoked cigars while women birthed made a big mistake. Now that I've witnessed the spirit inflating the pink and purple little bodies of my children, transforming them into real human beings, and now that I've seen my panting wife transformed into an awesome horse, whipping her long mane through the air, there will be no keeping me out.

15

CORD-CUTTING

A few months after Bryn was born, I lay in lithotomy position, the conventional birthing posture used in hospitals. If the truth be told, it is identical with the missionary position. Staring up at the ceiling, I lay on the operating table with my legs spread. The reserved British-Canadian doctor and his cheery Pentecostal, Caribbean-Canadian nurse had just covered my nakedness with a surgical sheet that had a large hole in the front of it. I almost made a joke about the size of the hole. I was going to protest that no man could possibly fill it. But other impulses welled up and took over. I felt humiliation, a rare sensation. I quickly transposed it into anger. Then I imagined I knew what women felt like in this position. For them, it is a repeated experience; for me, this was my one and only time.

The surgeon took hold of my parts and rolled his eyes to the ceiling. I was appalled. He should be watching what he's doing down there. I thought of Dysart, the psychiatrist who dreams he is an initiator cutting up young initiates.

I changed my mind. The urologist must be exercising modesty. As one man about to slice through another man's private parts, he was trying to minimize my embarrassment. Vincent Crapanzano's study of circumcision among Muslim males flashed into memory. I recalled how the young boy's penis stung as he was carried around victoriously on his mother's sweating back. Moroccan boys become men by becoming symbolically associated with women, Crapanzano says. So such initiation rites do not transform a boy into a man at all.

No, it's not modesty; the surgeon's a tactiphile like me. He sees with his hands—the way I drive and divine direction. Eventually, I relaxed, watching him search the map of the scrotum at the top of his brain, up in the direction of the ceiling. For most of the surgery, his attention was upward, like a yogi approaching trance. During the actual cuts, he would look down momentarily. When he stuck the needles in for deadening and stitching, he would glance down in order to hit the right spot, but as soon as the needle was in, up would roll his eyeballs again—high into intuitive space, I hoped.

I jumped.

"Did that hurt?" he asked.

"Yes, of course it did."

"It shouldn't have."

"It did. Not a lot. Go ahead."

"Are you sure? We can give you another injection."

"How many more stitches do you have left?"

"Two or three."

"Go ahead. They're no worse than shots."

"Did you feel the incisions?"

"Yeah, but they just gave me chills; they didn't quite hurt—not like these stitches."

"The scrotum is a funny thing," he began. "Because of its ruffles and ridges, the nerve endings are scattered. Sometimes there are pockets, and the anesthetic doesn't reach one of those pockets. Then it hurts even though everything else is dead."

"Dead," I thought to myself.

The doctor sewed me up but had difficulty. Four or five more stitches were required. Somehow the pain made the event real. I needed the pain to inscribe the event into my psyche, because the whole ceremony was over so quickly. The doctor would not have thought of this minor surgical procedure as a sacrificial rite, but I did.

"Consider yourself fertile for two more months," he advised as I pulled up my shorts, "even though in all likelihood you will not be."

"May I have my parts now?" I asked sheepishly.

"Sure, okay. I can't give you much. I have to send the pieces in so the lab can be sure I got the right thing." He smiled for the first time.

"The right thing? You could have gotten the wrong thing?"

"It happens. Never to me. But it has happened."

I handed him a small blue film canister. He scissored off a couple of centimeters of vas and deposited the two pieces with tweezers.

"I gave you some from each side—one from the right, one from the left. I thought you might like the symbolism," he teased.

"Symbolism? How did you know I was interested in that?" I asked.

"You said you taught religious studies, didn't you?"

"Oh, yeah. Sure." I said. "You catch on fast."

He exited for another vasectomy. He performed them in batches on Friday afternoons so men would not have to go back to work with humiliation on their faces. They had two days to recover from sterilization.

The black nurse escorted me to a bed, handed me a sugary orange drink, and commanded me to down it all and wait fifteen minutes so I wouldn't faint when I stood up. I bargained for apple juice and got it.

Sitting with men on either side, with only the thinnest half-length curtain dividers between us, I was unprepared for my tears. Only a few days before the operation did I begin to sense that I was making an important transition. The first sign was that I complained to Susan that she was treating the occasion like a visit to the dentist. So was I, she pointed out. She had asked several times how I felt about the impending operation, and I said I didn't know. The event seemed important, but I couldn't identify my own feelings about it. Was I worried about potency? No, I didn't believe so; I knew two males who still romped with vigor after theirs.

The nurse came through, fogging the air with a sickeningly sweet aerosol spray. Did she think we needed perfuming or disinfecting? A white nurse came in shortly after. She sniffed, frowned, and snorted, "Who sprayed that?" We men looked innocent but kept our humiliated silence. The black nurse heard the query.

"I did," she said, unabashed.

"Well, that's awful smelling stuff. What is it?"

"Just something that smells good," the black nurse countered. "We use it all the time at our church. Lifts the spirits!"

The white nurse rolled her eyeballs, smiled indulgently, and walked off.

I did not expect to have to mourn the passing of my own child-spawning capacities, since I had two children. Having two children later in life contributed to my sense that a late date, age forty-seven, was my life's midpoint. In my twenties I doubt that I would have mourned the loss of fertility.

I didn't anticipate any regrets, and I don't have any now. A friend, both a male and a nurse, expressed doubt about my decision. He said he thought it fatalistic (I think he meant presumptuous)—as if I knew what the future would bring. What if my wife or my kids died? "What if?" I said. "I would still do the same thing." The decision had nothing to do with divination of the future but with carrying my share of the responsibility for birth control. If Susan, Caleigh, and Bryn were to die, I still would not want any more children, even though I was much more interested in fathering in my forties than I ever was in my twenties.

Turning thirty was insignificant. So was becoming forty. But in the middle of the forty-seventh year, I was sure that I was becoming middle-aged, that I was passing over into the second half of life. A philosopher friend said I was playing a trick so I could live to be ninety-four instead of the usual seventy-two. Maybe so.

I left the hospital and walked toward the car but kept on going past it. I felt a desperate need to walk even though I hurt. Walking, pain flows. A nearby cemetery drew me. I tried to hide my tears from passersby. A woman and child strolled by, going in the opposite direction and oblivious to my weeping and new state of sterility.

An unmistakable compulsion led me directly to the back of an unremarkable tombstone. I wondered what had attracted me. Why this stone? I walked around front. It said, "Prof. E. A. Aksim, 1876–1930." Beside it was a newer stone engraved, "AKSIM: The Rev. Professor Eduard Friedrich (1876–1930) & His Beloved Wife, Maria Elisabeth (1887–1982)." I had never seen a stone with a professorial title on it or one man's grave marked with two stones. Who put this man's academic title on his burial monument? Who later amplified it with his clerical title? Why did he have two stones, one shared and one not?

I offered one snippet of my severed vas to Aksim and his wife and walked away, wondering what I had done. Who was he? Did I want to carry professorial status to the grave? Certainly not. Why not? Why did he?

This is it, I thought; this is a big turning point. In April the house will be paid off. For the first time in my life I will be a home owner, free and clear. Yeah, I argued with myself, but you are also a motherless child now and a fatherless one to boot. You have two kids and a wife, but you are a spiritual orphan. Your parents are gone, your kids will think you are old enough to be their grandfather, and your Zen master despairs of your enlightenment.

Standing there in the cemetery I began to realize how tired I was of being in the position of judge. Every day some new article to edit, some paper to grade, some colleague's research proposal to assess. Everyone seems to want my evaluation. I have come into my own. I have authority. *Life* magazine wants to interview me about its rites-of-passage issue. Someone from the New York Assembly has called for advice about rites of passage in public institutions. The Minnesota Humanities Commission wants me to do a workshop on ritual for public school teachers. What do I know? I can't even handle this minor transition. I am afraid of all of this responsibility, even though I have put myself in this position of power.

I kept ambling up and down the little hills of the graveyard. Here I was; I had authority, but I was sterile. The word *sterile* stuck in my throat. It was too metaphoric: To be sterile is to be lacking in creativity. Literal sterility didn't concern me, but spiritual sterility did. Having authority and spiritual sterility—a dangerous condition. Are we men to blame? I doubt it; we did not invent the scenario. Nevertheless, we are responsible for it.

It has been a while since my walk in the cemetery. The scars healed. Spring came. I disposed of the other piece of my sperm-bearing tube. I had recurrent fantasies about going out at sunup on Sunday mornings to plant pumpkin seeds everywhere—along the railroad tracks, in the parks, along the curbs where the dogs make their masters pause to scoop poop. "Ronnie Pumpkinseed," I called myself. I read and reread *The Man Who Planted Trees*. I found an old copy of *Johnny Appleseed* and read that too, not having done so since I was an adolescent. When Halloween came, I felt compelled to bake the jack-o-lanterns, freezing their meat for pumpkin pies in the winter and saving their slick seeds for the next spring.

A vasectomy reminds a man of the proximity of propagation to decline, sterility, and death. A decision not to give birth is a way of embracing the fact of death. Women who give birth know they face the possibility of death, even though many of them choose not to dwell on it. Since a man is not a birth-giver, he does not face death in order to give life. He has no monthly reminders or menopause to signal that he is foregoing life. He may be reminded of death by a birth, but he is not threatened with dying as a woman is. So the surgeon's cold steel knife in close proximity to the family jewels, as we called them when we were teenagers, is likely a man's most vivid reminder that life and death are bedfellows.

Men and women alike have appropriated birth as a metaphor for their initiations and funerals as well as for creativity in general. We give birth to paintings, books, new directions, and ideas. These and many more activities are spoken of as new, or second, births. In some societies—and Western, Christian culture is no exception—men have tried to convince both themselves and women that these rebirths were higher, and therefore better, than mere physical births. They have implied, "Once you were born of mere woman; now you shall be born of the spirit (by implication a male domain)."

As always, at least two interpretations are possible. One is that in making such assertions men are trying to steal the thunder of women. The other is that men (and also women) are paying their respects to biological birth by making it the metaphor for spiritual renewal and artistic creativity. We cannot solve the historical question: We do not know what happened to make second birth seem like the real birth. Whatever happened, the result has been demeaning to biological birth and to women. The displacement of value from first to second birth has functioned as a seriously damaging religious invention. So we should be suspicious of the notion of two births, one spiritual and one physical, especially if the implication is that one is higher than the other. We ought to nurture instead the spiritual birth that can coincide with biological birth. The spiritual birth that is supposed to happen later and that uses birth imagery for its own "higher" purposes will continue to be a ritualistic travesty until there is sustained effort to integrate the two kinds of birth. Physical birth *is* a spiritual event. So, rightly attended to, there may be no need for some second birth later in life. Let us men therefore tend with care the seeds we scatter.

PART FIVE

PRACTICING

Life is a heavy rite.

—Martina Takalo[22]

From age eighty-nine on, he [Jacob Koved] regularly used his birthdays as occasions to reflect upon his life and revise his interpretation of its sense and worth. He wrote pieces for the rites of passage in the lives of his children, relating their history to his own.

—Barbara Myerhoff[23]

In their rituals, we see persons dramatizing self and culture at once, each made by the other. There is a satisfying replication: Jacob [Koved] made up himself and his interpretation of his life through his autobiographical writings. He performed the final chapter when he died [in the middle of his ninety-fifth birthday party].

—Barbara Myerhoff[24]

"Mostly what I am objecting to is how they [the group of elderly Jews of which Jacob Koved was a part] make everything up, from bits and pieces," he said. "What do they end up with [when they invent a ceremony], but a schmatte *[a scrap of cloth], not a well-made cloak, a rag. Look how they are always deceiving themselves. And for this you expect me to be full of respect."*

—Schmuel[25]

16

THE POETICS
OF MONOTONY

Wisdom has it that life's a circle: You're born, you grow up, you marry, you age, you die. Then someone else is born. Like you, that person too grows up, marries, buries, and births. Then he or she dies. And on it goes. It's all very seasonal, this round of coming and going. Nothing is lost; nothing, gained. All is complete in the great cosmic recycling project, because every death is replaced with a new birth. Life so conceived is like a tree growing in layers. Earlier, inner layers are not lost but enshrouded.

However, wisdom also has it that life's a line, an arrow, a path: You're born, you grow up, you marry, you age, you die. That's it. The arrow hits the target, never to return to the archer. The pilgrim arrives at the destination at the end of the journey. Unlike nature, which we fondly picture as dying every winter and rising every spring, the human body doesn't recycle, and the birth that follows a death neither justifies nor completes it. Everything is lost. Nothing is gained. All is forever incomplete. Life's a river. All is flow; all is fire.

There is a third possibility: life as a spiral. The image allows one to avoid the dilemma of having to choose between a life going nowhere (life as circle) and a life that is forever slipping away from itself (life as line). Conceived this way, the lifecycle goes around again and again, but it also goes somewhere. Spiraling, one overcomes the split between circularity and linearity. The metaphor of the spiral lets us have it both ways. Spiraling, we climb upward while pressing outward. The image fits with a progressivist ideology: Upward is better; outward is more.

But the victory of having found a mediating metaphor in the spiral is short-lived. A tornado, after all, is a spiral. Surely its getting bigger and taller is not a virtue. The image too readily fosters spiritual expansionism; it is useful but not perfect.

People argue whether life's *really* a circle, *really* a line, or *really* a spiral. To argue is useless. Life is itself, not a geometrical construction. Circles, lines, and spirals are metaphors. All three cast light upon the faint paths people follow, but all three also lead astray. Human beings never escape making metaphors, but metaphor is never enough.

Whether a life is a circle, line, or spiral, it is inevitably disrupted. Life's rounds—daily, monthly, yearly—are crosscut, often through the very center. The lifeline—hurtling from the remote past, through the eternal now, hell-bent on the future—is inevitably shattered, rendering it a series of ellipses, a string of dashes. Verticals—accidents, failures, crises—punctuate the presumed solidity of lifelines. These vertical slashes crisscross and double-cross lifelines. Such breaks in a lifecycle disrupt its symmetry, and once-reassuring circles, lines, and spirals seem utterly incapable of rendering life meaningful. The appealing geometrics of such imagery become chicken scratchings. Who has eyes capable of divining them?

Wednesday, September 2, 1992. Boulder, Colorado, home of Celestial Seasonings Tea, the Boulder Creek Path, and the Flatirons. Boulder, where no one—even among the elderly—is over fifty. Boulder the beautiful. Boulder, ever-biking, perpetually climbing, always healthy, forever young.

I have arrived here on sabbatical to turn fifty next spring and to complete Marrying & Burying. *Sabbatical: "the seventh," the concluding moment of a seven-part cycle. (Why did Christians come to regard the first day, rather than the last day, as the Sabbath?)*

We have just moved into a downtown apartment provided by First United Methodist Church in exchange for acting as theologians-in-residence. Acting is the right word. When describing what we do, Susan and I put our dubious title in quotation marks. What am I doing in a Methodist Church, turning fifty, and playing theologian? I've not been in a Methodist church in over twenty-five years. What a peculiar circle! Have I come home?

Church members here are unsure what theologians do, but now they imagine they have two of them. Susan and I do not think of ourselves as theologians, but the job provides us with a home and enables us to lead a project on lifestory writing.

The stone church building, having seen better days, holds the fort across the street from Karma Dzong, originally the fountainhead of Tibetan Buddhism in North America. Our apartment is just around the corner.

The day we move in boils break out on my calf and thigh. "Boundary problems," Susan chortles. I go to see a doctor. The nurse leads me to a waiting room and weighs me in at 186. I am appalled. Dad weighed that much when he died. But he was seventy-two; he had an excuse. It has been ten years since I weighed myself, and I am twenty pounds overweight. The nurse, not in a white uniform (this is Boulder), takes my blood pressure. "One twenty over ninety," she an-

nounces, as if I know what that means. I inquire and she says, "Borderline. It means your blood pressure is borderline. We like to keep it below ninety." She exits.

The doctor enters and greets me. I point to the Tibetan Buddhist calligraphy hanging on his office wall. He explains that it means "confidence!" Examining my oozing blisters, he exclaims confidently, "Poison ivy!"

"Are you sure? That's all? They aren't psychosomatic?" I tell him that the last time I had poison ivy was twenty-five years ago in south Georgia. I had sat in a bed of poison ivy while deer hunting with a bow. That was my last hunt—for some animal other than myself.

"I am sure. That's all it is. Relax. I'll give you some free samples and a prescription." He writes it out in a doctorly scribble. "I could knock it in the head with pills, you know. Some people prefer that," he offers.

"That's okay," I reply. "I'll take the creamy, Buddhist way rather than the violent American way, thank you."

He grins.

"Now what about this one-twenty over ninety business?" I inquire.

"Oh, yes, that. Well, you're almost fifty, it says here. That's when it all begins to slide, you know. Life is suffering." He watches to see if I get the Buddhist allusion. "I see from your medical history that your father had high blood pressure. You've got the gene, so you'll have to watch your eating. And you'll have to exercise. The problem can be controlled."

In a day or two I am jogging like everyone else in Boulder. Unlike the inveterate exercisers, I don't like it. It is boring. And painful.

The day is alternately hot and cool. Autumn is setting in. A few leaves on the sumac bushes are beginning to turn scarlet. As I bounce and trudge, noticing how far down I have to reach for breath and how fiercely my heart pounds, I begin to imagine dying. I recollect bits of conversation between Mom and Dad: Would they meet over there? What kind of a heaven would it be if they didn't? Would we kids miss them? Would we miss one of them more than the other?

I have died. Susan, Caleigh, and Bryn are carrying on without me. I envy them.

I hate the idea that they can go on without me. Sure, I am glad, but that doesn't keep me from being mad. I am disgusted at the thought of aging. Trevor didn't want to turn thirteen and become a teenager. Do I want to turn fifty and begin old age? Dying I can take; I am not much afraid of it. But aging is another matter. Why did I choose to come to Boulder, of all places, to confront the inevitability of aging?

Coming up the steep hill that leads to campus, I feel tears cutting a muddy path through the dust on my face. As usual, I am surprised. I pause, sitting breathless atop a boulder and looking across the city toward the Flatirons, magnificent vertical slabs of rock, thrown up, shields against the plains. Ancient, they have witnessed aging males before. They are unmoved. And their impassivity is a relief.

I return to my office, climbing the stairs to the second floor lounge. I am heating lentil soup, wishing it were brownies, when I spot a new book on religion and sports. I flip it open and happen upon an article that asks, "Is running a religious experience?" It is about the high of running. The author says nothing about aging or mortality, so I put it down and scrawl a note to Susan offering her six more hours a week so she can work on her book Domestic Mysticism. *I say I will look after the kids. That evening, when she discovers the note under her dinner plate, she is surprised and very grateful. So are the kids. So am I.*

Ordinariness and routines are givens of domestic life. We get up, eat breakfast, brush our teeth, do some work, down a quick lunch, drift across the midafternoon, slump into supper, imbibe some TV, and sack in for the night show (the one that circles and cycles in our heads while we sleep). Then it starts over again. What does it all amount to? The routine can become so deadening and the body and mind so habituated that instead of fleeing breaks, we court them; we need relief. The daily round and the lifecycle not only suffer breaks; they also require them. Ritual interludes offer a break from the grind. There are the breaks that punctuate lives uninvited, and there are those that we court. For those that we invite we build ceremonial bridges: weddings, funerals, initiations, birthdays. A rite is a rope bridge of knotted symbols strung across an abyss. We make our crossings hoping the chasm will echo our festive sounds for a moment, as the bridge begins to sway from the rhythms of the dance.[26]

Rites of passage are simulated markers invented to make breaks in lives. Rites of passage are culturally stylized crises that reinforce a society's belief that the phases of a cycle are real and natural. By providing orientation points, they break up a life so its drudgery can be endured, maybe even transformed. Rites of passage both nourish and consume those who enact them. A rite is not only the bridge over which folks pass; it is also the troll beneath, its stomach growling to devour all who dare cross. Rites bridge; rites threaten to consume. We don't get to cross without paying the troll. There is good reason to weep at funerals and weddings. Having passed through a phase, we can't return.

With the invention of the idea of a lifecycle it is tempting to imagine that everything is in order. People derive comfort from such an order just as they do from schematizations of historical eras or schedules that chronicle stages in physiological or intellectual development. According to the generic ritual scenario, you're supposed to have your first birthday, then a graduation or two. Then you marry a person of the opposite sex, make progeny and money, live long, and die of old age. But some wise guy inevitably skips a grade, refuses to marry, puts off dying, or likes boys better. So the lifecycle, duly organized and punctuated properly with rites of passage, only partly works, part of the time, for part of the human race. The reason is that rites of passage are conventionalized, and the conventions may or may not fit actual, always idiosyncratic persons. You are supposed to become a woman at age twelve, but you get your period at ten. Your wedding works like a cookie cutter shaped to fit the contours of someone else's profile. Your initiation reveals that there is nothing to reveal: The god was but a human animal sporting a mask. Your child has to be hospitalized on the day of your graduation. And the funeral proclaims that your dead friend, who in his last twenty years despised Lutheranism, is a now member in good standing of the church triumphant.

Rites are imperfect means of marking significant transitions. However important, by themselves they are incapable of making a life meaningful. The ceremonies, homely or grand, with which to negotiate threshold crossings are, in the cosmic scheme of things, pretentious or paltry. But they are all we've got. Big and little ritualizings are made of the most fragile, ordinary stuff: breathing, sitting, lifting up, eating a lot, eating a little, walking around in circles, being quiet, making noise. The list is long, but the success is partial. Marryings and buryings are fragile deeds. They fail as readily as they succeed, leaving us to face life's rounds, ready or not.

The great wheel, whether turned by Buddha or Jesus, is forged of steel and studded with diamond dust. It *will* grind us down. We hope the wheel will polish, rather than crush, us, but no one can offer guarantees. The principalities and powers refuse to write warranties.

Harley sat, exiled to the sandbox. For a long time he sat. In the box he was free; he could grow tired; he could drift. To this cubicle he retreated for repose. He both hated and loved this crumbly, crusty pile of sand surrounded by its twisted, gray siderails that greeted his calves with splinters. Mom had said if he didn't get out of the house, he was going to turn into a girl. Outside was where a man belonged, she and Dad insisted. Harley didn't want to turn into a girl, even though he liked listening to women's stories better than to men's. He was a cowboy, not a cowgirl. Cowgirls were like Dale Evans, and they wore skirts. He wore pants. With a zipper.

Harley hated the photograph of himself and Kittysue Hamilton in newspaper hula skirts, lipstick, high heels, and bobby pins. Mom had dressed them up when Harley was three, just a baby. Now he was eight and already promoted to the third grade. He was a boy. He knew it. He had a wienerschnitzel and jungle berries. That's what they called them. At school weenies were not just ketchup-covered things to eat. Stokey Horner had informed Harley about weenies.

Harley was not sure what to think about his dad's response when he asked what a wienerschnitzel was. Harley didn't want his yingyang to be German. He wanted it to be American.

Sitting in the sandbox under the apple tree was what Harley the cowboy preacher always did. Always, always, always. That's what he told his mom when she refused to let him help her cook supper. He didn't know how to say "bored" or "monotonous," so he just spewed, "Always, always, always" at her instead.

Harley much preferred snappily paced weekends to the interminable string of weekdays. And he craved the cool indoors as much as he dreaded the heat of the outdoors.

There were only a handful of trees, and they were clustered between the chicken house and the windmill. Sand was everywhere, with a few clumps of grass, cactus, or weed clinging by their toenails to the earth's belly. Harley stomped the sand and swatted at the buzzing gnats that kept biting little chunks out of his earlobes and neck.

He hated hot days for being so long. Nothing ever happened in the summer except the Shadow Nose and Green Hornet on Sunday radio. He hated life when nothing happened. When school was on, at least Bobby Benson and the B-Bar-B Riders and Sergeant Preston of the Yukon entertained him.

Harley's tongue was sticking out in a long, sharp point aimed at his mother. Her eyes were just regular eyes, so she did not see the insult. "I don't want to be a girl, but girls get the best deals," he complained. "They get to bake cookies and sit inside where it's cool, and on Thanksgiving and Christmas they get to scrape the bowls and pinch the cakes, while the boys have to gather eggs and let the chickens peck them and sit in the living room with the men where the smoke burns your eyes."

Harley was adrift. "Daydreaming," Dad said, "you are always daydreaming." Harley ignored the voice in the back of his brain. He was having a vision: Jesus was wearing a dress. But how, Harley wondered, would he get on his horse?

Harley was a sheriff locked in jail. A robber had done it. Unannounced, his deputy arrived and yanked the bars out with a rope and horse. Sheriff Harley walked right out of the sandbox and mounted his palomino. He set off in a cloud of dust to catch the Wanted Guy who had locked him up. He didn't know why he wanted the guy.

When his Mom peeked out the screen door, Sheriff Harley was hanging the outlaw from an apple tree by the neck until dead. The tree was full of rusty nails that Harley had pounded in with a bent monkey wrench that Dad had given him from the tractor's toolbox. Old Nettie Skaggs had assured the boy that a tree needed iron before it could make tasty pears, so he had made designs—a circle, a square, a cross—by pounding tenpenny nails through its bark.

At first Harley had been afraid the tree would cry, because when he got a shot to make him well, he did. So he asked the tree, Mr. Tree, if he could give him a shot. When the wind rustled its leaves, Harley knew that meant go ahead, so he gave it iron-nail vitamins every week or so.

Sometimes Harley's boredom would incubate a song. He crooned hymns to make Mr. Tree bear juicy pears. He gave it human fertilizer, sometimes still wet and mushy, so sin would not make it grow crooked. He thought maybe they nailed

Jesus to the tree, right where the crook had hung, so the Son of God could have an apple when he was hungry and so the tree would have some iron.

Harley remembered a time when Stokey had come over with his folks. He helped Harley make a cross of nails so Jesus could go to heaven to be with his Heavenly Father. Harley announced that the tree was Methodist, but Stokey insisted it was a Catholic, because Methodists don't wear crosses. The boys got angry and threw sand in each other's eyes. They stung, because theirs were not the super, X-ray kind.

The routine that marked my existence as a boy straining to outgrow a New Mexico dirt farm (which we dignified with the label "ranch") was the daily round with its unending alternation among chores, school, and play. The routine felt interminable. It concluded every Friday evening and started again relentlessly the following Monday morning.

Weekly cycles framed the daily ones. Without weekends, weeks would have been intolerable. Saturday and Sunday were aunt and uncle. The gifts that attended their arrival kept me going. Monday through Friday were parental—excessively present and promising little that counted as excitement.

The long succession of weeks would have been impossible without the seasons. Summer terminated school and changed the agenda of farm work. Holiday cycles transformed and framed the daily and weekly ones, spicing them with occasional events of high excitement.

Still, as an adolescent in the late 1950s, the word *bored* fell easily from my tongue. The child who had been taught that an idle mind was the devil's workshop entered the gateway to hell, the workaday world, not knowing the difference between monotony and boredom. Only as a middle-aged adult learning to meditate did I understand the difference and sing the praises of the former.

THE POETICS OF MONOTONY

Monotony, the unappreciated drone,
the worker bee of solitude,
abuzz in the din of human traffic.
Mama monotony, the hum and spin
without which repetition
loses its ground.
Magnificent monotony,
the whirr that draws the soul down
where eddies and deep currents swirl.

Without monotony
no insight dawns,

no breath is bated,
no knee is bent
to leap or kneel.

Monotony is not boredom.
Boredom fragments the soul
into a nervous clutter
of pieces
too at self-odds for rhythm.

Monotony, the fundamental rhythm
of inwardness and outwardness.
The same thing said over
and over,
again and again,
the same bend of neck and curve of arm,
the ever-repeated tune that
badgers the body into paying diffuse attention.

Hoping to be taught
what something in me
thought it had forgotten,
I mumble in earth's sandy ear,
and for a moment
the meanings I intend
make a difference.
I chant and make sameness
sit up, erect,
where a moment ago
it slumped
and almost swayed off its axis.

Wrapped in a blanket of monotony
barely colored
foggy-morn gray and wiped-out white,
I for a moment
sigh the frenzy from my bones
and lean into a sacred laziness
from which I need not flee
and on whose bosom the fretful meaning-search is let go.

When the old stuff
of a creation ever-sprouting things anew
leaves my face dirty
and elbows scraped,

I scratch the earth's belly
for treasures the storyteller
says are there;
I flee to the breast of monotony.

She could care less.

Life as a parent and teacher is no less cyclical or taxing than doing chores as a farm boy. I have not escaped sandboxes, only built a bigger one with several bedrooms. I am torn, trying to preserve felicitous routines unchanged while hungering for serendipitous interruption. I use routines and schedules to protect my time from the dissipation of continual interruption. My schedule is a bludgeon with which I drive interruption from the door. But my success is also my prison. I crave interruption as surely as I do battle with it.

As a kid, I was grateful for the intrusion of Saturdays, with their promise of relief. Baths and Saturdays were inextricably linked. Water, a precious commodity in eastern New Mexico, marked the transition. Now that I live in the city and delude myself into thinking water is plentiful, bath-taking has lost its capacity to mark my week. Bath-giving, however, has become a promising substitute. It is both a delight and a chore. I use a tub of water to transform the kids. The weekly baptism changes them with a peculiar magic from demon-possessed imps into humans.

When Caleigh was two, she developed a marvelous, though probably not uncommon, routine. It was profoundly ritualized. After her bath she would make a beeline for the living room. There, under its cathedral ceiling and amid toys not yet picked up, she would lope in circles. Susan and I saw her as a filly in a field of prairie grass. She would toss her strawberry blond hair, sometimes lifting one foot in the most fascinating and peculiar way, and keep on circling—inevitably counterclockwise. The beauty of her step was so compelling that I would sit entranced, sometimes for a quarter of a hour, while she played out her celebration. As far as we knew, she had never seen a filly in a field or a unicorn in a Disney movie. We had not taught her the dance, and we marveled at its constancy and kinesthetic energy.

I am a professor. Predictably, I began to drum up a classroom presentation based on her circling. I would videotape several minutes of her postbath routine. There would be a split screen with her filly's lope gracing one half, while my Zen prostrations occupied the other. At the time I was performing 108 of them each morning in compliance with my Zen teacher's orders. Caleigh's routine would be spontaneous; mine, traditional and commanded. Hers would be unauthorized; mine, authorized. On screen she would be enjoying hers; I would be alienated from mine. Her circling would illustrate monotony—sameness and repetition embraced. My bowing would illustrate boredom—sameness and repetition resented.

The sound tracks of the video would contain her breathing and mine. On the right channel the viewer would hear spirited panting punctuated by occasional outbursts of sheer exuberance. From the left channel would issue labored muttering and the cracking of knees each time I bent to the floor, stretching out on my belly and reaching up to receive the feet of Buddha. I had no doubt which half of the screen would be the more interesting to viewers. Both actions would seem pointless, but hers would be obviously meaningful (though I could not decide what the meaning was), while mine would seem meaningless (even though I could say what the 108 prostrations symbolized).

I asked my Zen master why I should do what he required. His answer was simply that it was part of the practice, like sitting meditation or chanting. Other students had better sense than to press such inquiries. I know queries like mine neither deserve nor get straight answers in Zen. I asked again what the prostrations meant or accomplished. He said I should just do them and stop worrying about what they meant or accomplished.

At age six Caleigh continues the tradition, but now she sometimes stops as I enter the room. Another year and self-consciousness will likely mark the end of her choreographic innocence. Caleigh does not keep a journal. But her dad has a visual record of her circling. For better or worse, she will not be allowed to forget her inspired lope. Someday she will inherit some of the family videos, and there she will be, naked, circling, and oblivious to questions of meaning and function.

I did not follow through on the project, because I got stuck. What could I say about the significance of these two routines? Were they both ritual, or was one of them ritual and the other not? Was one of them meaningful and the other not? Was my daughter's activity the root of authentic ritualizing and mine the dead, latter-day branch of it? Or is this view just an example of ritual romanticism? How rooted is authentic ritual in the spontaneous repetitions and routines of children? Are the compulsive habits of adulthood—smoking, overeating, taking notes, foot-tapping—also unrecognized seedbeds of ritual?

SMOKE

This pipe
I have lit and returned to
time and space again.
Its smoke burned in neolithic caves,
blackening them ceiling to wall.
It colored my father's teeth,
his father's hair,
and their ancestors' high and raised-up statues.
This is not one pipe I am lighting,

nor am I merely lighting it one time.
The taste of the world's smoky fires
is packed deeply in the embers of its tobacco.
I have done this before.
Not that I ever lived before,
nor will again,
but that this smoking event is not mere.
It is not itself only.
This smoking is a flourish of lightings.
This is not the first pile of ash
lifted in the name of monotony
to chase a nervous demon
scurrying to a change-hungry god's side.

Whatever is smoked again and again is holy.
Doing the having-been-done-before,
whether the deed of a lifetime's mere years
or of the ages temples collect,
is a ceremony-in-the-sleeping.
All such smoking is a leaning into wakefulness,
a dawdling on the full belly of breath.

To draw on this bit
warms the hand and
nips at the tip of the tongue.
Let-go wisps sting
the eyes in a downwind,
fill the beard
with odors of barn and field.
October hangs in the mustache.
I blow a bluish-white billow:
visual chant,
winter frost in the summer light.

Even if this smoking were a bad habit
in search of a cancer,
or an oral fixation
in quest of looser genitals,
we should grant it
its proper trajectory.
Our hands and tongues remember,
even though our brains and eyes forget.

My smoking,
your nervous twitch,

her overdrinking—
these are unwitting advertisements
dangling virtual food
before the mouths of the spiritually hungry.
The one is as meaningless as the other;
the one as cosmically pregnant as the other.
Ritual is for the practice of it,
and our little boredoms,
done mindfully, bear immense possibilities.

The body continues to vibrate
after I cease paying it attention.
Regardless of our instructions,
it gestures its idiot prayers
without ceasing.
And the habits of its boredom
signal the insufficiency
of our gratitude
for the humdrum rounds
of which holy monotony is made.

Rites of passage, which tend toward linearity, typically occur in a system along with other kinds of ritual, some of which are more circular. In North America the most obvious circular ones are seasonal rites, holidays organized into an annual cycle. Some are religious: Christmas and Easter, Passover and Hanukkah. Others are civic or ethnic: Thanksgiving, St. Patrick's Day, the Fourth of July, Black History Week.

Seasonal rites are yearly, not once-in-a-lifetime events like rites of passage. Still, they are special. Their tone is typically elevated and expansive. Participants look forward to them. In some families and traditions they are big events.

When I was a child, weekly worship was boring and rites of passage, few. By contrast, seasonal celebrations were exhilarating but confusing. I would anticipate Christmas and Halloween for months; Thanksgiving, for maybe a week; and Easter, hardly at all. Combining my short emotional memory with the year-long seasonal cycle, I would forget the inevitable disappointment of holidays: The shopping bag full of Halloween loot would inevitably make me sick. Easter sermons would go on forever, and a glut of sugar eggs was not adequate compensation. Overeating at Thanksgiving would leave me in pain, and what about starving kids in foreign lands? Christmas toys were *almost* what I wanted, and Fourth of July fireworks—the sort that actually exploded—were legal only in Texas.

When Christmas came and Jesus was a baby again and not a man, the cousins from Texas arrived. Everybody ate and played at Uma and Big Papa's. Harley was excited, hungry, and sporting a new cap gun with plastic, pearl-white handles. On one side of the pistol butt was a star like the one over Bethlehem that a sheriff wears so he can shoot Bad Guys. On the other was a Texas steer whose pointy long horns gouged blood blisters on Harley's hand. The cap feeder only half worked. Even so, the smell of smoldering gunpowder was incense to Harley's nose.

Bibber arrived from Dalhart, a Texas town with a name that made Harley think of Valentine's Day. Which was next, he asked an aunt, Valentine's or Easter? He lived from holiday to holiday.

Last Christmas Bibber had said that he lived on a cattle ranch but that Harley just lived on a dirt farm. They fought about it. And this Christmas was going to be no different. Bibber arrived brandishing two pistols—not guns, he was quick to declare—and a rifle, too. Harley knew a rifle was a long gun you put to your shoulder while you squinted at the other end of the barrel. So he told Bibber he knew how to shoot a real one. But Bibber didn't believe him; besides he had a hat and vest and boots.

Harley wanted to go to the show and not play cowboys and Indians anymore. But Uma said that it was the Lord's day and that none of the grandchildren could go because Jesus would be sad if they did. Saturday was show day. Sunday was God's day.

Harley begged his mom, who had turkey juice and dressing crumbs all over her hands. She said, no, please honor your grandmother's wishes. Harley bet her the baby Jesus didn't even know what a cowboy show was. But Mom was stubborn as a mule and declared that Jesus knew everything, so go play.

Harley hid in a clump of prickly bushes. It was an outlaw hideout for when you were mad at in-laws. He told Jesus that he wished he could hurry up and become a man so he could be a cowboy with two real guns for shooting crooks and cousins. He waited to hear what Jesus would say, but the only sound was the wind beginning to howl around the corner of the house. So he went inside to ask Aunt Chris and Aunt Barb whether the newborn Jesus was naked and cold and who would clothe him and what was swaddling—did it mean waddling like a duck? On Christmas day he wanted to know, with a desperate urgency, was Jesus a man or a baby?

As an adult I have come to distrust seasonal celebrations. The reason I usually give is their crass consumerism and sticky sentimentalism, but the real reason is probably closer to home, since domestic and seasonal rites are, in my experience, so tightly woven together. I dread the thick glut of family obligations and the swamp of predictable domestic trouble that inevitably mark seasonal rites. They mark rites of passage too, but at marryings and buryings at least one doesn't have to anticipate suffering through them again next year.

On holidays people work overtime at producing a joyous atmosphere, symbolized largely by the variety and amount of food served. The facade always collapses. Mom is overworked and moody. Dad is displaced and withdrawn. The siblings begin to fight and the relatives, gossip. No longer in the mood to eat, everybody overeats; those that don't are objects of jealousy and therefore scorn. Stuffing is the only acceptable means of self-defense.

I dread holidays, but when I ignore them, I feel dislocated. I complain that Easter is seasonally misplaced, that it would be more believable if timed to coincide with the emergence of flowers and newly hatched birds. I would refuse to celebrate it, but if I were to do so, I would be out of sync with both the natural and cultural world. (Even the seasons are made to serve culture.) To miss celebrating the seasons is to be religiously lonely.

Disgust with seasonal ritual does not disarm it. It has enormous power, especially with children. Stores, schools, and television make it so. The big holidays are hard to escape or resist. Because of their cultural pervasiveness, they are capable of overwhelming merely idiosyncratic or merely domestic rites. So in our family we try to co-opt them. We play with the imagery, reframe the themes, and let the kids take initiative. It is not a mere pious wish to say that they teach us more than we teach them.

December 25, 1993. Last night the family performed Posada, a ritual-drama about Mary and Joseph's attempt to find a birthing place for their son. Caleigh was Mary and Bryn, Joseph. Since this Christmas tradition is Hispanic in origin and part of our family's Santa Fe experience, the kids took appropriate names: Maria y José. Susan and the kids pieced together costumes during the afternoon. The virgin wore purple and her spouse, black. They insisted on sandals even though their child was to be born midwinter. They added cheesecloth and bandannas to contribute color and mystery to their vestments. The carpenter-father carried a big stick, his peculiar magic being that of transforming plowshares into swords. The unwed mother's miracle consisted of getting so many donkey miles out of the stuffed gray dinosaur, which she "rode" by carrying the beast awkwardly between her knees.

Susan choreographed the scene and played the several inhospitable innkeepers. Reversing our daily personae, I got to be the wonderfully generous soul who offered them a place in the barn so they might deposit their famous baby in a manger.

Joseph sporting his staff, Mary heavy with child, and donkey

As darkness settles around Nederland, Susan and Caleigh sprinkle the house with candlelight. Bryn hovers around my knees. "Looking for instructions on fathering?" I tease.

Maria and José become impatient. Soon they are singing their song in Mex-Tex: "Somos Maria y José buscando posada" ("We are Mary and Joseph looking for an inn").

Alternately fondling and then fighting, Joseph and Mary, a typical married couple, bang on the doors—bathroom, playroom, upstairs bedroom.

"Please, sir, I mean, ma'am, may we come in?" pleads the Virgin.

"What for? What do you want?" booms the nasty old innkeeper guarding the oak doors of Eldora Swiss Resort Lodge.

"I'm pregnant. I'm about to have a baby," complains Maria in her most feminine voice.

"Yeah, yeah, a baby," echoes José, trying to sound like a bus driver.

"No, there is no room in the inn. Go away. Try the Nederland Peak-to-Pit Motel down the road," advises the surly innkeeper.

"But it's snowing," says Maria.

The door slams in her face.

The displaced but holy couple tries several more doors in search of shelter. After several excuse-laden rejections, the two arrive at a rundown ranch in southern Colorado (the dining room) owned by an old Anglo rancher married to a Hispanic woman from the San Luis Valley. The mother and father of God are invited in for a meal and offered the barn for lodging. As it happens, the rancher's wife has prepared too much Mexican food. "Come in. Welcome," says Jake the rancher, trying to exude hospitality. "Do you like red Swiss enchiladas?" asks Juanita solicitously.

"Sure," announces Maria, with José looking doubtful.

Here the role-playing part of our family Christmas enactment is supposed to end, but the roles stick. José is drooping as he contemplates what had been extolled as special holiday fare.

The rancher, not too good at making small talk, tries to help: "Well, son, I mean, Joseph, we're pretty poor here. This is poor people's food. Better eat so's you won't be hungry out there in the barn."

Joseph looks him straight in the eye and spits out words with a contempt worthy of an adult: "I'm poor too, but I don't eat this stuff!"

"Are you and Mary married?" inquires the rancher's wife, trying to avert a crisis.

"Well, yes," says Joseph with less than joy in his voice.

"Yes, of course," exclaims Maria with utter certainty.

"How come you fight so much then?" taunts the rancher.

"That's just how it is," says Maria, her voice full of saintly compassion. "People sometimes argue, but we really love each other. It's Christmas, you know."

Weddings need not be the only occasions upon which to contemplate marriage or other forms of coupling and multiplying. Our children now marry each other, us, movie characters, and their classmates with almost daily frequency. They act out scenarios that give us pause to contemplate our own marriage and to reflect on mythic ones. The advantage of studying the weddings of heroes and children is the humor and perspective one can muster in doing so.

In our family we teach about burying the same way we teach about marrying: by ritual play. We started death play with a kite given to us at Trevor's backyard funeral. It has the names of our dead on it, along with their expiry dates. We fly it in the spring, sometimes at Easter. We also fly it in October or after funerals. At

Halloween we invoke the dead. Like everyone else, we trick or treat and carve pumpkins, making pies out of their carcasses. But we also play with dead leaves and stash bulbs in the soil. We play, tease, tell ghost stories, and talk about death. Sometimes I dress up as Old Death. We build and rebuild Polunk Boritz, the effigy who wears Dad's old hat and his black and red plaid jacket. Boritz greets visitors who knock at our front door. Sometimes I haul out Shorty and Cow, the two bleached skulls that declare my mythic roots and evoke Georgia O'Keefe paintings. I give Shorty a cigar to smoke and stick tiny paper umbrellas through the bullet hole in his head.

Good Friday, 1991. I am busy writing Marrying & Burying. *The stores are closed. The day is miserable. By midmorning Susan feels like observing Easter and goes to a local church. It is closed, so she drives to a monastery but does not go in, because the kids' noise would disrupt the silence. She drives to another nearby church, hoping it will be open and uninhabited. People are lining up for confession. So she returns home feeling like doing something in the attic without being sure what it might be. As she begins to gather things in the kitchen, she tells Caleigh about Jesus' having been killed. Bryn is still too young to understand, though he rides out the afternoon in a backpack peering over Susan's shoulder. She and Caleigh make nests out of melted marshmallows and shredded wheat. Then they gather a tray of things without any premeditated sense of what they might be for. Some things Susan suggests; some Caleigh chooses. Among the items that find their way to the tray are Band-Aids, crackers, a bunny cup full of water, flowers, candles, a blue and green clay snowman, Yoda, gauze, handkerchiefs, and postcards with pictures of the saints on them.*

On the way into the attic Caleigh gets to pick one of the crucifixes off the wall. She chooses the cross of Saint Francis, which I bought when we were in Spain and Susan was pregnant with Caleigh. They put the crucifix on one of our meditation mats, where it becomes the focus of activity.

Mother and daughter begin to collaborate and improvise. Susan tries to convey the sense of the story, focusing on the single point, Jesus's suffering. She tries to link it to kid pain: "What do you need when you are hurt? How do you feel when people are mean to you?" And finally, "What do you think we should do?"

Caleigh: "Uh, give him some tuna." They give Jesus invisible tuna, since there is none of the other kind on the tray.

Susan: "Anything else?"

Caleigh: "Well, how about a Band-Aid?" They put a Band-Aid on Jesus' knee.

Susan: "Is that all?"

Caleigh: "Well, I cry. How about a hankie?" They give him one. Then Caleigh seizes the initiative. She thinks Bryn would want to give Jesus some chicken; he likes chicken wieners. So on Bryn's behalf Jesus suffers the little wieners (also in-

visible) to come unto his belly. Susan gives Jesus a cracker, the only real food the crucified man ever tastes.

Susan reminds Caleigh that Jesus' mom and friends were there. So they pull out some birchbark figures that become the two Marys. Yoda, Frosty, and the postcard saints join them, so Jesus in his pain will have comforters. Frosty would be good, Caleigh says, because he's used to the cold; Jesus is lacking proper clothes. One of the saints, Rose of Lima, has a guitar. It evokes a proposal to sing. Caleigh suggests "Baa, Baa, Black Sheep" without having the slightest idea that Jesus is the lamb of God and that Good Friday is a black day.

When I arrive home, I hear the story, two versions of it, over supper. The initiative has been taken, and it is up to me to join it. At other times initiative might have come from me or one of the children, even Bryn, who on occasion will call out, "Dwum, dwum" or "Buddha, Buddha" and point to the attic.

The next day, Holy Saturday, Bryn and I climb to the attic and begin making dirgelike, thundering sounds. He and I are banging on things, some of which are drums. By the time Susan and Caleigh join us, we have hauled out a porcelain-faced clown and wound him up. He is playing "Send in the Clowns." The clown's whiteface seems an apt mask for Jesus, who is now descending into hell, which he will harrow.

We paint Easter eggs, cover them with gauze, and bury them with Jesus. A pot of flowers is put in the middle of the dead man's belly. The theme slowly emerges. It is no longer pain and suffering but burial, and Susan asks what we should sing. Caleigh requests "Baa, Baa, Black Sheep" again. We deter her by asking what songs she would sing at a cemetery. She puzzles a while and then begins, "Oh bury me not on the lone prairie." Startled with delight at her choice, we join her, marveling that she has lifted the song from Michael Martin Murphy's tape, Cowboy Songs. *Little did we know how many of the words she had heard and absorbed.*

At supper we talk about where we would like to be buried. I would like nothing better than burial on the lone prairie. Susan can think of nothing worse than either burial (she prefers cremation) or setting up eternal residence on the lone prairie in a narrow grave six by three.

On Easter Sunday we unwind Jesus, freeing him from his gauze grave. We haul out musical instruments and circumambulate the attic, dancing and making lots of noise to wake up Jesus. What does resurrection mean if not waking up? We crack open a painted egg. One is eaten, one is kept, and one is given away. Bryn trashes a fourth. We peel the foil off chocolate and peanut butter Easter eggs, knowing that boiled eggs don't taste festive to either the adult or child palate. Gustatory memory sometimes requires a sugary boost even in the best of families.

Our family's ritual improvisation was a kind of doll play, shared by adult and child, in which there were no qualms about linking figures of different sorts: sacred, homemade, commercial, and imaginary. The question of belief did not arise. In our experience things either take hold or they do not, regardless of the

Susan, Bryn, Caleigh, and me at the end of our Colorado sabbatical (photo by Claudia Putnam)

intellectual assent we give or withhold. So we do not insist on making metaphysical distinctions among Yoda, Jesus, and Frosty. Nor will we do so when the kids are older. The playful sensibility is not a strategy for evangelizing children but an expression of our own religiosity.

Lone Prairie Easter remains a high point in the repertoire of family ritualizing. So far we've not tried to repeat it, though we may decide to keep parts of it, because we want to consolidate family traditions. Caleigh's appropriation of an old cowboy song as a Holy Saturday hymn dramatizes what is lost if children are not actively involved in ritual processes. If parents are not too hamstrung by orthodoxies and orthopraxies, children can make profound connections that render adult ritual prosaic by comparison. Susan and I provide parental direction in ritualizing, but more important is learning to follow the leads that the kids provide. The inclusion of children in the process of incubating ritual exposes cultural assumptions about which moods are acceptable and which ones are not. For our family, humor, paradox, noise, and glee are proper ones for dealing with what we adults like to define as serious concerns: pain, suffering, death.

I doubt that North American families will succeed on a massive scale in taking back their dead from the professionals. Nevertheless, I hope a few disgruntled families will insist on laying hands on their dead—washing, dressing, and saying farewell to them in a way that ensures a wedding of the quick and the dead. Serious knowledge is embodied knowledge. No touching, no teaching. Not necrophilia, but tactiphilia. The dead have much to teach, but their knowledge requires contact. Viewing won't do. Funerals will not fune until we make olfactory and tactile contact. We need to embrace the dead, for death is the soil in which life grows.

Domestic life is the crucible in which ritual attitudes are formed and fired. Even if rites are completely absent from the home—having been relinquished to school, religious institution, and state or else given up altogether—childrearing practices establish the baseline for ritual competence as surely they do for intellectual and moral competence. Ritual learning, like language learning, is most effective when participants are young, not yet having separated work from play or tradition from innovation.

17

RITUAL
PRACTICE

Groups and individuals have asked me to help design rites of passage, often for use with their children, sometimes for themselves. Occasionally, I offer a hand, but more often I decline rather than do battle with the unspoken premises of such requests—for example, that decisions should be made by committee, that training should require only a weekend workshop or two, that start-up costs be kept to a minimum, that the time required be modest, and that I supply an easy-to-read manual.

I leave how-to books to others. Although ritual learning is possible, manuals are not the way to accomplish it. The way of the handbook is the way of Don Quixote. From such books we learn to ritualize about as well as Quixote learned to be a knight or Dysart, a priest. For Quixote knighthood was a nostalgic dream imitated with comical and dire consequences, much as supposedly primitive rites of passages are by us. We learn ritual from books about as effectively as we learn to make love or raise children from them. Manuals can't evoke, much less teach participants to embody, ritual knowledge. Ritual is fundamentally tactile and kinesthetic, so how-to books are of use only as reminders of what has already been learned elsewhere in a hands-on, feet-to-the-fire fashion.

Workshops are no better. They are more dangerous than manuals because of the readiness with which participants claim them as experience and add them to their spiritual résumés. For the most part, they are fodder, feeding pretensions to spiritual leadership. Current American-style vision quests, for instance, are spiritual alcohol for the white middle-class. They inebriate the power-hungry. Their weekend fare is spiritual junk food.

I don't believe in manuals, and I distrust workshops. I am convinced that ritual has to be cultivated or incubated rather than outlined or invented. The difference is attitudinal and therefore enormous. But surely I plan to offer something better. Haven't I found some exciting new path? Otherwise, why write?

Thursday, October 15, 1992. Jogging down the hill to Boulder Creek path, I set out dutifully, doing exercises as the doctor recommended. I don't want to develop Dad's high blood pressure.

The pain in my right knee is excruciating. It's that short right leg. Damn the tractor that smashed it! Running, I taste the watermelons we'd have harvested if I hadn't landed in the hospital. They said I would never run again.

Why weren't you watching, Dad? I was just a kid.

I leave the stone steps and concrete path for a trail that parallels the creek on its less populated side. I wear my glasses, eyes open wide for creeping poison ivy. I intend to see it before it sees me. I am grateful that there is an alternative path, because the bicycles are thick as flies and the bicyclists are worse speeders than Jeep drivers.

Soon I become irritated at having to follow someone else's alternative path; for some idiotic reason it has been marked with red powder. Following it, I have joined the herd. We are individualists here. Boulderites, like most Americans, hate other people's paths. We would blaze new trails up and down the creek, deep into the Rockies. Inevitably, however, we find that someone else has gotten there ahead of us. Forests are crisscrossed with trails cut by Americans, all of whom hate crowds and tourists, especially other American tourists. We're not tourists; we are pioneers.

But the rules are changing for the sons and daughters of pioneers. We are learning to worry over the appearance of new trails as much as we despise the old ones, because the new ones are destroying the ecosystem. The geographical frontier is gone, and the spiritual economy is no longer expanding. Tourism of the spirit, no longer spiritual pioneering, has become the latest form of imperialism.

I cut back to the concrete path. Eventually, it takes me to a football field surrounded by the black rubberized track of Boulder High. In the hot sun it smells like the burning tread of dragsters. The odor almost turns me back, but it evokes memories of high school days, then a drag race on a country road in which I beat a souped-up Chevy pick-up with Dad's turquoise-and-white Ford station wagon. Station wagons are domestic vehicles; they don't usually win races. Beware, oh you hot rodders, of the power of domesticity.

I round the reeking track. High school students are at one corner of it, shooting arrows into a six-foot-high stack of hay bales. A Tibetan—so I imagine him—is jogging ahead of me. Could he be the son and spiritual successor of Chogyam Trungpa, whose alcohol and reputed philandering, they say, brought about his death and threatened to dismantle Tibetan Buddhism in North America?

Can you inherit enlightenment from your father?

I begin to set little goals. I'll run from this 50-yard line around to that 50-yard line on the other side. That's 220 yards, if I remember correctly. Dad used to run the 220. He won the New Mexico state championship. I barely make it. Short leg, short wind.

I attend to my breathing. Let this onerous workout become spiritual exercise. I transpose the jogging into Zen practice. Running, I just run. Breathing, I just breathe. Hurting, I just hurt.

But the "just" doing doesn't last. A conversation breaks into the running. At breakfast this morning Susan admitted that she had an irrational fear of what she called the great cosmic balancing mechanism; it governs the universe. She confessed that she is sometimes afraid when things work out too well. Something— who knows what—will come along and balance out all this happiness, she speculated.

We like the mountains. We like our marriage. We like our kids. We are content in our work. But what if, without knowing it, I have come here to die? "What if you croak?" she asked. Bryn is not even three. What if I age and die the way I became an Eagle Scout—too early?

Here I am doing my spiritual exercises, jogging to beat death, whom I claim not to fear. After all, haven't I have played Old Death? Why should I be afraid? I know why. It's because I can't find my way back home. Religiously, I am not quite lost, but neither do I have a home. Like a scout in a grade B black-and-white cowboy movie, I push ahead of the family-filled Conestoga wagons and then return, push ahead and return. The train is moving ever so slowly. I move quickly, surveying the horizon with a keen eye, but I ride in circles. I check out everybody's campfire, but at night I sleep alone between camps. I work the edges of traditions. Religiously, I am a landed immigrant, unwilling or unable to take out citizenship papers.

Another conversation interrupts these reflections, which are beginning to evoke too much anxiety. "If this running is not a religious experience, I don't know what is," I mumble in a tone of special pleading.

"Give me a break," I object to myself. "This running might be religious if you'd quit all this chattering in your head and just run."

"Well, maybe you're right. This jogging, done the way you are doing it, is merely boring, too meaningless to be religious."

"Just run, Grimes."

"I can't just run. When I run, I think. I feel. I sit eight hours a day at my desk writing. My heart clogs. My brain jams. But when I move, things break loose and I can't help thinking, remembering, feeling. Not running is a courtship with death."

"Don't get attached to life—to goals, fears, or feelings about yourself. You can't take those things with you. You will die. Your kids can't accompany you. Neither can your wife."

"Don't preach at me. I need my little attachments and goals. They are brownies. They energize my passage."

"They will put an early end to your passage."

I am a man riddled with the conundrums that trouble other men. I want to beat aging and take my family with me. I want to eat brownies and keep my thirty-two-inch waist, too. I want my dad to take notice even though he is dead. Like everyone else, I wish I were not like everyone else. I want to cut my own trail to enlightenment and wisdom. Yet I want to be wrapped in the arms of a venerable tradition and coddled by a supportive community. I long for a distinctive practice of my own. But I pine for a wise master who, relying on intuitive insight and venerated canons, will advise me how to live my life.

If my wishes were fulfilled, I would probably become rebellious. My longings are too self-contradictory. The result is that my practice is piecemeal and my spirituality, makeshift. My passages are troubled. I worry that I will not do a good job on the last Great Passage. How shall I pass that Final Exam?

Passages fail for many reasons. One of the most basic is that they lack grounding. Invented rites-of-passage and the customary seasonal rites in North America are too often superstructures without foundations. They are extraordinary events. They photograph well, and their expansive scale suits the North American sensibility. But they neither permeate nor ground. Because they are limited in number and restricted to specific days on the calendar, people trust them not to bleed shamelessly into everyday life, but this seemliness is part of their weakness. Even if the rites of passage repertoire were richer, a problem would remain. Such rites thrive only if integrated into the rounds. Otherwise, the shift from the big rites of the lifecycle and the holiday seasons to the little ritualizations and minor practices of the workaday world is experienced only as a loss.

Most of life is not lived in the high drama of major transitions but in following routines. Rites of passage may punctuate a lifecycle with peaks and valleys, but other sorts of ritual are necessary for weathering the plains of ordinariness. Whereas rites of passage and seasonal celebrations are desserts, daily meditation, weekly worship, and other such rites are staples. A serious distortion would occur if we were to assume that a life is adequately ritualized by major passages and their attendant rites. What about everything else between the passages? Even though hundreds of weddings may be conducted in a week, an individual typically weds only once or twice in a lifetime. For most of us, funerals, weddings, initiations, and births are special, not quotidian, occurrences. Without a connection to the routines of mundane existence, ritual loses its basis. The big moments of passage need to be shaped by practices that precede and follow them. Otherwise, they become isolated—precious moments shrouded in nostalgia—rather than determinative events that inscribe meaning on body and soul.

Ritual itself is sometimes defined as idealized activity performed in a special place at a special time. This view emphasizes ritual's difference from ordinary activity in ordinary time and space. Such a definition highlights the tension be-tween the ritually ideal and the ordinarily real. But this view is a half-truth. The other half is that ritual should shape the reality outside its boundaries, permeat-ing it so that living itself is suffused with ritual values. The capacity of ritual to determine reality outside its own boundaries is what we call its paradigmatic function.

Grounding is accomplished by what I call ritual practice, spiritual exercise, or just practice. Anything, absolutely anything, can be done ritually. Marrying, burying, birthing, and coming of age are not the only events of ritual signifi-cance. One can stand ritually, or sit, run, or walk ritually—even breathe ritually. So ritual is not only a *what* but a *how.* If one cannot enact the more basic biologi-cal events (such as breathing, eating, or sitting) ritually, the ceremonial perfor-mance of high-profile social events will likely fail. It is a serious mistake to try constructing large-scale, once-in-a-lifetime, or seasonal events without first lay-ing a foundation in more familiar human routines—those sometimes deni-grated as housekeeping details.

It is essential to notice the domestic ritualization already going on in one's life—after-dinner walks, tooth brushing, bedtime stories, Saturday night mov-ies—activities that provide order and predictability. After following and observ-ing them, it can be revealing to amplify, play with, or stylize them. A simple act like drinking a glass of water becomes special when one pours the water into a wineglass. There are other ways to ritualize, of course. Elevate the glass; then drink. Or just drink slowly and deliberately.

Two things can happen after drinking a special glass of water. One is that sub-sequent, ordinary glasses can taste bland, leaving one longing for the special. But there is another possibility: Ordinary drinking can become extraordinary, even without the wineglass or the toast.

Ritual practice is the activity of cultivating extraordinary ordinariness. It is necessary, because human activity has a kind of entropy about it; life, like love, runs down. Things gets tiresome and difficult. Body and soul cry out for some-thing different, hence the impetus to ritualize. But if the ritually extraordinary becomes a goal or is severed from ordinariness, it loses its capacity to transform, which, after all, is what rites of passage are supposed to do.

So practice ought to precede performance. To practice is to engage in se-lected, quotidian tasks as if one were new to them. It is to begin with the premise of ignorance rather than the assumption of knowledge. To practice is to assume the questioning and receptive attitude of a beginner and to refuse the presump-tion of expertise. Some of the most compelling images of ritual practice are to be found in Zen.

In the mid-1970s I spent part of a summer on retreat at the Minnesota Zen Center. My time with Katagiri Roshi was short. The few weeks don't make much of a story; they did not constitute a rite of passage. I slept sometimes in the basement, sometimes with Zen students who lived nearby. I ate. I meditated. I strolled around Lake Calhoun. I talked with Katagiri. I got up the next morning and started over again.

Not long ago Katagiri died. I miss him. I began missing him before he died. Unenlightened soul that I am, I probably missed him even when I was with him.

Katagiri remains one of my most influential teachers. How can that be? He is dead. What did I learn from him? His students taught me to wash dishes; his wife, to sew cushions. He taught me what he taught them: ordinariness and attentiveness.

One morning I remarked how ritualistic Zen was. "Yes," he agreed, "Zen is very ritualistic." Immediately, he turned the conversation to tooth-brushing and shaving. This was the sort of ritual practice he considered essential, not the elevated and elaborated sort (of which he was also capable). For him, ritual was "nothing special"; it was how one did what one did all the time—standing in the yard, brushing teeth, shaving, dishwashing. For him, ritual did not consist of the drama of big events but of the attentiveness with which one performed small tasks. The notion was not new to me, but a person capable of embodying it was.

An image of Katagiri remains, and it still teaches. I enter by the back gate. Katagiri is standing in the yard. His standing is not dramatic or mystical. He is just standing there. I notice the back of his shaven head as the wind catches a fold in the sleeve of his robe. He is not leaning forward, as if awaiting the future; he is not tipped backward, as if tethered to the past; he is right here, right now, facing the wind.

If I had to summarize my religious aspirations in an image, this one would be on the short list. Katagiri was known for his ordinariness, which he embodied in an extraordinary way. If I were to live up to the aspiration, I would be fully present to my children (who are at this moment whining and fighting), to the suffering that just presented itself in the phone call that interrupted this writing, to the robin presently sucking water from the dripping icicle that hangs outside my window. I would practice ordinary routines in an extraordinary way.

Once I was asked by the editor of a Catholic liturgy journal to write an article on a peculiar but provocative question: What should be done with liturgical spaces when worship is not going on in them? Liturgical spaces are extraordinary, not functional in the way that houses or office buildings are. Did the editor want me to recommend some morally respectable use for such places? Was the question based on the values of a morally minded Christian activist? Did it assume that we *should* do something rather than nothing and that such doing *ought* to take the form of putting things and places to good use? Did it assume that churches were better full than empty?

Ours is society in which fullness is a treasured metaphor: "fullness of life," "fullness of heart." The very thought of an empty or unused space, especially one located in an overcrowded city, strikes us conscientious moralists as an affront. Surely the poor or children or the homeless could occupy it, thereby help-ing it earn its right to be. Such use would make it functional. We associate un-used spaces with the rich, who do not walk on their grass, sit on their porches, or wear old clothes once they begin to look used. Consistent with the value we place on usefulness, we suppose that sacred space requires continuous use, which we can rationalize morally and justify economically. But ethical acts are not the generative source of religion. They are its consequence.

Ken Feit, my long-gone, wandering-fool friend, and sometime colleague, taught me this Japanese haiku:

> *See this flea.*
> *He cannot jump,*
> *And I love him for it.*

When I try to explain what I mean by ritual practice, I invoke Feit's flea. For me, ritual space is where fleas are not required to jump, prove themselves, or achieve something. It is where we, whose nature it is to act, do not have to so act. At the heart of this haiku are silence and stillness. The one who attends to flea behavior is characterized by an attitude of deep receptivity. Between seer and flea there is no difference. In ritual practice we seers-of-fleas learn to become re-ceptive—even to creatures we dislike, fleas that bite. We try to become receptive to those we oppress, to ourselves, to the earth, to whatever or whomever ani-mates the universe. All rites, including rites of passage, are, in my view, off center unless they have this contemplative attitude at their core.

Differentiating ritual passage from seasonal ritual is commonplace. But dis-tinguishing both from foundational ritual is not. In my view, the staple of ritual is practice, which takes a variety of forms depending on one's tradition. Weekly worship, daily prayer, and hourly meditation are among the more traditional forms. I am not so much recommending one of them as espousing an attitude. These forms are means of cultivating a basic, contemplative attitude character-ized by receptivity and reverence. Contemplation is a posture in which practitio-ners do not judge things by their usefulness. Rather, they let them be so practi-tioners can experience their connectedness, if not identity, with those things. As I aspire to engage in it, right ritual action is predicated on this reverent, nonachieving, non-goal-oriented attitude. Contemplation is a way of valuing the givens in life. Without it all the drum-beating and organ-playing in the world is noise.

I sometimes call such foundational practice "nothing-doing," since to hu-mans, whose nature it is to jump, it looks like nothing is happening when one is doing it. The practice of doing nothing is not the same as inertia, laziness, lack of moral resolve, or mere lack of direction. It does not result in avoidance of politi-cal and ethical issues. It is not identical with the usual clutter-mindedness that in ordinary parlance we speak of as "having nothing to do."

The phone rings.

I answer, "Hello."

"Hi, this is ... What are you doin'?"

"Oh nothin', just watchin' TV and munchin' chips."

This is not the sort of doing nothing I have in mind, because in this instance my nothingness is utterly cluttered. TV and chips are the tip of an iceberg. Inside my head there are conversations, fragments from the day. My foot is tapping, anticipating tomorrow, even though I am still not finished with today. The ritual practice of doing nothing is not the same as the muddleheadedness that results from being between tasks—remembering the one just finished and anticipating the one on the horizon.

Dad used to complain that I was lazy, a daydreamer scouting out too many faraway lands, most of them in my head. He got angry when he had to tell me twice to do the chores. He thought the point of life was to work, to engage in productive activity. Wasn't I a farmer's kid and he, a Depression dad? During long summer days I would complain that there was nothing to do. As punishment for not being gainfully employed, he would assign some senseless, goalless activity. His proof-text was the familiar proverb, "Dig a hole. When you finish, cover it up and then dig another one." To my detriment I sometimes hear his voice when my Zen master tells me to sit or to do prostrations without attachment to either goals or meanings.

Mom used to quote her mom, "An idle mind is the devil's workshop." By means of parental proverbs I absorbed the manly virtues and came to feel that work itself was an ultimate value. I would probably be unable to give it up even if I tried. It has done me well. It may also do me in.

Ritual is an activity that most men find hard to understand. It does not accomplish much. Where does one list it on a résumé? To participate in it we have to reconceive the work-driven life. North American sacred spaces too easily become tracks and fields of the spirit, arenas for the exercise of religious labor and the display of spiritual capital. Musclebound by our virtues and driven by goals, we profane them.

Goals and accomplishments, doing and planning—these are the activities by which we white American males measure our worth. These, and not snails or puppy dog tails, are what we are made of. If we engage in ritual at all, we employ it as a tool for accomplishing some definitive deed. Practice is made into a means of preparing for life's big play-off. It is not allowed to be a daily discipline valued in itself like play. Our sense of the term *practice* is like that of *baseball practice*, not like that of *ritual*, or *spiritual*, *practice*.

So what is this do-nothing ritual practice if it is not like baseball practice and not like digging a hole and then refilling it? It is the action of attending—without clinging, anticipation, or attachment—to what presents itself. It is the act of attentive waiting, of just sitting, or standing, or. ...

As a Methodist, I thought religion was something to be believed. In seminary I learned to speak of faith instead of religion. I said, "believe in" rather than "believe." But the difference didn't make much difference. When I took up Zen and began to think of religion as practiced rather than believed, the difference was immense. I learned not only to engage in *the* practice, that is, sitting meditation, but also to conduct other activities such as walking, toilet-scrubbing, or diaper-changing as practice. Anything could be done "as practice." I continue to conceive of foundational religiosity as requiring ritual practice or spiritual exercise. Doing so reminds me of its bodiliness and earthiness.

Not only have I largely given up believing for the sake of practicing; I have also had to learn the difference between practice and work. Work demands results—good health, enlightenment, peace of mind, salvation. I do not claim that I am free of result-seeking, only that I wish I were. Religious work eventuates in items on a list:

- Work nine to five
- PTA on Tuesday evening
- Aerobics on Wednesday night
- Shopping on Saturday afternoon
- Meditation on ...

So conceived, ritual is just pious busywork, and the lives of the religious, like the lives of the nonreligious, become organized like shopping lists. In this model religious ritual is just another item stuffed into a Friday evening or Sunday morning slot.

As I like to tell the story, Jesus drives the money changers out of the temple, not because money pollutes sanctity, but because he thinks people are turning sanctuaries into places of religious busywork. The Jesus of my version of the story allows the do-nothings to remain. He drives out religious overachievers.

Some of us enter empty downtown churches open at noon for prayer and meditation with the same attitude we enter health clubs. The aim differs only slightly: spiritual health rather than physical health. Framed this way, prayer becomes the ethereal equivalent of pumping iron, and meditation, an activity governed by how-to manuals and progress charts. We discover by accident that an empty sanctuary can be a place where nothing needs to happen.

BORROWED CRANNY

I borrow a cranny at high noon,
making a hut of the place,
a smoky, damp abode of
One whose speech is silence.

A guest,
I make myself at home,
huddling the back tight
against a cool column,
a tree of marble
whose boughs arch into a cathedral.

Sitting ravenously,
the ears continue to hear,
and the half-closed eyes strain to see.

This cosmos in concrete and buttress
hollows me too, too wide.
I snuggle
closer to the tree
and tuck my feet under.
Shoes, do not mar the pew.

This great grandmother in stone
is chilled and immense on the whole,
warm and receptive in part.
"Intimacy needs the heart of a nest,"
mutters a French philosopher
somewhere in the loft of my brain.

Over this architectural edge
one can peer into immensity,
make the stations without moving,
test the envelope of silence.

Others meander.
Saints are tucked among the pages
of a voluminous space.

Nameless things peek out from cracks,
bowels in holy mortar.

A beam drifts on a wisp,
then skids off a brass cross.

Souls float among cherubs,
less naked than we.

I am wrapped in empty arms,
garments of awe.

The column cools the spine.

Somewhere behind, a coin clinks
with a silver ring.
The man at-one with the tree
starts at the sound
but drifts back to contemplating his predicament.

Hush settles to her knees
and begins making silence of the routine.

For a bare moment
nothing at all transpires.

A herald's voice
whispers sharply from a stained window.
I shuffle.
The lids flutter and the thighs ache
—almost asleep against the hard leg
of this architectural mother.

"Time," whispers the voice.

The hour has passed
with less than nothing done.

I do not suggest that religious institutions get rid of formal religious liturgy, only that participants need to hear its essential silence and embrace its lack of means-end reasoning. One way to facilitate this is by learning to occupy sacred space for the disciplined practice of doing nothing. In North America recommendation of such a thing borders on the bizarre. Someone once remarked in a sarcastic tone, "Why don't you go all the way and recommend sleeping in church too!" I admit that incubation, the ancient rite of sleeping in a sacred place, is attractive. Is there a better way to enact the human hope of receiving a vision or undergoing healing?

Even though ritual practice is a little like sleep, it is not sleep. The practice of diffuse attentiveness enacted in a matrix of silence and stillness leaves the spirit alert. Some traditional rites have a place for silence. But the silence is seldom silent, and if it is, we aren't. Religious ritual should be permeated by sustained, not token, silence and emptiness.

In Christian liturgy, for instance, one is fed with the bread of heaven. However, when participants are not being so fed, the proper state is hunger, the emptiness of belly, heart, and mind. Hunger creates anxiety (the same sort that imperceptibly arises when one exhales). The impulse is to grab and gasp. If the real thing is not available, then embrace a substitute. Rush to fill the felt void. It is human nature to eat and breathe, to want to be filled and fulfilled. As surely as it is a flea's nature to hop, so it is ours to hunger and thirst. But surrounded by a culture of affluence and abundance, we are tempted to leap over moments of silence, emptiness, and hunger. Not embracing them as practice, we become possessed by them.

The practice of doing nothing can be excruciating, but the alienated body and spirit cry out for it. There is a desperate need to heal the breach between Monday work and Saturday play. We need the kind of work and play that converge in ritually sustained stillness and silence, in agenda-free space. Religious ritual should be an enactment in which we set space, both natural and institutional, free from agendas.

Although I am using both work and play as metaphors, religious rites ought to manifest some of the kinesthetic and auditory earmarks of literal work and literal play: for example, the sweat of labor and the noise of celebration. Liturgies should be the most palpable, not the most rarefied, forms of ritual. In liturgy, as in work and play, the feet cry out to touch the ground. Bread, not wafers. Wine, not grape juice. Sweat, not perfume. Dancing, not handshaking.

We ever-pragmatic souls want to know what ritual will do for us. We are adept at devising strategies to make empty things full and silent things speak. Instead, we need to stop doing for a moment, quit despising the flea when it does not hop, no matter how sure we are that it is the flea's nature to hop. The conundrum of religious ritual is how to hear its silence and embrace its peculiar form of inactivity. And there is no better place to do so than in a truly empty sacred space: It is the only place in town where Nothing is going on.

Although I recommend doing nothing, have no laudable plan, and am uncertain where home is, I should at least say what sort of practice I long for. I envision one based on the premise that the process by which rites are created determines their outcome. *How* we proceed to revise or cultivate ritual may be more important than *what* is actually done in it. I would like to be able to integrate search (in the spiritual sense) with research (in the scientific sense). But search for what? Research for what? What is the question that animates such exploration? Among the candidates are these:

- What is worth practicing?
- What gestures, postures, and exercises can best ground fundamental values?
- What practices best prepare us for birth, death, marriage, divorce, failure, or other major life crises?

Sometimes I wish for a small group devoted to such questions. Because I am not a groupie, I know well the difficulty of solitary practice. Alone, one easily loses heart, becomes self-deceived, or fails to be morally responsible to the larger society. This group would share uniform, yet-to-be discovered, core practices. These minimal practices would be "canonical," the lowest-ritual-common-denominator of the participants. Core practices would allow for the least improvisation and would be rooted in the most fundamental human activities, such as walking, standing, sitting, lying down, or drinking water. As I imagine them, they would have both active and receptive aspects, as well as serious and ridiculous ones. They would have to be utterly elemental.

A second set, at the other extreme, would be free-form. We would try to develop an ethos and minimal framework capable of facilitating both individual and group ritualizing with a minimum of direction and prescription. This kind of research would function as the group's growing edge. I imagine it as a kind of "Quaker" meeting in which people, individually and collectively, move, rather than speak, when the spirit moves. Free-form research would aim at locating a kind of emergence place, a zone of openness in which gestural and postural responses could emerge as if into a midwife's hands. Ultimately, this research would be the ground for developing the core practices.

Mediating between these two extremes (core practices and free-form research) would be a third layer that one might call mnemonic exercises. This series would consist of a series of movements and postures loosely analogous to tai chi movements or katas in the martial arts. It would be physically demanding and spiritually evocative. I imagine several sets for various purposes and for various constituencies: a fast set, a slow set, a woman's set, a man's set, a set for grieving, a set for celebrating, and so on.

A summary of the premises of practice would look something like this:

1. The premise of *processual primacy:* The form of ritual exploration more profoundly shapes attitudes than the content of it does. Process is determinative. If ritualists care about their sense of ritual, the process is what shapes basic attitudes, which are always both bodily and spiritual.

2. The premises of *enactment and embodiment:* Action is the primary form of engagement; talk is secondary. Posture, gesture, and placement take priority over verbal interpretation. Cultures, societies, and groups do not merely surround bodies. Bodies incarnate but also transform, and even undermine, cultural values.

3. The premise of *ordinariness:* The ground of ritualizing is ordinary human life, with its routines and circularities. Ritual practice is the enactment of ordinary activities in extraordinary ways or with extraordinary attentiveness.

4. The premise of *attunement:* Attunement is a metaphor for activity typified by responsiveness to the environment and interdependence with others. Attuned, ritualists' sense of separation from the objects of their contemplation becomes minimal. Attuned, ritualists move together like a flock of geese or school of fish; they exhibit flowing order.

5. The premise of *receptivity:* Receptivity is open, empty waiting. It requires exertion and attentiveness and is not the same as passivity. Without practiced receptivity, ritual creativity is necessarily shallow.

6. The premises of *silence and stillness:* The spirit of silence and stillness is essential to ritualizing and should pervade even the noisiest of celebrations. Thus, contemplation is the mood that most appropriately prepares one for other kinds of ritual attitudes—celebration, for instance.

7. The premise of *mystery:* Mystery is wonder coupled with reverence. Mystery is not the result of secrecy or of hiding truth either from oneself or from others. It is the outcome of attentiveness to whatever presents itself.

8. The premise of *play:* Play is detachment from ends and a willingness to explore possibilities for no particular reason. Ritualizing should be open to, and nurturing of, inversion, foolishness, clowning, and other forms of play.

9. The premise of *improvisation:* We have no choice but to improvise. And we have no choice but to structure what we improvise. Structures are but long-standing improvisations. Improvisations are but fast-moving structures.

10. The premise of *imagination:* Ritualizing is a form of imaginative activity. Imagining eventuates in dreaming and ritualizing; dreaming and ritualizing, in imagining. The human imagination is at once revelatory and deceptive, a source of vision, as well as of projection and stereotype.

11. The premise of *criticism:* Ritual must have a critical component. Reverence should be held together with iconoclasm. Participants should test and question each other. Criticism, however, should not be premature. It should follow, not disrupt, ritual practice.

I worry about lists. They are the poisons of vision. But I am a pragmatist reared by pragmatic parents to live in a pragmatic society, so I set the poison and the medicine side by side on the same shelf. In the dead of night, when the sleepy hand gropes for what it needs, it is sometimes hard to tell which is which.

Harley boasted that this hike in the desert was to be a quest, a ceremony Indians do when they want to dream dreams and have visions—like in the Bible and the movies. He had had a dream the night before. In it he shot his friend Chico, an Indian boy. The boy began to cry. So did Harley when, as sometimes happens in dreams, Harley was transformed into Chico. The cry became church music, then drumming, the sound of which was as disturbing as firecrackers exploded in a Methodist sanctuary.

At school Harley had read about crying for a vision. At first the word had puzzled him, but now he was flying a chicken feather in his baseball cap. He was a Sioux warrior sporting two pearl-handled pistols and a Superman cape.

The day had started out bright and sunny. Mom had packed some Fritos, cold beans, a tuna sandwich, and some sasparilly (a drink Harley had invented by mixing cinnamon, vanilla, cloves, Welch's grape juice, and a dissolved, green Life Saver). For short, he also called it Clovis Tea. The sasparilly was sloshing happily in a U.S. Army canteen. Nestled in his backpack were "survival implements" (a newly learned phrase) that now comprised a pocket knife, mirror, Gideon New Testament signed in blood with a flag inside the front cover, three smooth black stones called Apaches' tears, a Vis-Queen (a plastic sheet for covering wet cement), salt pills for sunstroke, a dead Mexican jumping bean, and a small glass vial of El Skunko perfume purchased at the curio shop in Hotel Clovis. The El Skunko was in case he was accosted by a polecat on his journey.

The walk to the sand dunes had taken almost two hours and had led by an abandoned corral with a rotten gray loading chute, across several barbed-wire fences, and finally up the face of a rocky escarpment strung with wires and strewn with stone platforms used each year by the Cattlemen's Association for performing the sunrise Easter pageant. In the summers they put on a Billy the Kid show there using local talent.

Last year Harley had skinned his boots by falling off one of the platforms on which he had climbed after the show to adjure Pontius Pilate to keep his hands clean or suffer the lash and cringe before the silver bullet. He remembered last year's pageant with disgust at the Roman soldier who had been played by some rancher's nephew who was visiting from a drama school back east. He had ridden English style. Even Jesus was disgusted. Harley could see it on his face.

Harley picked his way through the rocks, keeping in mind what he had been told about blind rattlesnakes and hoping to see a bobcat—in the distance. He carried a staff to comfort him, for such was the armor of faith. He bathed in the sun and solitude as he made his way sneezing through the ragweed and sage on top of the escarpment. He looked around to be sure no one was watching. Then he lay down in the warm sand wiggling and hissing. He was a snake. Then he stood up, a yucca—tall, still, barely swaying in the breeze.

Big Papa had said sidewinders made waves in the sand. Harley had never seen a sidewinder. But he kept his eyes open, sweeping the dunes in front of him with frequent sideways glances in case, true to its name, one came slithering at him sideways, nailing him with venom in the ribs. Harley wondered if both eyes were on one side of the snake's head and whether they were on the left or right side. He laughed at the thought, "two left-eyed sidewinder." Big Papa would have chuckled to hear that one, since he liked exaggerated, cockeyed ways of naming things.

The sand and wind held off their duel until the afternoon. Harley was on his way back home when the sandstorm hit. Like a brave, he cried and hollered for a vision but couldn't raise even a dust devil or a tear. He was not sure if you had to cry real tears before the Great Spirit heard you, but he tried anyway, without success.

Weary of trudging in the sandhills, Harley was beginning to feel beaten up by the wings of the storm. Scraggly patches of Johnson grass, like wisps on a balding head, began whipping at his bare knees. His canteen had begun to leak, soaking his hip pockets. A swirling wind hoisted the tiny grains of golden pepper off the ground. The sand pelted his skin and burned his eyes.

The wind tied Harley's hair in tangles like dry cornsilk. He squinted and went on trudging even though he had sand in his left boot. Since his lips were cracking, he licked them often. Soon his face looked as if he had weathered a devil's food cake fight at a birthday party. The grit around his mouth reminded him of burnt toast and sawdust. He swallowed, hearing Randy Joe's voice chide, "Dirt is good for you—has minerals in it."

"Yeah," muttered Harley, "and besides it is where you came from and go to, so it can't be all bad."

When the sandstorm had begun to announce its impending arrival, Harley turned in the direction of home. He pondered whether his prayers had stirred up the Wind Spirit. At first he pulled down the brim of his John Deere cap, squinted his eyes, and kept on trudging toward the escarpment ledge and home. Gradually, though, his skin began to redden and his eyes water from the pelting of the sand. His feather flew the coop to accompany the wind over a high dune.

Harley was forced to give up. He sat down to wait out the storm, hoping enough light would remain for him to get home before dark. He covered himself with the plastic sheet and lay belly to belly with the grainy earth. Far from being frightened, he was comforted by his plastic shell and the sound of the wind, so much so that he eventually fell asleep and dreamed: Seeing a wrinkled old man with long hair, he followed him into an abandoned shack. Soon the place was filled with an eerie presence and strange light. The man addressed him as grandson. Then the presence became a rainbow-colored mist, hovering like a flying saucer and shining brilliantly, with rings like Saturn. Harley fell off a bench trying to look at it.

Falling, he noticed his shoes. They were floppy like those of a clown. If he flapped them, he discovered that he could fly, but just barely. Then he noticed something soaring above in the clouds. It was Chico, his Indian buddy. He, too, was flying, and he began teasing and spitting watermelon seeds at Harley. Harley awoke with a start when one of the seeds hit him squarely in the eye.

The world was pitch dark. Harley heard the faint sound of a familiar bell. He blinked, jumped up, and ran in the right direction with a certainty only boys and antelopes know. In less than half an hour he was standing at the edge of the escarpment, bouncing the beams of his flashlight off a mirror toward the tiny lights of home far below. His brother, who had been set to sounding the old 4007 bell, returned the signal by ringing wildly. Soon two more flashlights, one of them very bright, appeared near the bluish porch light. Harley scrambled down the cliff, stopping only long enough to touch for good luck the huge boulder they called "the one that got rolled away."

After a token bit of scolding, Mom informed him that the Sioux sometimes had to cry several nights before they got a vision; she had read about it in National Geographic. *Harley said he couldn't stay awake or sad that long.*

Because practice is regular and repetitive, there is a danger in it: Whatever is a structure can become a cage. The point of practice is to connect, not to separate, practitioners from the world. So practice has to be open in ways that make serendipity possible. In my family walking is one way we extend practice beyond the home.

A quarter of a mile behind Nederland Elementary School is an open space on a hill. It is not quite a meadow, but I called it that when I lived near the place, having moved there from downtown Boulder. From that spot we could see a mountain that I came to call Mountain That Makes a Man Cry. I discovered it by accident. One day I walked up the hill and paused, short of breath. It was then that I noticed the mountain, looming and white, to the southwest. Without thinking what I was doing, I laughed and shouted, "Yes!" I don't think I noticed the feelings that ensued from the affirmation until the next week. Standing there again, this time with tears in my eyes, I remembered the impulse to cry that had arisen in the same spot the week before.

I continued returning to the meadow. Each time my experience was the same. A yes would arise coupled with an urge to cry. I didn't actually cry on every occasion, but I always felt like it. A cloying, knotted sensation would arise in the throat. I recognized it well: Something in me wanted to cry; something else blocked the crying. When I was in my twenties and thirties and felt the need to cry, that would be it—end of story. Nothing would happen. But now that I am fifty-something, I have a choice. I can play with the incipient need for tears. Like a Greek widow's practiced ritual keening, which sets a community to wailing and mourning, I have discovered that pretending to cry can trigger the real thing. In middle age I have learned to cry. It has taken practice.

So when I saw the mountain from the meadow, I sometimes cried; I sometimes didn't. An option was just to stand or walk with a knot in my throat. Weeping-walking, I called the practice. Since I didn't always cry, I once considered changing the mountain's name to Mountain That Makes a Man *Want to* Cry, but the original name has stuck. The optional title was too long.

Why I couldn't cry when I was younger and why I had to learn to do so, I understand well enough. But why the mountain made me cry was a mystery. I am not a nature buff. I don't get sentimental about mountains or meadows.

After several visits to the mountain-viewing meadow, I made a discovery. Early one morning I glimpsed the mountain from another hill and felt no desire to say yes or to cry. Puzzled, I tried gazing at it from several vantage points outside the meadow. Nothing happened. Then the obvious dawned on me. It was not the mountain that made me cry but seeing the mountain from that particular meadow. It was the relationship between the meadow and the mountain that created the evocative circumstances. For a while I toyed with yet another name: *Meadow* That Makes a Man Cry. But the name was less than perfect, because if I stood in the meadow, turned around, and looked in some other direction, I felt no lump in my throat. In the end it was too much trouble to name the meadow. So it remained nameless, just as the mountain remained Mountain That Makes a Man Cry.

Occasionally, I rebuked myself for indulging in such blatant romanticism. I would go after myself like a boorish Gestalt therapist. "Grimes," I would chide, "*You* cry. The mountain doesn't *make* you do anything. You yourself do the crying. Stop riding this pathetic fallacy so hard." But this attitude came to seem arrogant, as if neither the mountain nor the meadow had anything to do with the event.

Was I the sole actor in the universe?

Surely not.

What was the source of this impulse to cry? And what was its meaning? It didn't appear to be linked to any particular frame of mind that I carried with me on my walk. Whether I was happy or sad or preoccupied or content, the result was the same.

I considered the obvious psychoanalytic angles—mountain as father, meadow as mother. The ideas were fun to play with, but they didn't get me anywhere. Mountain and meadow did not evoke childhood traumas, and I had no persistent set of associations with either. Well, that's not quite true. When I focused attention on where I was, the meadow, I sometimes imagined building a home there. When I attended to where I was not, the mountain, I sometimes wanted to climb it. The fantasy got out of hand once or twice, and I imagined circumambulating the mountain, looking it up on the map, discovering its real name, and calculating its altitude. I was a little ashamed of my fantasies and so resisted the temptations to build and climb. Well, if the truth be told, I couldn't have built a home in the meadow anyway; the spot was in a national forest. I probably could have climbed the mountain, but did I want to? What would I gain—or lose—by such a symbolic conquest? I left open the possibility of going there, but only on the condition that I be able to find the proper attitude for doing so.

What was the proper attitude?

I wished that I knew.

Looked at religiously, rather than psychoanalytically, the mountain could have been interpreted as a symbol of transcendence. It was high and I was low. Sometimes it was bright and sunny when the surrounding mountains were dark and cloudy. It got my attention. It would likely get yours. But lots of other mountains in the Colorado Rockies attract attention.

Transcendence is a bad word these days. Feminist theology has made it so. Perhaps we do need a moratorium on the term. Even so, the experience of something other, something above that both draws and repels, does not go away. Maybe this is not the best or the only experience of holiness, but I remain unconvinced that it is bad for spiritual health. And even if it is bad for women, it was not bad for this particular man. Was the relationship between the mountain and me hierarchical? Did it condition me to become an insensitive bureaucrat, lord on high, oppressor of females, children, the poor—in short, others, those whom I am not? I don't think so. When I would come back from a walk in the meadow, I often wanted to hug my wife or daughter and son—maybe even a tree if no one was looking. Sometimes I would just sit on a boulder thinking nothing, saying nothing. I didn't want to bomb, make more money, earn another title, or assert my superiority. After crying in the meadow, I did not feel superior.

Why did I return? Was going back to the site some latent form of masochism? Was that mountain the "over there" of the evangelical hymns I used to sing? Was my trek to the meadow a romanticized expression of the death instinct? Why would anybody other than a fool or a masochist return to some crying place for an unexplainable experience of good pain?

The impulse to cry was at once joyful and torqued. "Yes," I would exclaim. Maybe I should have renamed the mountain, Mountain That Makes a Man Say Yes, but it made me say no too: No, I am not you; no, I am not there. Torque is power that twists or turns. I was in the meadow and the mountain was there, over there, other. Yet in the meadow, I felt related to the mountain. I felt safe in the meadow, at home in it. It was open enough that I did not feel claustrophobic and surrounded enough that I felt protected. So there was torque: no/yes, other/ same, over there/here, could never be home/feels like home.

Yes to the torque.

Part of the mountain soared above the tree line. So when it snowed and the other mountains looked like baking moms with flour dust in their dark hair, this mountain was snowcapped. Even so, there are many snowcapped mountains in the Rockies. What then was the source of the crying, and what was its meaning? Why that mountain? And why only from that meadow? The crying did not seem to *belong* to mountain or meadow, Mom or Dad, God or self. Ultimately, I was unable to know the source of the crying, and I could only guess at its meaning. Because I can only guess, I enjoy being a man. And because I am unable to know, I remain a religious animal.

18

THE POLITICS
OF PRACTICE

Ritual is not only cultivated by practice but also negotiated by action. The world is not just a field in need of tilling but a political arena ringing with conflict. Without contemplative practice ritual easily becomes the pawn of cultural fads. But the meditative root of ritual practice is not identical with its ethical fruit. To attend only to the source of ritual without noticing its consequences would be irresponsible. Practice must be both contemplative and political, and the political is not limited to parties and governments but has to do with distributions of power and uses of authority.

Since my ritual sensibility is largely determined by the academic study of religion, my Protestant background, Zen practice, and domestic ritualizing, my attitude toward ritual authority is often iconoclastic and ironic. Although I play seriously at ritual, I am wary of its misuses.

My intellectual formation coincided with the 1960s. In that decade we discovered that iconoclasm and ritualizing were not mutually exclusive. My doctoral defense, the culminating moment in an academic rite of passage, was temporarily dislocated by protest activities provoked by the U.S. invasion of Cambodia. My days and nights were filled with the drama of marches, picketing, building seizures, and other forms of ceremonial protest. My most sustained training in the uses of ritual power was not in seminary liturgy courses but in the streets of New York City. At Columbia University and Union Theological Seminary issues of gender and race were sacred topics of debate and motives to action.

Gender and race, therefore, were not mere factors in my ritual formation; they constituted identity. As a man I have been able—at least until recently—to garner degrees and pay raises faster than most females who were my classmates. That I am middle class has provided me with sanctuaries in which to explore traditions, also with time in which to experiment on models. My choice as a white academic has not been *whether* to have authority but *how* to use it. We who have, or claim to have, authority need to remind ourselves daily that all authority is ritualistic and all ritual, political. Ritual is a primary means of identifying ourselves with, and defining ourselves against, others.

During a leave of absence from the university where I've taught since 1974, I was asked to teach a course on Native American religions at the University of Colorado in Boulder. Ritual is foundational for most Native American traditions, so its study constitutes a large portion of any course most religion scholars would teach on the topic. But ritual knowledge is hotly contested these days. The politics of ritual are nowhere more evident than in the teaching of Native American religions. At first I considered declining the invitation. Later, I accepted it on the condition that I be permitted to comment publicly on the situation facing me. I posted the following E-mail message to three electronic discussion groups—one on religious studies, one on anthropology, one on Native American issues. I invited reflection on three questions:[27]

- *Should or should not European Americans be teaching courses on Native American religions?*
- *If we should not, why not, and what would be the results of our deferral?*
- *If we should, how best can we proceed?*

I am giving much thought these days to the question of cultural imperialism, especially religious and academic imperialism. While on leave from another university, I have been asked by the Department of Religious Studies at the University of Colorado, Boulder, to teach a large, publicly visible introductory course on Native American religions.

Vine Deloria teaches here. So do Sam Gill, Ward Churchill, and Deward Walker. This is a sizable concentration of authorities on indigenous culture, politics, law, and religion. Ordinarily, I teach a course on indigenous religions at Wilfrid Laurier, a small Canadian university where I can consider such topics in relative obscurity. I teach at considerable remove from indigenous populations of the American Southwest, where I do most of my fieldwork, and at a safe distance from high-profile scholars whose names are regularly associated with Native American studies.

Currently the Boulder campus is the locus of a highly charged stand-off that no one talks much about, at least in public. In part the issue has to do with academic, religious, and cultural turf. It does not have to do simply with who is right or wrong on a given issue, but who has the authority to talk about indigenous ritual and religion. Anyone who has read Churchill's critique of Gill's Mother Earth *or heard Deloria's reflections on that book knows there are good reasons for European American scholars not to rush in, fools, where angels fear to tread.*

In fact, some are rushing in the other direction: out. I know several white male colleagues who are giving up long-standing research and teaching commitments to Native American, black, or feminist religion. For most, leaving is the result of feeling embattled or unappreciated. Exiting white guys feel they will never get respect or credit for attending to Native American concerns. Some may find this minor exodus an occasion for joy. I do not.

I have to ask myself—as a colleague asked me yesterday after seeing the video Gathering Up Again: Fiesta in Santa Fe—*"Shouldn't we just abandon such topics [in this case, the conflicts among Native American, Hispanic American, and Anglo American religious traditions]? Isn't scholarship, like art, just another way of appropriation, just another form of cultural imperialism? Why do you keep teaching on the topic of indigenous religion and ritual?" he wanted to know.*

This was the question of a non-Native colleague; Native ones are raising the question as well. The notion of abandoning academic turf as if it were bad land and giving it back to "the natives" as if it were a gift we previously owned seems to me a piece of bad choreography to which we have danced several times before.

The question of cultural imperialism is especially acute when the subject matter is religion rather than, say, law, economics, or politics. Religion is, after all, supposed to be a protected domain. We religion scholars ought not to be desecrating what we study. In Ritual Criticism *and elsewhere I have written about the act of desecration that occurs when indigenous cemeteries are excavated or sacred objects are put on display in museums. But the questions I must now ask myself are no different from those I have put to archaeologists and curators. Does teaching about rites indigenous to the Americas desecrate them?*

I have violated sacred domains. Reared a cowboy American Protestant in the Southwest, I could hardly have done otherwise. I violated the sanctity of my grandmother's religion when I began to study it critically. Had I not done so I would still believe that Indians, blacks, Catholics, and communists are all in league with the devil. I cannot say that I regret my decisions to talk religion with religious studies teachers and not just my grandmother.

But it is altogether a different matter when the object of study is somebody else's religion. In religious studies we like to feel that we honor a religious tradition by taking it seriously enough to teach it. The very act of paying attention is, or ought to be, a way of valuing. So what are we to make of the accusation that our teaching of religions, especially Native American ones forced by historic necessity into linking sanctity with secrecy, is really a way of appropriating or desecrating? Our first line of defense is to argue that we teach about religion; we do not teach religion. Unlike those New Age wanna-bes in California, we responsible scholars do not put on plains garb or do the Santo Domingo Corn Dance. Surely we are blameless.

But we do read the ethnographies (some of them distorted, some of them in violation of confidences) and contemplate museum objects (some of them stolen, some of them falsely named and ritually underfed). We may not be guilty for the sins of our forbears, but we certainly make intellectual capital on the basis of their colonial activities.

An anthropologist friend said to me a while back, "Grimes, if we took all the stuff you say seriously, we'd be paralyzed—like the proverbial centipede suddenly made aware of its own legs and completely immobilized by that fact. You would paralyze us with self-consciousness and guilt." I said I thought he was right but that being stilled and silenced for a while might not be a bad thing. He accused me of being a Buddhist.

Reflecting on the conversation, I had to ask myself, What form should this immobility and silence take? Should we white folks give up teaching about Native American religion and ritual, leaving such topics to those who can teach it from their own hearts and traditions? (In many cases such given-up courses would not be taught, because there are not yet many Native American Ph.D.s in religious studies.) I can hear the religion scholars object, "Surely you don't think that only Hindus can teach Hinduism, only Muslims, Islam," and so on. Academic study always requires the sympathetic exercise of imagination. If we taught only that which we embodied by virtue of our upbringing, gender, class, ethnicity, and so on, we would all be reduced to autobiographical confession or mere reiteration of our traditions. I'd be teaching Grandma's peculiar brand of frontier Methodism, which would insist on the unquestioned superiority of my kind.

So I have chosen not to exit. I continue to write and teach about rites and other religious practices of groups in which I do not hold membership. Some of them do not object to such study, but others do. Scholarship, I have come to believe, necessarily incurs guilt. We should not pretend otherwise. Scholarship, though it can be a kind of honoring, is also a kind of hunting as well. So scholars should do it with great care—identifying their fate with the fate of what they hunt, taking only what they really need for survival, and hedging their activities with considerable ceremony. The hunting analogy is less than perfect. I am, of course, borrowing this particular version of it, which is more humane than the hunting tradition I grew up with; we did it for sport. I invoke the hunting analogy as a way of reminding our (white) selves of the violence of scholarship even when we intend to be nonviolent. Though we may not experience scholarship as violent, thus not a form of hunting, we are being told that others experience our study as violation. We need to pause and consider this charge, because some of our colleagues, students, and friends are making it. So the question is not, What is the nonviolent way to study religion? Rather it is, What is the least violent way to do it? What are the limits and ethics that bear on the teaching of Native American religions by non-Natives in public institutions? Whatever the answer to these questions, we should do what we do with humility and open ears.

The politics of ritual are intense and complex if the context of instruction issues from a history of ethnocide and the instructor is a descendant of its perpetrators. Among European Americans there is a strong feeling afoot that the knowledge and attitudes encoded in Native American ceremonies hold the key to the world's ecological future. A student said in my American Indian Religions class, "If we don't have that knowledge, and the Indians don't want to teach us, then we whites will destroy the world—us and them together."

"Suppose you are correct?" I replied, "Then what?"

Her answer dumbfounded me and outraged Indians in the class: "Well, then, we have a right to that knowledge! They owe it to us." She spoke aloud the presumption held by many non-Indians. In view of it, our actions are just as politically motivated as any action taken by Native Americans.

Native Americans are not the only ones responsible for politicizing the study of religion. We European Americans are as well. The white conviction that we have rights to sacred ceremonial knowledge—like the god-given claims we lay to Indian land and the minerals beneath it—is a fiercely political stance no matter how apolitical its advocates may feel in articulating it. This dangerous presumption of rights currently drives much of the fascination with American Indian ceremonial knowledge. Instead of pilfering other peoples' ritual knowledge, we ought to be examining our own ritual ineptitude.

The politics of studying ritual mark not only interethnic debate but also discourse on gender. Not long ago Wilfrid Laurier University, the place where I teach, was in the news across Canada. There was a panty raid. Afterward, women's underwear, smeared with fake blood and feces, were found hanging in the cafeteria. These trophies, displayed as banners, were labeled with slogans demeaning to women.

The ritual illiteracy of the ensuing debate resounded on both sides of the argument. Among the supporters of the raids were those who claimed it was a harmless tradition, a getting-acquainted ritual—as if labeling something tradition made it harmless or as if calling it ritual made it innocuous. "No one takes these things seriously," several male students insisted. Obviously, somebody did. Rites and traditions are like that: One moment they appear empty, the next moment they erupt.

Among the critics of the raids were those who considered them not only morally reprehensible but also senseless, meaning by this term not rational, achieving no real end. They used the ax of rationality and the bludgeon of moralistic pragmatism to smash a botched rite.

Such weapons are not commensurate with the enemy. Both responses—pro and con—were telling expressions of the university's tradition of studied ritual illiteracy. Evaluated by the standards of this tradition, panty raids were par for the course.

An academic year is littered with symbolically laden events: orientation, final exams, chapel services, convocation, wine and cheese parties. The list goes on. Some of the events are pap. Their rhetoric is innocuous, and they are designed to mask the boredom of participants or to disperse the passion of intellectual engagement into mere politeness and civility.

In the efficacious ones—those that actually transform—power is regularly mishandled, and the ones that are explicitly taught contradict the values actually symbolized by behavior. For example, my university's mandatory, herd-style final examinations, patrolled by strolling faculty proctors, achieves the opposite of the honesty, cooperation, and good character extolled by official rhetoric. The examining system institutionalizes mistrust of both students and faculty.

The university's convocation, like that of many institutions of higher education, is likewise dishonest. With its singing of supposedly generic hymns and praying of supposedly generic prayers, it dragoons participants into a pseudo-ceremonial piety that offends atheist and Christian, Hindu and Jew.

Panty-raiding students were just acting out of the ritual ignorance into which faculty and administration had initiated them. Students at least knew enough to call panty raids ritual. What neither faculty nor administration had taught them, however, was that they were bad ritual. How could students have known the difference when we provided them with no good examples?

An interviewer asked an anthropologist on campus if the panty raid wasn't like a primitive initiation. She said she thought not. Of course not. She was right. Those "primitives" aren't as ritually illiterate as we are. They know that rites, packed to the hilt with the black powder of symbols, can blow up in your face just when you think you've defused them or gotten them under control.

A student at Queens University was involved in a fiasco in which men posted a sign reading, "No Means Dyke" (to parody the "No Means No" campaign). He moaned, "I think a lot of us are still in shock that it went this far. It was supposed to be a joke." No one taught him that symbols are not toys for grown-up boys.

Besides being morally reprehensible, the panty raid was a botched rite. It failed to achieve ritual inversion, that dicey business of turning social roles and statuses upside down. The WLU panty raid didn't turn anything upside down; it just reinforced the already oppressive status quo. What's wrong with panty raiding has little to do with shorts, panties, ketchup-as-blood, and mud-as-shit. What's wrong is that men have so few elders to teach them that if they want to splash blood, dish out shit, or otherwise play the ritual clown, then they first have to be baptized in shit, spill some of their own blood, and be subjected to sustained symbolic lessons in humility. Pueblo ceremonial clowns are initiated in just such a fashion, but, we imagine, they have nothing to teach us; we're beyond the filthy stuff of primitive rites. And our civilized ones are harmless.

What we need is not just to squash panty raids with moral outrage. This is only a first step. If it is also the last step, we can expect a return of the repressed. A second step is that of providing alternatives. And these must be in a symbolic medium, not in a didactic one. To take this second step, moralizing will have to give way to dramatic enactment and ceremonial creativity. It will not do to be satisfied with public proclamations of virtues, hoping they will counter our few—oh, so very few—vices. Nor will it suffice to co-opt the raids by officially sponsoring them; our administration tried that. What is needed is serious education in symbol-using and worthy examples of ritual-making. Moral principles, even the strongest ones, are insufficient to counteract symbolic assault rooted in unconscious fears.

Some people don't think panty raids are very serious business, certainly not enough to warrant railing about them as an initiatory element in the educational process. But near the same time as the infamous panty raid, the Montreal massacre occurred. That event exposed the ritual politics of gender even more dramatically. On December 6, 1989, a lone male[28] entered the engineering school at the Ecole Polytechnique in Montreal, complaining about the damage that feminists had done to him. By the time he was finished, he had killed fourteen women with a rifle:

> Geneviève Bergeron
> Hèlén Colgan
> Nathalie Croteau
> Barbara Daigneault
> Anne-Marie Edward
> Maud Haviernick
> Barbara Maria Klucznik
> Maryse Laganière
> Maryse Leclair
> Anne-Marie Lemay
> Sonia Pelletier
> Michèle Richard
> Annie St-Arneault
> Annie Turcotte

Spontaneously, ceremonies sprang up across Canada. Annual commemoration services continue to the present. Largely organized by women, they were expressions of outrage, hope, and fear. For some participants, the ceremonies were funerals. For others, they were rites of solidarity with women, consolidations of feminist consciousness. For still others, they were mourning rites or ceremonial occasions for public reflection on sexual abuse.

I witnessed more tears during the week of December 6 than in any other week of my academic life. Many women, and some men, far removed from Quebec, feminism, and ritual-making mourned, held candles, marched, had bad dreams, sang songs, observed silence, and jumped when someone stumbled over a trash can in a classroom. Men met, examined their consciences, and declared themselves guilty or not guilty. Some joined women. Some did not. Some women wanted to be joined. Some did not.

The rites we constructed and experienced were inept—wordy, hurried, and self-conscious. But they did their work; they enabled the enactment of outrage and grief. They were the best the academic community could do with no warning and so little preparation. We were awkward together, and it was good.

I am a professor, so I imagined the murderer's invasion of my classroom. In one version I am teaching Love and Its Myths, a large introductory course. I am heroic, leaping into action with my decades-old karate training coming back on cue. No one is killed. Only a few stray shots hit the blackboard near some diagrams explaining the image of the androgyne that Aristophanes paints in Plato's *Symposium.*

In another version the murderer charges in and dashes wildly about the class, shooting women. Fourteen lie dead on the floor of my classroom. Like other men, I am helpless and inept. We are unheroic, utterly incapable of rescuing damsels in distress. The damsel-and-knight scenario collapses completely. The heroic fantasy proves futile in the face of charges made by women that all men, knightly and villainous alike, were implicated by the massacre.

In my university's first ceremony, performed shortly after the massacre, I was assigned the job of beating a drum. I did so—slowly, not very well, in the background, with considerable ambivalence. Some women thought I should not have participated. So did some men.

In another rite I read a poem expressing my fears about being a father to a daughter and a teacher of female students:

NO SAFE PLACE

Come, daughter dear.
You're only two,
and it's just three.
Come close,
next to me.
Snuggle into a safe place,
here,
in the cubicle
of your dad's heart.

What do you mean,
it's crowded in there—
that your mom
and her mom
and her mom,
that my mom
and her sisters
and my sister
are hiding away in there?

Hiding from what,
dear daughter, only two?
Hiding from what
in the cubicle
down the long corridor of my heart?
What do you mean,
there are fourteen or more
huddled there,
cowed by a little man
with a big gun?

Oh, my God, dear daughter, only two,
it's three,
and you're frightening me.
Tell me it's just a dream or a nosebleed.
I'm your dad,
and this is my haven,
my cubicle,
down the long corridor of my heart.
Don't, please don't,
tell me there's a man
with a gun down there.
Not in the cubicle of my heart.

I am a man,
a real man,
a religious man,
a professor man,
a man's man,
a woman's man,
a daughter's dad.

Scoot over, daughter of mine.
Now it's my turn
to huddle in bed with you
even though it's only three
and you're only two.

Remember when,
not so long ago,
you cried, "Dad, Dad?"
When you fell thundering
head-first in the night?
Oh, my God,
I prayed,

I swear,
I heard you,
I swear,
before you hit the floor.
There's still blood there
deep
and brown in the carpet,
but it was just a nosebleed
hanging on the tail of a dream
when it was about three,
just after you turned two.

Let me crawl,
let your daddy hide
in the purity
of your two-year-old heart.
Daddy's scared
of that bad man
hiding in the cubicle
down the long hall of his heart.

No?

What do you mean,
the gate of your little girl's heart
is too tiny
for a daddy
big and bearded and booted like me?

Oh, my God,
there
is
no
safe
place.

No safe place, not in my heart,
not in yours.
No safe place.
Not in the library,
not in the bookstore,
not in the toilet stall.
Not in Central Teaching 4201.
Not in S205,
or P2102.

Not in the library,
not in the bookstore,
not in the toilet stall.
That mean man's everywhere,
in here, out there.

And there is
no
place
to hide.

But I am a man,
a man's man,
a woman's man,
a spiritual man,
a scholar man.
And only a man
can stop a man
if that man
is down the dark corridor of his own heart.
What man
is man enough
to make a space safe enough
for a dear daughter
only two when it's dark and three—

or even when she's twenty-three
and it's broad daylight?

Still,
one day,
a long ways away,
you'll come, daughter,
older than two
and long past three,
down the dark corridor
on floor four
into the heart
of this university,
into the sanctuary
of your dad's last class,
the one on love,
the one in 4201.
And you'll sit where she sat,
the girl who said,

> *"Are there many of them out there?"*
> *"Them?" I said.*
> *"Them," she said,*
> *"you know, feminists."*
> *And this time*
> *when I say,*
> *"Not only are they out there,*
> *they are in here too,"*
> *I won't be lying.*
> *There will be at least two*
> *in this dangerously safe place,*
> *this university,*
> *this sanctuary of the mind,*
> *where, daughter dear,*
> *you and your friends*
> *and other engineers of the spirit*
> *will have raised floodlights*
> *along the dark corridors*
> *of the human heart.*

I wrote a second ending to the poem, which I did not read, because it spooks me. Whereas the read version ends hopefully, this one does not. It is a meditation on the dangers of the protective instinct of the man who resorts to violence to protect those he loves:

> *But I am a man,*
> *a man's man,*
> *a woman's man,*
> *a spiritual man,*
> *a scholar man.*
> *I'll make it safe, daughter dear.*
> *You'll come—*
> *older than two*
> *and long past three,*
> *down the long corridor*
> *on floor four*
> *into the heart*
> *of the university,*
> *into the sanctuary*
> *of your dad's class,*
> *the one on love,*
> *the one in 4201.*
> *And you'll sit where she sat,*

the girl who said,
"Are there more of them out there?"
"Them?" I said.
"Them," she said,
"feminists, you know."
And this time
when I say,
"Of course, not only are they out there,
they are in here too,"
I won't be lying.
There will be at least one.
And it will be a safe place,
daughter dear,
for you, your friends,
and other engineers of the spirit—
even if I have to post
at the door
a big man with a big gun.

If we combine the body politics of gender with those of ethnicity and then frame both ritually, the result can be both sobering and hilarious. One afternoon during African dance class I shorted out. The feet and hips couldn't remember their assigned movements. The ass wouldn't shake rightly, and the drummer's fine rhythms refused to animate this untrained body. So I sat the session out, brooding, with the teacher, an African American woman, and the other participants, all female, snatching glances at me.

The next day I complained to colleagues, "You know, the white man just can't dance." With voices in my head either pronouncing judgment or offering false comfort, I accounted for my kinesthetic ignorance in several ways:

- The man can't dance, 'cause he's white, and white folks got no rhythm.
- The guy can't dance, because he's a male, and males are socialized to be rigid and controlling.
- The old guy can't dance, because he's middle-aged; at fifty-whatever the spine grows tired and the muscles, flabby.
- Dr. Grimes can't dance, because he's an academic, and we all know that scholars live in their heads and grow fat asses from excessive reading and writing.

For the next few days I desperately wanted to drop the course, but for reasons beyond my ken I persisted. By the end I had been dubbed Old Faithful. Despite

Gender formation: What it feels like to be a girl; how to become a man (photos by Milton and Nadine Grimes)

my ineptitude, I enjoyed being a student again, even if I was the oldest person in the class.

Foolishly, I enrolled in a second African dance course, this one on healing ritual. After my first two or three sessions I complained to the teacher, "I am in kinesthetic culture shock." She rolled her eyeballs at such high-flown rhetoric. Trying to explain, I went on, "The body is a little world. Cross its boundaries and you go into culture shock. You know, move it, shake it, and bake it in some way other than that to which it is habituated, and it goes into somatic culture shock. Learning African dance is like crossing an international frontier into a new territory where they speak another language, and the food, currency, and manners are different."

She agreed but didn't feel much pity for me.

I finished the second course, too. Now Caleigh, Bryn, and I dance regularly. We dance African, country and western, Celtic, and the portions of Peter, Paul, and Mary that Bryn insists are rock and roll. We are unabashed. Still, I quip, "Nope, 'the white man,' he just can't dance."

The refrain disturbs friends, particularly other white males. They find the self-parody demeaning. Why do I persist in it? Am I white-male bashing? Aren't I one of them? If I don't mean literally and absolutely that all white men, for genetic reasons, can't dance and that all black people can, what the hell do I mean?

In my ritual glossary "'The white man' can't dance" has become a metaphoric way of speaking about ritual ignorance. By "the white man" I mean something like "the ritually inept." And by "dance" I mean something like "ritual rightly performed, religiously significant, and culturally integrated." We white males, I believe, really are the most apt symbol of inability to do the dance.

I know I'm playing with a dangerous stereotype, "the white man," which is why I put it in quotation marks and do not say, white men (without quotation marks). I readily admit that some white men can, in fact, dance. There was one in my class who could. Built like Michelangelo's *David*, with a bronze face resembling a raven on a Northwest Coast totem pole, he could shake his behind in a most astonishing way.

I am also aware that not all black people dance so well, which is to say, "naturally." Two African Americans, about my age, one male and one female, danced with as much difficulty as I did. The man was quiet, serious, gray-haired. He was unflappable; he just persisted, no matter how stiff his limbs or confused his sense of direction. The woman, a grandmotherly, gourd-shaped social worker, laughed at her inabilities and joshed me for fretting about mine. She too persisted, undaunted.

Nevertheless, it is hard to deny that certain kinds of performance are learned by certain kinds of people with enormous difficulty—perhaps not at all. Why? What factors inhibit ritual learning? I doubt that every culture successfully teaches all of its members to ritualize. Ritual knowledge sometimes fails to take root. Why is it so extraordinarily difficult, I wonder, for that peculiar class of humans whom we type "the white man" to dance?

Claiming that blacks dance naturally whereas whites can do it only unnaturally would be racist, but even if we argue that culture, rather than genes, is the ultimate cause of one's dancing well or badly, we still have not said much. We need to be more specific about the circumstances of learning: What is it about European American, male kinesthetic culture that renders it irreligious in face of the maxim "Religion is danced, not thought?" This is an urgent question. What divides us into blacks and whites, Natives and non-Natives, perhaps even into women and men, is not just economics, land, and politics but also "the Dance." There is a deep rift between those who dance for reasons of recreation or health and those who do it as a way of embracing the world. Making ritual ineptitude a matter of culture, rather than genes, does not get us off this hook.

When we enact rites, we are not merely illustrating knowledge that exists somewhere else, say, in a book or in someone's head. Ritual is a kind of knowledge. Specifically, it is somatic knowledge. Because ritual is a sort of knowledge, one can be ignorant of it—ritually illiterate, we might say, ritually disabled.

Ritual learning, like language learning, may be most effective when it happens early and proceeds by immersion. But immersion is not always possible. Even some traditional people are now having to learn at a considerable distance from their cultural homelands. Increasingly, neither they (in this case, black folks) nor we (white folks) have the option to absorb ritual knowledge through the pores or dissolved in our mothers' milk. However attractive it may seem *not* to have a choice among ritual practices, a growing number of the world's population have no choice but to participate by choice. And choice often implies learning by overt instruction in a classroom, in a faraway place.

So my question is not merely, What is ritual knowledge? Rather, it is, In what cultural spaces is ritual knowledge best cultivated? What are the difficulties of pursuing it cross-culturally in classes rather than in villages among tribes? What is the epistemology governing ritual knowledge when the circumstances are such that it is fractured and the site for it is socially or geographically dislocated?

We need to be at once more specific and more general in answering such questions. We need to be more specific about the dances, for example. My proverbial white man, though he stumbles through the *focodoba* (a dance performed by children in Guinea), can, if he persists in practice, whirl through the waltz. In any consideration of ritual ineptitude, we need to take into account specific choreographic sensibilities and the politics of learning. In addition to being more specific, we need to be more theoretical in identifying social, psychological, and bodily conditions that engender ritual ineptitude or facilitate ritual competence.

My clumsy attempts at learning African-inspired ritual dance helped me become aware of conditions that inhibit such learning. *Self-consciousness*, for instance, is a major obstruction. Self-consciousness is not identical with self-awareness. Self-consciousness inhibits action. Self-awareness facilitates it. The Space for Dance, the refurbished wing of a milk plant where we practiced what was called Healing Dance, had mirrors down one side. Their presence defined the south wall as front. No one ever faced the opposite wall. The mirror helped us see the teacher, as well as ourselves, but we could have done without it. The dance space itself elicited considerable self-consciousness. In my view the mirrors militated against the ritual dimensions of the class by evoking a performative self-consciousness.

A mirror might have enabled us to become self-aware, but self-awareness lapses into self-consciousness when a second inhibiting factor is at work: *competitiveness and goal orientation.* Some of us did not merely see ourselves there in the mirror. We saw ourselves being awkward. I saw so-and-so dancing with a lot more finesse than I could muster. I noticed someone else dancing without effort. I wanted to do well. I wanted to learn something, not look like a klutz. Even when I was not being overtly competitive with others, I was competing with myself: I wanted to do better than I had done the last time.

In addition to self-consciousness and competitiveness there is a third reason "the white man" can't dance: *individualism and the lack of a supporting social context.* Why was I looking at myself in that mirror and not, say, at all of us? Why was I not worried about how we as a group were doing? The answer, I suspect, is that we were not a community. We did not depend on one another outside this hour-and-a-half context. We were merely bodies moving together. To be sure, we occasionally reached golden moments of attunement and rapport; the drums would pound us until we pulsed like the beat of a single heart. For a moment we cared. But the moment always evaporated, and we were a collection of individuals again, going our separate ways. "The white man's" dance is not very communal, so in one respect it is no dance at all but an exhibition or exercise. "The white man" can't dance, because he doesn't have the right ethic. He doesn't have the right ethic, because he does not live in the right social circumstances. If this way of putting it sounds too normative, there is another way to say it: "The white man" cannot dance, because he can enact only the social circumstances in which he dwells. And they define him as an individual over against—often above—other individuals. They teach him to imagine initiative as coming from inside, from the will, rather than as arising from the social and physical environment that surrounds him.

There is no clear separation between social and bodily reasons for ritual ignorance. *Habituation* is one way to name choreographic, or kinesthetic, reasons for ritual ineptitude. By habituation I mean the repetitive baselines of posture and gesture that constitute the framework of a person's daily existence. For several hours a day I, for example, sit—writing, eating, talking. I cultivate an erect posture hoping to avoid curvature of the spine and rounding of the shoulders, staring at a computer screen in order to write things such as this. One evening a week I bike over to the Space for Dance hoping in vain to dance my way down out of my head. The way I choreograph my day and week is dualistic, despite my anti-Cartesian theory of ritual, which leads me to reject any ultimate separation of mind and body. My theory holds that they are one, but my lifestyle splits them in two. The "erectitude" of my workday predisposes me to choreographic and liturgical verticality: I sit up straight and walk with my shoulders back. But these habits are ill-suited to African dance. Kinesic dissonance arises because "the white man's" kinesthetic habits predispose him against the circuitousness of ritualistic and choreographic movements characteristic of African and many other kinds of dance. I discovered in myself what I came to call ritual resistance. By this phrase I mean a bodily, kinesthetic trajectory that runs counter to other ways of moving. Although I was a most willing participant in African dance—I had no conscious resistance to it—resistance arose. The body groaned and fought against other habits of being. Practice, when it is sustained and habituated, has biogenetic consequences.

In African dance class we literally had to stick our necks out. Simultaneously, we had to stick out our behinds—in the other direction. Having "erected" myself for eight hours prior to class, an hour and a half of undulation hurt. To make it all worse, I have practiced Zen meditation for fifteen years, learning to be still, keeping my spine straight, and making my attention one-pointed, as they say. In African dance we became snakes and birds. The spine swayed this way and that, and one's attention needed to be diffusely focused. African dance demands ambidexterity of all four limbs and the torso as well. My only habitually ambidextrous activity is typing. The aesthetic of African dance is such that dancers move with multiple rhythms in multiple vectors. I, who can barely pat my head while rubbing my stomach, had to practice polyrhythm. Polyrhythm: polytheism. I grew up a monotheist. At best "the white man" is monorhythmic; at worst, he suffers a-rhythmia.

Of African dance routines I often could not remember much, either during a session or when I went home and tried to replicate there what I was supposed to have learned in class. "The white man" can't dance, because of his *uncultivated kinesthetic memory*. To put it in Cartesian fashion, my mind can remember the titles and authors of books (even where they are on the shelf), but my body cannot remember whether to lead with the right foot or left, whether to jump and then turn or to turn and then jump. The movements were too complex, and they came too quickly. There was too little repetition. Often I could not recognize repetitions, because they were of patterns rather than of discreet, single movements.

The differences between religious traditions are as choreographic and kinesthetic as they are conceptual and doctrinal. In fact, kinesthetic ones may be the more fundamental and enduring. Religious competence in many traditions is fundamentally choreographic, not verbal. And ritual ignorance is the necessary side effect of ritual competence. To incarnate the values, or dance the attitudes, of any one tradition is to create psychosomatic structures that resist those of other traditions—no matter how open we aspire to be to them.

Learning ritual in classes, rather than in more integral settings, may be our only option, but it is a troubled path. The gulf between learning by immersion and learning by deliberate, formal instruction is enormous. Though ritual knowledge may arise in classes, ritual wisdom probably arises only in traditions. So even if I should not claim with such resounding hyperbole, "'The white man' can't dance," I would still have a serious reservation: Sure "the white man" can learn to dance—but only as a second language.

ENDING

Big Papa drove Harley to the stockyards in the elder's ancient pink Cadillac, which reeked of sweltering cow dung. Mashed peanut shells clung like devil's claws to the driver's side carpet. "Portales peanuts is the best," Big Papa boasted, shoving a handful toward Harley's belly. When grandpa and grandson arrived, Big Papa led his grandson to the catwalk. They climbed its steps and began to stroll above the indifferent heads of cattle awaiting sale. Harley tried to walk smoothly, imitating Tilly's gait when sneaking up on a field mouse. But the heel of his boot kept snagging on splinters or sticking in the cracks between the planks. More than once Big Papa was left with Harley dangling in his hand like a sack of chicken mash.

His grandpa pointed out a ghostly gray bull with a terrifying hump on his back. A gleam in his eye, Big Papa asked the boy if he wanted to ride the animal. "Meaner 'n hell," Big Papa declared. "Them goddamned Brahmers is from India and meaner 'n hell, not like American or Mexican bulls."

Harley knew Uma would not like for something that mean to be in Clovis or Portales or anywhere else on American soil. She had preached on the devil at a WCTU meeting, and Harley had listened to her speech on the radio. "The Devil in New Mexico," it was called.

Harley wanted to say yes so he could brag to Bibber, but he knew the devil was from hell and would take your soul unless maybe you were in a rodeo and had a clown to help you in case the bull wanted to stomp your butt into the ground where the devil was.

Harley hesitated, "W ... e ... l ... l ..."

While he was still drawling out his consideration, his granddad spirited him up by the shoulders and rump and hung the boy's dangling, much too short legs directly over the Brahma's back.

With a suddenness approaching the apocalyptic, horns and clowns were flying everywhere, shouting, grinning, cartwheeling, teasing. Harley was a rodeo cowboy. He was a man. He was a baby. He was a ripe apple ready to fall. Hallucinat-

251

*ing, he was paralyzed with fear. Hooves thundered like a hundred curly-haired
preachers. Beneath their weight Harley felt his ribs crumple like egg shells,
crushed like Adam's when he gave birth to Eve the hard way. Harley's head was a
watermelon in a bushel basket.*

*Big Papa, whose sense of humor Harley had learned to fear, pulled the trem-
bling cowboy out of danger with an ease characteristic only of God. "Scared you,
huh? Ah, someday you'll ride one of those damned things. Meaner 'n hell. You'll
get yourself a trophy buckle if you stay on one of 'em and then get off without
gettin' your brains mashed out."*

Harley was gasping for breath.

*"Don't cry, boy. He scares me too," confessed Big Papa, offering his awkward and
insufficient consolation. "Just wanted to learn you some courage. You'll need it
when you're a grown-up."*

*Harley forced a laugh by imagining a scoop of mashed potatoes in the shape of
a head. But it was a year before he went again with Big Papa to the stockyards.*

*When he told Randy Joe the story about dancing above a Brahma's back, he omit-
ted the part about having to make several dashes to the bathroom later that day.*

In Zen tradition there is a series of bull, or ox-herding, pictures that depicts
the unfolding search for enlightenment. The bull is a symbol of one's true nature, from which the herder in his ignorance thinks he is separated. He treks after the self as if it were some stray animal. In search of himself, this cowboy of the
human spirit is in danger of being trampled. But who is his real enemy—himself
or the bull? His journey is recursive. In the last picture the cow herder, now enlightened as to the nature of the self, returns to the city. There is no trace of enlightenment about him. As they say, "He does not stink of Zen."

Rodeo cowboys and Zen practitioners, despite their obvious cultural and religious differences, share a common aim: to become inseparable from the bull.
They break their bones and egos attempting to become one with it. Even though
cowboys hanker after barbecued beef, and vegetarian Zen students vow not to
harm sentient beings, both have powerful affinities for this beast. In rodeo tradition bulldogging (now called steer-wrestling) and bull riding are the two most
dangerous pursuits. They are the ordeals most in need of the rodeo clown, who
keeps cowboys from being gored or trampled.

Serious and dangerous pursuits evoke the antics of fools. Zen myth provides
them in Kanzan and Jitoku, two wandering idiots whose foolishness is wisdom.
Contemporary cowboy culture finds them in rodeo clowns such as Skipper Voss
and Wick Peth. On the margins of zendos and arenas, these tragicomic figures
appear draped in the regalia of full paradox. These underdogs put their quixotic
ways on public display. The top dogs, the rodeo champions and Zen masters,
need them for their very lives. Whether in ritual meditation, which cuts the human tendency to cling, or in ritual combat with animals, which teases cowboys

into regarding themselves as lords of the beasts, the foolish clown in masterly backwardness is not in the least worried about the contradictions inherent in the notion of a Zen cowboy.

BULL

1. searching

bitching the while away,
i sniff pasture and sky
for what i do not know
or am.
i remember; it hides.
i forget; it pursues.
i have no choice
except always
to be leaving this desert.

2. traces

wading these dunes
dappled with fibrous piles
of beastly residue,
my encrusted boots
bear the only sign
that i am in it already.
the stuff
is everywhere—
to my nostrils
a testimony of absence.

3. seeing

i am spotted
by the shaggy bull's eye,
not my dream's mirage
(a charging buffalo),
but a granddaddy Brahma bull.
he glimpses, dodges,
and is gone.
i am left staring into desert space,
a drugstore cowboy,
a dude,
belly to belly with earth
and hungry
for steak and more.

4. catching

driven
by his two points
of horn
into a cactus-strewn
box canyon,
i lay hold
of a muscled neck
and humped back.
with rope and knot
i bulldog the beast,
exposing
his very upside down.

5. taming

elder bull,
dance you to the crackling tune
of the whip's curling lash;
lumber to the music
of singing leather taking on wings.
open the spaces
between your very ribs,
and tune your bellowing
to the drum
of these two banging, clanging
noisy knees.

6. riding

between the beast's breath and mine:
no difference.
between hoof and boot:
no distance.
in this homecoming parade
there is neither
rider nor ridden,
player nor played.
all breathing is harmonica.
all stomp-and-thunder is drum.

7. no bull

just walking
this way in the desert.
no path, no whip, no rope.

just this way
is home.

8. no cowboy

no bull, no cowboy.
no light, no dark.
a horizon so empty
that no hand or trace
can cling.

9. source

a flash of desert rain:
the cactus flower springs yellow,
the sage breathes purple,
the rattler is bathed
in one fine hour
of liquid sun.

10. entering

in clown-patched cowboy rags
he enters the city's circuit
of burger and dollar.
eyes do not recognize him
as he hands them
their lives
by the seat of his pants.

The curse of autobiography is that you can't narrate your own conclusion. All you can do is envision it. Because my life continues, its story cannot close with either a dramatic death or a peaceful demise. Much is left dangling on or above the horns of some dilemma or other. Even if I were to ride off into the sunset, leaving readers to contemplate the south end of my northbound stallion, they are smart enough to suspect that the hardest part of my life is yet to come. I am aging. And immortality is not an option. In the Western world narrative endings, like sexual orgasms, have traditionally invited contemplation of death and reflections on eschatology, the study of so-called last things.

I want to be a wise old man, a holy fool, a rodeo clown rolling around in a barrel through that arena of intellectual combat, the university classroom. But I would settle for being a cantankerous grandpa, a perfectly ordinary old coot with interesting stories to tell the grandkids. Having fathered Bryn and Caleigh late, even the more modest wish is probably overstepping my bounds.

Do I have time? What exercises should I do or not do? How should I sit? What should I eat? On what should I train my vision? What practices can prepare me for the hairpin turns?

Crooked is the way and narrow is the gate.

The search for a worthwhile ritual practice is endless. Since I can barely envision it, I expect to die not having found it. Likely, I will not arrive at the place to which I aspire. Or having arrived, I will discover, if I am especially blessed, that I am in the sandbox of my own backyard.

This journey into the far country of manhood hasn't led me anywhere special. Even the mountain peaks I've glimpsed have been contemplated by others; I was not their discoverer. Assuming I complete the journey, the trophy I shall receive will likely be a mere pot, perhaps worthy of a cactus plant or handful of ashes. Wherever this place is at which I've arrived, other men have been here before me. I am not the only religious animal to have brayed such primal noises, not the only male to have suffered from an overdose of authority, not the only white man to have tried dancing someone else's dance, not the only educated person bedeviled by too much distinction-making. Other people's tracks are everywhere.

As an adult I still ask the same questions I posed as kid: the perennial, easy-therefore-difficult ones. They are the ones that require myths as answers. Such questions make me think of home. They transport me back to the beginnings of things.

At home they remark that I've gone a long way from home. They wish I were closer by. How did I get where I am anyway? You know, I mean, what's the path that led you from Methodist fundamentalism, to academe, to Zen, to domestic ritualizing, to sabbatical on the Continental Divide? My sister pleads on the phone: Will I ever come back? Do I like living on the Canadian side of the border better than this side? Her questions inflate the border and divide into metaphors. She asks bigger questions than she knows.

The farther away I've gotten, the more home beckons. But where is home? If home were ever—even for an instant—exactly where I stood, the foundations would shake. I am still a long way from home. I don't believe in cowboys anymore, or in Santa Claus or Jesus or Buddha or clowns or manhood. No matter. I dream clown dreams. I wear cowboy clothes like a real man. I sit on cushions as if enlightenment were possible. And I hum along with Emmylou Harris and Brian Bowers as they croon old hymns about going home.

So belief can't be all that important. Maybe the "I" that is supposed to do the believing isn't either. Is it too a fiction? What kind of spirituality is this—no belief, no self to do the believing, no proper tradition in which to practice? What is left? The doing, of course—the practice.

"And what is it that practices?"

When I ask myself the question, I do not have to be evasive like a Zen master, so I have a clear answer, "The bones. The bones practice. And the blood. And the heart. They do the doing."

"Ah, but they must be returned; they are on loan," says the master, refusing to stay out of the conversation. "Returning is the stuff of ritual," he reminds me, trying to beat me at my own game.

In the end I, a mere mortal male of bone and blood, must return. So be it. Let me then be carried home, packaged in pine and spruced up for burial on the lone prairie. Let there be a few stubborn coyotes to howl. Let there be a sandbox and an unlatched door, maybe even an apple tree.

We run in circles: daily rounds, seasonal cycles, journeys that go afar in order to return home. We Westerners, cowboys of the spirit, fear this circularity. To compensate, we armor ourselves with eschatology, the fantasy that one day things will be different. Tipped forward, we long for the kingdom to come and the new age to dawn, for progress and evolution to reach the ends we desire. We never quite give up our millennial hopes; they have burrowed deeply into the bone.

A few years ago when my students inquired why I was flying to the States to meet with Dan Noel (who was writing about neoshamanism and sacred space) and a colleague (who was writing about the ritualization of nuclear confrontation), I replied, "To plan the millennium, what else?" The brighter ones laughed. The slower ones looked puzzled. The business students quipped that my plan would never survive a cost-benefit analysis.

I had joined a project instigated by Dan. The collective aim was to imagine and then celebrate (or mourn) the turn of the millennium in 1999. My job was to construct a rite for the occasion. Whether I will actually do so remains to be negotiated. I found myself playing ritual contrary, disrupting the decorum of our discussion by inverting its values. I discovered that I didn't quite believe in the project, but then I was not asked to believe, only to imagine.

Imagining, I began to remember. I told Dan how as a kid I had spent hours, days, and years, it seemed, exiled to a sandbox a few miles south of Clovis, a desert island too damned close to Texas for comfort. Indoors, I recalled, Mom was baking brownies. (Now in bliss, she no doubt continues to do so.) I wanted in, but she said I had to stay out, or else I would be turned into a girl. Dad corroborated her prediction. Boys need sunshine; the outdoors bakes them into men. The sand toughens them. The irony of sitting in a sandbox in a land of sand (not enchantment, as the New Mexico license plate boasts) did not occur to me until I was thirty-something.

My New Mexico is not that of D. H. Lawrence and C. G. Jung. It is not the land of artists, tourists, and New Agers. They haunt Taos and Santa Fe, not Clovis. My eschatological sense is conditioned by the flat geography of Clovis, by sandbox exile and the distance between me and the Great Baking Mother. Primal alienation from the source of nourishment controlled by female hands conditions my vision of the future. Since childhood I have longed for a motherly hand to swing open the door of the universe. Being locked out probably prepared me well for the dawn of feminism, because it taught me that the sources of ultimate power are seldom male. Mother Earth could withhold rain; Mom controlled the cookies. The males of my New Mexico childhood could boast only sweat, work, smoke, and money. And money was not good for anything but buying chocolate for brownies or wells with which to court the watery favors of Mother Earth.

Before I was ten I learned that I was always going to be waiting for something, which, if I got it at all, was probably going to be doled out in measured bits and pieces. And likely it would not taste as good as I had fancied. Getting everything I wanted, I had to learn, was bad for my health. Whatever I might get as a reward for waiting impatiently in the sandbox was going to be just enough to whet my appetite. That way I would be dumb enough to wait in the sandbox for another round.

On the farm, waiting in the sandbox, there wasn't much to do. If in the spring the bee martins had young in the nest above, they would dive-bomb my head. Sitting under one of the three trees within several square miles, I had lots of time to contemplate the horizon around Clovis. If I looked at it for any time at all, I knew nothing ever happened here. I longed for the future, because there was nothing much in the present, at least not here, not in the place where I sat. I didn't believe that anything would ever come over that horizon. It never approached. In fact, it seemed always to be receding.

Once when I was twelve, I strapped on a couple of army surplus canteens and set out to hike to the horizon; someone had recently taught me the word. I got as far as the paved road four miles away and had to borrow a farmer's phone to call home for Mom to come get me.

So for me, future-orientedness, in whatever form (millenarianism, progressivism, eschatology, jogging to beat death) is neurotic. There is nothing whatever to be gained by longing for or anticipating the turn of the millennium. Doing so is an infinite hike in search of a receding horizon.

The millennial crux, 1999–2000, is probably miscalculated anyway. A Mennonite colleague explained to me the vagaries and politics of the Gregorian calendar. The turn of the millennium will not, he instructed me, occur at the end of 1999, because of a historic glitch in calendar-making.

Well, what the hell? I still wait for cookies. So I joined Dan Noel and other fools in this nonsense. If nothing else, it makes good dream fodder.

In Dan's vision the 1999 project is supposed to culminate at Land's End in Cornwall, the westernmost portion of the British Isles. But I objected: There is nothing special about Land's End. Why not Water's End? That would be Clovis, New Mexico. Why not Waterloo, Ontario? Isn't a waterloo where you meet your end? Why not in Nederland, Colorado? Nederland—the hinterland up near the Divide? What's so special about where land ends and water begins?

At heart, whether dwelling near the Great Lake shores or squatting on the Continental Divide, I remain a desert rat. My vision is prairie-glazed. I mistrust

Turning fifty at the canyon's edge (photo by Sam Gill)

water, though I long for it. I married a water woman. Susan plunges into Lake Ontario in the coldest of weather, her ecstatic lips turning a frosty blue. Not me. If I must meet the millennium, I'd rather do so in the desert with my trusty army surplus canteens at my side. Let Dan and those who can afford the trip gather at the water's edge, where a flood might at any moment make Atlanteans of those Cornish Methodist farmers and their New Age American pilgrims.

I have trouble walking when I walk, shitting when I shit, eating when I eat. I am always off in the future looking for a better job, cheaper repairs, tastier food, or a more centered self. This searching, even if I imagine the millennium is a mere quarter-inch in front of my nose, is still an illness. My only remedy—which isn't much of one—is to breathe regularly and deeply while trying to remember that there is no place like this one and no time like now. Wherever I stand is home, even though I may be absent from it.

Of course, I *say* there is nothing special about the turn of the millennium or about Cornwall and other greener pastures in the same breath I say that brownies are not good for one's health. Trying to utter two things at the same time with the same breath, I choke on my own self-contradictions.

Giving in to the urge for brownies is deadly. Denying the craving is sick. So there is nothing much to do, no way to prepare for the dawning of a new age except to sit in whatever sandbox I'm in and hope the bee martins don't peck my head. Everything depends on the quality of the sitting.

Notes

1. David Gilmore, *Manhood in the Making* (New Haven: Yale University Press, 1990), p. 107.

2. Virginia Woolf, *A Room of One's Own* (London: Hogarth, 1954), pp. 159–160.

3. Robert Moore and Douglas Gillette, *King, Warrior, Magician, Lover: Rediscovering the Archetypes of the Mature Masculine* (San Francisco: HarperCollins, 1990).

4. In *Ritual Criticism* (Columbia: University of South Carolina Press, 1990), chapter 9.

5. Originally published by Cornell University Press, 1976. Reissued by the University of New Mexico Press, 1992.

6. Parts of the following account were previously published in my *Ritual Criticism.* They are reprinted here with the permission of the University of South Carolina Press.

7. Peter Shaffer, *Equus* (New York: Atheneum, 1974), pp. 6–7.

8. William G. Archer, *Songs for the Bride: Wedding Rites of Rural India* (New York: Columbia University Press), 1985, p. 46.

9. Machado de Asis, *Dom Casmurro: A Novel,* translated by Helen Caldwell (Berkeley and Los Angeles: University of California Press, 1966), pp. 38–39.

10. Søren Kierkegaard, *Journals and Papers,* 7 vols., edited and translated by Howard V. Hong and Edna H. Hong (Bloomington: Indiana University Press, 1967–1978), vol. 5, IV A 107.

11. Ronald L. Grimes, "The Lifeblood of Public Ritual: Fiestas and Public Exploration Projects," in *Celebration: Studies in Festivity and Ritual,* edited by Victor W. Turner (Washington, D.C.: Smithsonian Institution Press, 1982), p. 281.

12. Lance Morrow, "The Hazards of Homemade Vows," *Time,* June 27, 1983, p. 58.

13. Georges Bataille, *Eroticism,* translated by Mary Dalwood (London: Calder, 1962), p. 59.

14. Loring Danforth, *The Death Rituals of Rural Greece* (Princeton: Princeton University Press, 1982), p. 109.

15. I am indebted to Basia Irland, who allowed me to sleep several nights in her Toronto art studio among the pieces of her assemblage *Euhemeris.* Her art and that space incubated this poem, in the middle of which the ghost of my mother insisted on making herself a nest.

16. Jessica Mitford, *The American Way of Death* (New York: Simon & Schuster, 1963).

17. Philip Ariès, *Western Attitudes Towards Death,* translated by Patricia M. Ranum (Baltimore: Johns Hopkins University Press, 1974).

18. Margaret Mead, *Male and Female* (Harmondsworth: Penguin, 1950), p. 222.

19. Robbie E. Davis-Floyd, "Birth as an American Rite of Passage," in *Childbirth in America: Anthropological Perspectives,* edited by Karen L. Michaelson and others (South Hadley, Mass.: Bergin & Garvey, 1988), p. 153.

20. Jorgé Borges, "The Circular Ruins," in *The Aleph and Other Stories,* edited and translated by Norman Thomas di Giovanni. (New York: Dutton, 1970).

21. Davis-Floyd, "Birth as an American Rite of Passage," pp. 153–172. A similar but more general argument is developed by Janice G. Raymond, "Medicine as Patriarchal Religion," *Journal of Medicine and Philosophy* 7.2 (1982): 197–216.

22. An Old Believer quoted by Juha Y. Pentikainen in Ugo Bianchi, *Transition Rites: Cosmic, Social and Individual Order,* Proceedings of the Finish-Swedish-Italian Seminar held at the University of Rome "La Sapienza," March 14–18, 1984 (Rome: "L'Erma" di Bretschneider, 1986), p. 22.

23. Barbara Myerhoff, *Number Our Days.* (New York: Simon & Schuster, 1978), p. 220.

24. Barbara Myerhoff, "A Death in Due Time: Construction of Self and Culture in Ritual Drama," in *Rite, Drama, Festival, Spectacle: Rehearsals Toward a Theory of Cultural Performance,* edited by John J. MacAloon (Philadelphia: Institute for the Study of Human Issues, 1982), p. 155.

25. Quoted in Myerhoff, *Number Our Days,* p. 101.

26. This is borrowed and modified slightly from my "The Lifeblood of Public Ritual," p. 282.

27. I have edited the original posting for publication purposes.

28. The man's name was Mark Lepine. Some feminists refuse to write out his name. One, who loaned me Louise Malette and Marie Chalouh's *The Montreal Massacre* (Charlottetown, Prince Edward Island, Canada: Gynergy Books, 1991), marked out his name in red throughout the entire book, asking me if I didn't consider this ritually more appropriate. After reading her red-letter edition of the book, I was sure that orthodox Jews, who do not pronounce the name of God, knew what they were doing. Deletion highlights. The effect of reading her edited copy was to compel my eye to leap on every instance of his name on the page; hence, I write it out here. The man was nothing special. Like the rest of us men, he has a regular name. Unlike God's name, his name is not worthy of being passed over in silence.

About the Book and Author

Significant life passages are marked by ritual in virtually every culture. Weddings and funerals are just two of the most institutionalized yet troubled ones in our own society. A wide variety of rites, both traditional and invented, also mark birth, coming of age, and other major transitions.

In *Marrying & Burying* Ronald Grimes, a founder of the new interdisciplinary field of ritual studies, tells an intensely personal story about the role of ritual in his own rich and sometimes difficult life. His critique of ritual impoverishment in North America reveals the extraordinary potential that ritualizing holds for negotiating and enriching transitions, both exalted and mundane. Always aware that no two people's experiences are alike, he encourages readers to think critically and creatively about the role of ritual in their own lives.

As both subject and theorist, Grimes is unflinchingly honest as well as generous, unsentimental, and wise. Using an impressive array of genres, he examines the problems of inventing the self and of finding rites that can stitch together the torn pieces of a man's life. Fiction, poetry, journal, and essay create a multivocal text, a symphonic portrayal of the mysterious and intransigent human need to ritualize.

This is a book for anyone committed to untangling the meaning of life as actually lived. It offers the student of contemporary North American spirituality and culture a rare opportunity not only to follow an experiencing subject but to glimpse the humanity behind a well-known theorist's analysis of ritual. It will attract those who study religion—especially anthropologists, psychologists, and sociologists—as well as students of gender studies, men's studies, education, and literature.

Raised on a drought-ridden ranch in eastern New Mexico, Ronald L. Grimes now makes his home in Waterloo, Canada, where he is professor of religion and culture at Wilfrid Laurier University. He is a founding editor of the *Journal of Ritual Studies* and author of *Symbol and Conquest; Beginnings in Ritual Studies; Ritual Criticism; Reading, Writing, and Ritualizing;* and numerous other books, articles, and reviews.